Burning and Turning

THE AUTHOR

Dr James Begg MBE worked as a GP in Ayr until his recent retirement. His previous book, *Rescue 177: a Scots GP Flies Search and Rescue with the Royal Navy*, was published by Mercat Press in 2003. A prize-winning poet and short story writer in the Scots language, he is also the co-author of *The Dipper an the Three Wee Deils*.

BURNING AND TURNING

THE RESCUE 177 STORY CONTINUES

JAMES A. BEGG

MERCAT PRESS
www.mercatpress.com

First published in 2006 by Mercat Press Ltd
10 Coates Crescent, Edinburgh EH3 7AL
www.mercatpress.com

ISBN-13: 978-1-84183-111-4
ISBN-10: 1-84183-111-5

Set in Italian Garamond at Mercat Press
Printed and bound in Great Britain by
Bell & Bain Ltd., Glasgow

DEDICATION

To the memory of those aircrew from HMS Gannet
who died while serving their country
1986–2006

Contents

Illustrations

Photographs courtesy of the Royal Navy and Peter Sandground

INTRODUCTION

Burning and Turning, the ongoing story of the magnificent work done by Rescue 177—the Royal Navy's Search and Rescue helicopter at HMS *Gannet*—covers a most important and momentous five-year period from 1992 to 1997, during which the Prestwick Base finally established itself as one of the busiest in the UK. The ever-present dangers faced by helicopter aircrews were graphically demonstrated by the tragic loss of a Seaking off the coast of Islay; and medical care continued to evolve as the team worked hard to keep their expertise and quest for new equipment one step ahead of the pace.

Having flown my last SAR in November 1997, I remained at *Gannet* as the Base Civilian Medical Practitioner, and watched with interest the continuing evolution of SAR, as firstly my Medics and then the back-seat aircrews assumed, with great assurance and skill, the functions and responsibilities previously undertaken by myself—assisted on board by an increasing use of specialist paediatric, obstetric, and intensive care medical teams picked up from major Glasgow hospitals, such as Yorkhill and Southern General, to deal with seriously ill transfers. However, these support teams are seldom available on a heaving ship or a sub-arctic Scottish mountainside, and it is in those hostile conditions that back-seat crews perform heroic life-saving feats—often unsung and unreported.

Lt Cdr Roger Stringer who, as a young Pilot Lieutenant, first flew with me twenty years ago—and witnessed with glee one of my least edifying moments when I filled two flash gloves with the contents of a barbecue—is now the Commanding Officer of HMS *Gannet* SAR Flight. In view of the present controversial MOD review on the future or otherwise of military SAR helicopter operations, I am delighted that he has agreed to collaborate in writing the final chapter of *Burning and Turning*, describing the momentous changes which have occurred at *Gannet* in the past nine years, some of the exceptional rescues undertaken, and what the future may hold for Rescue 177, the SAR helo, in the years ahead.

But meantime, for any readers who may have not yet read the first volume of *Rescue 177*—the book—a glance through its introductory chapter, modified and repeated below, should be of great interest.

◉

Search and Rescue—or SAR to those in the know—owes its origins to the fast RAF Air Sea Rescue launches of the Second World War, sent out to retrieve downed fliers from the seas around the British coast.

Post-war development of the helicopter, a fast, extremely versatile aircraft, and with a much greater scanning horizon for visual searches at sea, quickly led to its adoption by the RAF and Fleet Air Arm as their ideal search and rescue asset for the recovery of aircrew. Strategically placed bases, from RAF Lossiemouth in the north of Scotland, to RNAS Culdrose in Cornwall, ensured that no part of the British coastline was outwith the range of Air Force or Navy helos. Early Whirlwinds were soon superseded by the agile Wessex, which gave superb service for many years, till phased out over the past two decades by the Westland Sea King, with its superior advantages of twin engines, radar for night navigation and a much greater radial range of 300 miles.

Though the rescue of merchant seamen, fishermen and yachtsmen had hitherto, for well over a hundred years, been the task of courageous RNLI Lifeboat-men and the Coastguards, gradually the unique capabilities of military helicopters, both on land and sea, led to their incorporation in a nationwide search and rescue service.

Operations in coastal waters involving lifeboats, assisting vessels, and latterly its own four Sikorski 61 helicopters, are controlled by HM Coastguard. Distant offshore, or maritime, rescues were initially controlled by two military Rescue Coordination Centres: the

Northern RCC at Pitreavie Castle, Fife, for operations from Latitude 32 degrees 30 minutes North (The Wash) to the Faroes—and the Southern RCC at Mount Batten, Plymouth, Cornwall, covering incidents from The Wash south to the Bay of Biscay. With advances in global positioning satellite communications (GPS), these two centres have recently been replaced by a single centre, RCC Kinloss in Morayshire, which now coordinates rescues over this vast area of ocean, backed up by long-range Nimrod aircraft, tasked to locate distressed vessels and provide top cover for any rescue helicopters involved.

On the not-infrequent occasion when there is an overlap of responsibility for a maritime incident, RCC and HM Coastguard operations dovetail very effectively, making maximum use of all assets: Lifeboat Stations; Royal Navy Sea Kings based at HMS *Gannet* SAR Flight, Prestwick, and RNAS Culdrose; and RAF Sea Kings from RAF Stations—Lossiemouth, Boulmer, Leconfield, Wattisham, Chivenor, and Valley—as well as Coastguard Sikorskis at Sumburgh, Stornoway, Lee-on-Solent and Portland. These SAR Stations all have a range overlap, allowing one unit to cover another if its helo is out of station on a long mission.

Initially conceived as purely military assets, whose use for civilian purposes was frowned upon and resisted for many years by the MOD, the enlarged role of the SAR helicopter has evolved in response to public needs, and a political awakening to the public relations benefits and goodwill engendered by each high-profile dramatic rescue. In addition to PR, there were obvious, tangible benefits to be derived from the superb training offered, as motivated aircrews honed and perfected their flying and medical skills daily in extreme real-life situations rather than on simulated exercises. Nowadays only 5% of SAR activity involves going to the assistance of endangered military personnel, and this statistic has recently given rise to a major MOD review of the future of military search and rescue bases, and a suggestion that they might in future be run by a civilian agency such as the Coastguard.

On land, over the past thirty years, the soaring popularity of climbing and hillwalking has led to a huge rise in mountain incidents, and generated a demand for increased provision of rescue services. After the War, the RAF had formed and maintained its own Mountain Rescue Teams to handle any military air accidents on land, while Police MRTs, aided by local volunteers, formed the backbone of the civilian effort. Very quickly, however, the RAF teams became heavily involved in climbing rescues, while at the same time, in all major UK climbing centres, local highly trained, superbly equipped civilian MRTs were being formed from the nucleus of farmers, stalkers and shepherds previously called out for their local knowledge and stamina, rather than their rock-climbing expertise. As climbing became more technical, so MRT members had to be able to respond to any situation.

It was inevitable that rescue helicopters would soon become involved in this challenging environment. Despite the flying constraints frequently imposed by appalling mountain weather conditions, they have proved invaluable in cliff rescues, airlifting casualties and MRT members, and in conducting day-long searches for missing climbers.

At sea, there were two separate perceived needs. On the leisure side, as in climbing, there had been a similar explosion in the popularity of sailing, sea angling, sailboarding and just messing about in boats, which had also led to greatly increased demands on rescue services.

There was also a serious gap in the provision of emergency transport to hospital for inhabitants of remote areas of Scotland, especially the island communities. This need had been identified as far back as 1933, when the Scottish Air Ambulance Service was born. Using small twin-engined aircraft able to land on short grass airstrips, or even island beaches, this unsung pioneering initiative has quietly continued to provide the primary, major lifeline service from the islands to mainland hospitals for over seventy years.

The service was greatly expanded by the Scottish Ambulance Service in 1992, with the introduction of three light helicopters and three fixed-wing aircraft, with the aim of reducing their budgetary expenditure and dependence on SAR helicopters. This has not happened, since fixed-wing aircraft and light helicopters are also affected by adverse weather conditions, unable to land on waterlogged grass runways, operate in severe gales, snow or fog, or attempt night landings on some airstrips. Some small inhabited islands have no airstrip. In such situations, SAR helicopters have still found themselves just as heavily involved in Medevacs of patients with serious medical problems as they were in the late 1970s and early 1980s.

In those early days, long-distance helicopter transfers—except on occasions when the patient was accompanied by an island doctor—were often undertaken without the necessary medical skills, or even adequate medical equipment to deal with potential inflight emergencies, since the MOD's only contractual responsibility to Health Authorities was to provide a transport vehicle for the patient, not medical expertise or equipment.

This was the situation in which I found myself in June 1986, when I took over the role of SAR Doctor at HMS *Gannet*, Prestwick, from my illustrious predecessor and friend Dr S.Y. MacKechnie MBE. Suddie had been the Base Civilian Medical Practitioner for the previous fifteen years, and had been involved in around twenty-five SAR missions during this time. Search and Rescue was then only a relatively minor operational part of the work of 819 Squadron, Fleet Air Arm, whose primary role was anti-submarine warfare. Since *Gannet* was not then a designated SAR Station, callouts were infrequent, averaging around thirty a year, and the response time—at 45 minutes by day, and 90 minutes by night—was more leisurely than rapid!

Worldwide, the skills and protocols for Pre-Hospital Immediate Care were still in their formative stages, and many of our present-day standard procedures were as yet unknown. I had been fortunate in being asked to help establish an Immediate Care Scheme for Ayrshire and Arran Health Board in 1976, and my experience of dealing with road accidents and other pre-hospital emergencies, and awareness of the new techniques and equipment being developed by the British Association of Immediate Care Schemes (BASICS) and the Scottish Ambulance Service, made me quickly aware that a Royal Navy standard Ship's Doctor's white plastic box, containing a couple of drip sets, some drugs, a few field dressings—(and a bottle of Smelling Salts!)—fell far below the standard of equipment routinely available on our frontline ambulances.

Since Rescue 177, our SAR Sea King, was becoming increasingly employed as a 'frontline ambulance' for the islands, ships, fishing boats and mountains, I felt strongly that it should be equipped as such, and as soon as possible.

The first book tells of early struggles to achieve simple objectives, like a second oxygen cylinder on board—'We've got to watch the weight, Doc!'—and the purchase of a set of cervical collars; and of the thrill of acquiring a thousand pounds-worth of surplus ambulance equipment.

It highlights the frustrations of dealing with Navy bureaucracy when trying to obtain 'non-standard' vital items of equipment, such as a Heartstart defibrillator and a Propaq vital signs monitor, once HMS *Gannet* had become a designated SAR Station in 1989—with the take-off response time for Rescue 177 sharply reduced to only 15 minutes from dawn to dusk, and 30 minutes by night.

Between 1986 and 1995, annual SAR total callouts rose exponentially from 30 to 230 per year, making HMS *Gannet* the second busiest Search and Rescue unit in the UK after RAF Lossiemouth. Finally, with 274 callouts in the year 2000, Royal Navy Air Station Prestwick overtook 'The Crabs', and achieved the distinction of being the busiest SAR base in the British Isles.

The first book tells of the constant learning curve, and of lessons learned and applied after encountering unexpected problems during a mission; like the quiet satisfaction on hearing that a newly installed incubator had saved another premature baby.

The lessons learned, the availability of first-class monitoring and resuscitation equipment on board, and a more professionally structured Service programme of Advanced Pre-Hospital Care training, gradually produced a build up of confidence and expertise among my Medical Assistants and backseat aircrew, to the extent that eventually they seldom felt the need to call in the Doc. By 1997, I was virtually—and happily—redundant, having participated in sixty-four SARs.

Most of these were Medevacs from the islands, inter-hospital transfers, or Casevacs from vessels at sea. Due to the nature of mountain rescue work, often involving long, exhausting searches, I was seldom called out to witness superb flying skills in extreme weather conditions, or experience the naked fear of flying within a few feet of a thousand foot cliff-face in blizzard conditions. Although unable to relate them first-hand, I have heard many tales, and can only marvel at the courage of those involved.

Despite the massive press coverage often given to those saved in major dramatic rescues, because of that self-effacing modesty which characterises the professional persona of aircrew (I'll say nothing about their Mess and Wardroom antics!), very little is usually learned by the general public about the background to each drama.

As a civilian, I was uniquely privileged to fly for eleven years as a member of a Royal Navy SAR Aircrew with some great lads—and lasses—and to observe, and participate in, many exciting, monotonous, humorous, tragic, challenging and mundane jobs. I was also (sorry lads!), in the words of Robert Burns—'a chiel amang ye, takin notes'—or at least, taking note and fascinated by all that happened.

The end result is intended to give a fly-on-the-bulkhead picture of the wise-cracking camaraderie of the SAR aircrews, often used to lighten a hazardous moment or a harrowing experience; and also to pay a personal tribute to the tremendous skill and team-work involved in getting there, doing a good job, and returning safely.

Because of the sensitive nature and tragic end to some of the tasks undertaken, and the need to preserve patient confidentiality, and where I have been unable to trace patients to obtain permission to describe their stories, I have in many instances used fictitious names and fictitious illnesses, and changed town or island names to protect individuals. Sometimes, especially where there was press publicity of an incident, and there was a happy outcome, I have not disguised identities, with the gracious permission of those involved. It was marvellous—and very touching—to speak again with many of these former patients, and learn of their progress and success over the intervening years. I hope that this format will offend no one, but in the unlikely event that it does, I apologise unreservedly for any intrusion of privacy.

Finally, there are two unwilling parties to this adventure, without whom it would never have been accomplished. Firstly, my partners who, under sufferance (but well remunerated!) had to absorb my interrupted surgeries when I shot off up the bypass with green light flashing—and occasionally to fly themselves in the early years—and secondly, but most importantly, my dear wife Helen.

Helen's suffering was greater than any other, and probably shared stoically by most of the wives and partners of our SAR aircrews nationwide. It is one thing to swan off on some Action Man stunt on a horrible dark night, getting your adrenalin fix in the sure company of a bunch of guys you can trust. It is another to lie awake with a mind running wild, as an Atlantic winter gale batters against the bedroom windows, worried sick and agonising as to whether you will ever see your husband again. And sometimes, when carefully arranged social plans went 'oot the windae', she'd wish I'd join them!

Thank you, love, for putting up with my selfishness and 'Boy's Own Capers'!

—James A. Begg,
October 2006

1

20th May 1992

SPOTTY YOUTHS

The surgery phone rang. 'Fiona here, Doc... just to give you heads-up on a signal we've had from HMS *London* to fly a doctor out to her tomorrow. Seems they've got several cases of chickenpox on board.'

My usual response to a mid-afternoon request like this for a house-call to something as trivial and self-limiting as chickenpox would have been to fast-talk myself out of it—Calamine lotion and Calpol, don't scratch the spots, and keep the bairn off school and away from other kids for at least a week!

I was already halfway embarked on this defensive, knee-jerk response, when it suddenly clicked that tomorrow was Wednesday—my half day. I would be out at *Gannet* anyway, the forecast looked good, and a fair-weather 'jolly' might be just the job. My principles did a quick u-turn. Don Clark phoned back later with an update. The briefing would be at 0815—and he was equally puzzled as to why a doctor was required, for the *London* should have a petty officer medical assistant on board.

At the briefing room next morning, I was met by the tall figure of Lt Andy Aspden, the OOD. 'We're on to *London* just now, Doc, just to see if you're still needed. POMA Clark will be flying with you.'

I glanced up at the crew list for Zero Seven, chalked on the duty board. It already had a six man complement, and neither Don nor myself was included... strange!

The squadron daily briefing got under way with the Met Officer's report. The weather forecast was good—bright and hazy, cloudy later, with a seven to ten knot NE breeze.

Then the Engineering Officer gave what was fast becoming a standard, par for the course report on day-to-day aircraft airworthlessness—only two serviceable out of nine.

The 'Peace Dividend' was apparently playing havoc with the supply of spare parts. A while back, some bright sparks at the MoD had put an embargo on the ordering of spares, having failed to grasp the basic practical fact that bits frequently break up, wear down, or fall off twenty-year-old helicopters. This blunder had now been rectified, but it would possibly take another twelve months before the shortfall was made up.

On the bright side, however, a new gearbox had arrived for Zero One, the designated SAR Sea King, which had been out of service for a month. Zero Three, the temporary SAR replacement, was serviceable, and was being tasked this morning to fly a Royal Navy bomb disposal team down to a fishing boat with a live mine tangled in its nets somewhere off the Antrim coast.

With these minor aviation operational details now safely out of the way, Jim Fergusson the XO rose to deliver a stirring 'England expects... all hands to action stations... man the pumps... and sod this for a bloody lark, chaps!'—peptalk to the Company on the operational burden to be endured by all at the Annual Cocktail Party later that evening. To a chorus of groans, grimaces, and derisory laughter, he delegated escort duties, and allocated sundry blue-rinse matrons and boring old farts to those unlucky single officers who had not had the wit, wisdom, or foresight to bring along their wives or girlfriends!

The CO of 819 put in his few words, then asked if there was anything from the floor. A 'subby' at the back stood up and announced he had spare places on a hang-gliding course—at which, Gurney Hickey, the chief fllying instructor, observed drily that under the present circumstances, it might be an ideal opportunity for aircrew to log up some flying hours!

On that light note the squadron briefing ended, and I sped off to get into my goon suit, unaware that our sortie briefing was scheduled to follow immediately afterwards. A few minutes late, and somewhat embarrassed, I slunk back in and dropped into a spare seat beside Don, just as Lt Martin Lewis slipped a transparency of the flight deck of a type 22 Frigate into the overhead projector.

'Have any of you guys deck-landed on a type 22 before?' he asked, to be met with a nap-hand of negatives. It slowly dawned on me. This was to be a training flight—and it wouldn't be Martin Lewis landing me on, but some laddie who had never done it before! A distinct feeling of unease replaced my eager anticipation, as I listened intently to the various reference points peculiar to type 22s being described and demonstrated on the screen.

'There are two bumlines across the flight deck... You must land aft of the forard mark, otherwise your rotors will slice the lid off the Lynx hangar... but don't go too far back or your tail wheel will drop off the stern of the ship!... And there are two vertical lines on the hangar door. You centre on the right-hand one—not the left, or you might tip sideways off the port deck.'

I began to develop an uneasy feeling that this 'jolly' might not be quite the jolly jolly I had originally envisaged.

'Doc,' Lt Lewis's voice broke into my thoughts. 'How long will you and the POMA need?'

'About ten or fifteen minutes, I would think... doesn't take long to diagnose chickenpox.'

'Fine. Well, you'll have to hang about for a bit longer. We're doing a HIFR—Helicopter Inflight Refuelling—exercise with the *London*, which will last about two and a half hours... OK with you?'

'No problem. I've never seen round a Frigate before.'

With Don still as puzzled as I was as to why we were needed for a case of chickenpox, we dutifully embarked on Zero Seven. It was a bonny, calm day, but very hazy, as we rose from *Gannet* on a heading of 250 degrees to seek out HMS *London*, somewhere in the Firth of Clyde.

Disappointingly, the Frigate turned out to be no more than eight miles off Prestwick, cunningly hidden from view by the sea haze, and it was only a few minutes before we had Harry Blackmore's jocular voice crackling from the observer's seat: 'Get ready for deck-landing. Everyone strapped in?... O.K. Doc?... and Baby Doc?' I couldn't resist a grin as I glanced at Don, all five foot five of him—plus beard!

Martin Lewis was in the left-hand instructor's seat as his pupil, linking with the winchman, talked himself down into the decklanding position. 'Am now aft of the forard bumline, lined up with the left-hand door line, now... set for landing.'

With a soft bump we landed on, just as it penetrated my brain that the pilot had in fact lined up on the wrong door marking. He was two metres off centre—it should have been the right-hand line... another few feet to the left and we'd be over the side! Flight deckhands rushed forward to secure the aircraft with anchoring straps, and Don and I nipped out smartly, relieved to discover that there were still three metres of deck between the left-hand wheel and the side of the ship.

We were shepherded into the Lynx hangar as the Flight Deck Officer signalled the Sea King to lift off and begin its refuelling exercise. Here, POMA Mackay, the ship's medic, introduced himself, and escorted us through the bulkhead doors and along a passageway to his office, where, in the stuffy heat, we were glad to get out of our goonsuits. En route, we were briefly introduced to the Captain, who was below decks, checking out the dhobi wallahs in the laundry—presumably scrounging a clean shirt.

'What's the story, then?' I eventually asked Mackay, eager to find out just why our presence had been so necessary.

'Several things, Doc. We had a couple of ratings sent sick on shore with chickenpox just before we left Devonport. That was a fortnight ago. Now we've another fresh case, who is just back from shore leave and probably became infected just before he went off ship. So the Old Man and the XO are a bit twitchy in case we might soon have an epidemic on our hands.'

'Possible, but hardly likely.' I calculated. 'What's the ship's complement?'

'Two hundred and eighty.'

'I don't know the exact figures, but I suppose there might be ten per cent of the crew who've never had chickenpox as kids. Maybe twenty-eight to thirty men.'

'That would really knock hell out of the running of the ship, Boss.' Don interjected. 'The Navy runs a very tight ship nowadays. Manning levels are critical. With so much hi-tech specialisation, there's not much leeway if any of the crew fall ill.'

The sick bay was a compact, well-designed, small room, crammed with neatly stowed vital equipment, an examination couch, spotlessly clean work surfaces, and a screened-off bunk area. In the latter lay an extremely spotty, slightly embarrassed, red-haired young rating. A cursory glance was sufficient.

'We'd better get you ashore, pronto,' I smiled, 'before all your mates are smitten and we have to run up the Yellow Fever Flag and quarantine the ship for a month.'

'And while you're here, Doc...' How often had I heard that gambit before! The POMA continued. 'We've a PO with a high fever and vomiting... Could you have a look at him, just in case he's developing chickenpox as well?'

The PO's pyrexia had settled, and he now had a dose of diarrhoea—definitely not chickenpox.

'And the XO would like you to do a witness report on a sentry found asleep with his gun across his knees inside the funnel last night. This is why you were called in. The request came from up top—not me.'

'Bloody hell! This is turning into a ward round!' I exclaimed laughingly.

'It's a serious charge, Boss.' Don informed me darkly. 'That sentry would have been shot if there was a war on.'

'Ach, we're too near Prestwick beach. A man walking his dog would have heard the shots and phoned the police!'

'Even in peacetime it's quite a serious charge.' Don persisted.

'What's the background?' I turned to POMA Mackay.

'He's a silly young bugger.' The offender's FMed 4 records were produced. 'I treated him six days ago with antibiotics for a chest infection and temperature, and told him to report back if he didn't feel any better. He didn't come for review, and obviously went back to full duties too soon.'

'Better bring him in, and I'll hear his side of the story.' I reckoned there might be a good plea of mitigation.

It was as I had suspected. Although his chest sounded clear, the lad still had a rough cough and dirty spit, and had hardly slept for a week. Last night, despite his battle-dress parka, he had felt shivery and cold, though all his mates were warm, so he had slipped into the funnel chamber for a heat—a common enough practice during night watch—but had unfortunately fallen asleep.

I had no compunction about rendering a sympathetic account in the official witness report—on pain of dire penal consequences to myself, should I not be telling the truth, the whole truth… This session took over an hour—so much for my 'ten to fifteen minutes'—but it still left time for a comprehensive tour of the ship after a word with Lt Cdr Colley, the Executive Officer, who was quite relieved to hear that his ship's company was unlikely to be decimated by chickenpox.

The *London* had been involved in the Gulf War, and its darkened ops room, with multiple glowing radar consoles, dials, and screened-off secret bits, was just as incomprehensible and scary to me now, as TV newsreel glimpses had been during the conflict. It was a claustrophobic place, and I was glad to get up on deck. Here, Don was in his element, pointing out Sea Wolf missile tubes and Oerlikon anti-aircraft guns.

'They call these the "Spotty Youth Guns"', he informed me, pointing to the Oerlikons.

'Why?'

'Because it's been found that seventeen-year-olds handle them best—best eyesight, best reflexes. Once they get to nineteen, they're past it.'

'Doesn't say much for you and me,' I observed wryly.

'Don't know about that,' he retorted with a grin. 'I had plenty of practice coming back from the Falklands. We had a huge amount of live ammunition still on board that was getting past its sell-by date, and would have to be dumped at sea because it was becoming unstable and dangerous. So every man on the ship got the chance to fire off thousands of rounds into the air… rifles, machine guns, Oerlikons, even missiles. Got a bit boring after a while. Every ship in the Task Force was doing the same. Must have cost millions, but what couldn't be fired off had to be dumped anyway.'

The Sea King was still buzzing around on its HIFR exercise, and from a vantage point at the Lynx hangar door I was able to get some good photos of the fuel pipe being hoisted up and connected while it hovered over the stern. From the flight deck it looked massive, compared with the compact yet lethal little Lynx folded neatly away in its hangar.

Twenty minutes later, Zero Seven landed on, and we embarked with our chickenpox case. Don and I went forard, and automatically strapped ourselves in for take-off. Suddenly it felt very crowded. I looked up to find all the four front passenger seats were now occupied. Apart from Harry Blackmore, everyone who could, had scrambled up-front to get as far away as possible from our spotty friend. Wimps!

When we met later at the Cocker's P (the annual cocktail party), I commended Harry for his courage above and beyond the call of duty in continuing to man his post. He laughed. 'Did you enjoy your first deck-landing, Doc?' I said yes, but expressed reservations about landing on the wrong reference points.

'Yeah. Just as well it was a flat calm,' was his laconic reply. 'Any swell and you can have a problem slipping off the side. The Sea King is not fitted with a check-hook like the Lynx has, to grab the deck grill, and,' he added for good measure, '...there's only six feet of clearance at the front, and four at the back!'

2

24th July 1992
HARD TO SWALLOW

I don't know what it is about Sod, but he's got it down to a fine art, that bloody law of his. Imagine the scenario. The first few days back at work after an idyllic fortnight of total relaxation in the warmth of the Dordogne—during which Craig had been called out on a SAR to Stornoway, to escort a deeply unconscious heart patient back to Glasgow—a long trip for nothing, as it transpired, since the poor man died only an hour after reaching the cardiac unit.

Monday night finished around seven o'clock, after a fraught morning at *Gannet* dealing with the aggregated problems of a three-week absence—accentuated by the frustrations of finding the foundations of my new sick bay much as I had left them. There was no sign of this marvellous, prefabricated building which they had promised would be up, if not running, on my return from leave. At Cathcart Street, the afternoon had been spent in identical fashion—discovering, likewise, that the building warrant for our new surgery extension had not materialised either!

Tuesday had been even worse. With two partners away on holiday, and a third still off ill a week after his return from abroad, the two remaining stalwarts, rather than splitting their joint half-day—which would have buggered up their weekly foursome—decided to bugger up my day instead, by swanning off to golf as usual, and leaving myself and the trainee in sole charge of the practice from eleven in the morning! Thank God there was no SAR callout. Young

David and I finally struggled out of the surgery at a quarter to seven, and I still had an hour's paperwork and a foul temper to dispose of.

Wednesday brought a pleasant surprise—a new sick bay, erected and ready for inspection—well, almost. Fiona gave me the nod that Ray Pike, *Gannet*'s Projects Manager, was on site, so I slipped in for a sneak preview.

'My, Ray, they've fairly knocked this up in jig-time. When did it arrive?'

'Monday afternoon, Jimmy. Five articulated lorry-loads of prefabricated modules, popped straight on to the foundations, and there you have it—ninety thousand quids' worth of sick bay, just like that!'

All around us, fitters were busy fitting fittings. The sink, bath and toilet units had already been installed, along with the carpets, at the factory. They even had the curtain rails up in my consulting room, which was graciously spacious, and had a fine view north over the practice golf and cricket nets to pleasant green fields beyond. What a welcome change from the opaque glass windows of my old wartime brick hut, which would now be converted back into officers' cabins to help overcome the serious accommodation shortage anticipated when 826 Squadron joined us next year.

The new sick bay had been designed with this expansion in mind, and I had advocated its dual role as a casualty clearing station, in the event of any major accident on the base, when I drew up the outline plans on which the final layout had been based. Having twice suffered a harrowing experience as 'Clerk of Works' overseeing big extensions to our own surgery premises, and with the dreadful prospect looming of a third major extension about to occupy the best part of the next nine months, it was a marvellous feeling to see a brand new sick bay spring up out of nowhere—and to have no worries or hassles over rectifying architect's errors, re-siting partners' plug points, or placating bolshie upstairs neighbours with blocked drains.

'What's the time scale for completion, Ray?' I asked, my eagerness tempered by a host of painful memories.

'Two weeks. We plan to have you moving in before *Gannet* returns from summer leave.' I was happily impressed. It really made my day—till Thursday.

Thursday was horrendous. Real back to 'normal', nose to the grindstone, non-stop pressure, from eight-thirty in the morning till eight at night, with only a twenty minute break for lunch. I was so exhausted when I got home that I went to bed after the nine o'clock news, leaving Helen and Fiona watching some awful American mini-series on TV.

There was ahhnn interesting aahh-rticle… I waahh-nted to read in… the BASICs Journahhl… ohhnn… defibrillat-ohhrzz… in… helicopter-zzzzz!

I awoke to the phone ringing. Bewildered, I squinted at my watch. Eleven-thirty. I wasn't on call! Was I? Who was?

I picked up the receiver.

'This is Captain Fairley, *Gannet*… Is that Doctor Begg?'

'Yes, Doug. What can I do for you?'

'We've word of a medevac from Arran. Can you come in? I've talked to RCC and they think we might be better with a doctor on board. It's a teenage boy with a fifty-pence piece stuck in his throat.'

By this time Helen was hovering anxiously at the foot of the bed. 'Don't worry, love. It's just a quickie to Arran and back… Shouldn't lose too much sleep.'

'You'd better not! You are exhausted! And I remember once before you said that about Arran, and you were away for six hours!'

I had some doubts about any real need for my presence en route to *Gannet*. If the coin was obstructing the laddie's airway, he would have been long dead by this time. If it was stuck in his gullet, his breathing should be unaffected, and there should be no requirement for my attendance.

Still, better safe than sorry. On arrival, I remembered we didn't have McGill's forceps in the SAR kit—handy tools for removing any debris from the back of a throat—so I found myself outside the SAR cabin, turning the contents of my immediate care box upside down in the car-boot, and groping around in the darkness for a pair. All the while I could hear the chopper revving up impatiently in the background. I was already late, having earlier stupidly pulled on my flying suit with the coathanger still inside it, and having to strip off again! Frantically, I located the forceps, stuffed them into a goon suit pocket, and dashed out to the aircraft.

The short flight across to Arran didn't leave us much time to prepare, but Fiona, quietly efficient, had brought all the kit aft, and my recent reorganisation of the grab bag after the ATLS course made it simple to locate the airway box and mini-tracheotomy kit—God forbid I had to use it! Suction and oxygen were to hand.

In ten minutes we had arrived at Knockenkelly, guided in by police car headlights. The island fiirc brigade was there; holiday makers with flash cameras were there; but no sign of an ambulance. As we hung around waiting, Fiona took off her helmet and held her head in her hands. 'My head's ringing!' she complained.

'Serves you right for having too much to drink last night at the Summer Leave Ball,' I remonstrated.

'Drink is nothing to do with it!' she retorted indignantly. 'It's my hair that's wringing—not my head. I was having a bubble bath when that bloody bleep went!'

Sod, it seems, has it in for more than me.

After five minutes I got worried. Had something gone wrong? Had the boy's airway obstructed at the hospital? Were we too late? Just as a policeman radioed the hospital to find out, the ambulance drew up.

The doors opened to reveal a very anxious mother, and a young boy propped up on the stretcher, who looked much happier than he should have been under the circumstances—in sharp contrast to his mum.

Angus Campbell, the local GP, approached with a large buff envelope containing x-ray plates. 'They show a fifty-pence piece lodged at the level of the bifurcation.' he informed me quietly.

'Not lodged *in* the bifurcation of the trachea, I hope!' I inquired, half in jest.

'No.' He laughed, and lowered his voice. 'His mum doesn't know it yet, but he'd swallowed three big glasses of wine before he got round to the coin… Holiday-makers!'

'So that's why he looks so happy. He's half-pissed.'

'He might not be so happy in the morning when his father finds out. He is at home in Glasgow, and on his way to Crosshouse right now.' And so were we.

It wasn't Fiona who merited a lecture on the evils of strong drink—at least, not this time!

3

29th December 1992

RUM DUBH

The long weekend off at Christmas had been a welcome break, after supervising three weeks of internal demolition work which had left the surgery looking like well-kept bomb site.

Our progressive practice, ever keen to be one step ahead of the field, had thought it a great idea to go fundholding, and consequently take on a huge administrative task previously done perfectly adequately by the Ayrshire and Arran Health Board.

The cart had, rather unfortunately, been put several yards before the horse. Thousands of pounds worth of expensive computer hardware had been installed, and an enormous gathering of statistics on all aspects of hospital referrals had been undertaken, before we had been able to purchase the two upstairs flats desperately needed to provide extra office space.

I had never been able to see any logic in applying this fundholding philosophy—an English answer to an English problem—to the already efficient, user-friendly, and co-operative hospital service we enjoyed here in the West of Scotland; and the political dogma which had inspired it left me cold. The bureaucracy and paperwork now involved in running our practice was reaching Royal Navy battleship-sinking proportions. So while the computer buffs and financial whizz kids of the practice were applying themselves to the complexities of negotiating and recording the price of haemorrhoidectomies, I had found myself acting as Clerk of Works for the third time in twelve years, overseeing a major extension project. The practicalities and problems of building work I could at least understand.

Everything had been sailing along smoothly, maybe too smoothly, as I went to pick up the *Gannet* bleep which I had passed over to the duty threesome for the duration of the Christmas weekend. There had been no callouts—which was just as well, for the bloody thing had gone AWOL! Scott didn't have it. Craig didn't have it. And big Paul, away at his Special Clinic, also swore blind he'd not got it. After twenty minutes of fruitless searching I phoned the SAR Cell, reported the loss to Jamie Paterson the duty POACMN, and asked them to phone the surgery if by any chance there was a callout.

True to form, at a quarter past four, Fiona rang. 'We've got a shout, Boss. There's a job on... a three year-old. Don't know what's wrong or where we are going, but RCC have requested a doctor.'

And equally true to form, the journey out to *Gannet* was hellish. The roads were jammed with homeward-bound Christmas sales shoppers, every traffic light was at red, and every wee green man was dawdling across the carriageway. When I eventually burst clear of the log-jam and put my foot down along the bypass, I became conscious of a beautiful, still, but bitterly cold winter evening, and a wonderful twilight.

The Sea King was revving up on the apron, and Jamie Paterson, the PO aircrewman, stuck his head round the locker room door as I got changed. Two vests, long johns, a sweat shirt, woollen bunny suit, pullover, flying overalls, and then my goon bag—six layers of clothing—I wasn't going to be frozen stiff this trip.

'Won't be long, Jamie,' I acknowledged him. Looking up quickly, with one leg in my goon suit and hurrying to slip in the other one, I pushed down with my right foot. There was a bit of resistance, and I cursed the way goon suit legs had of twisting back to front and making life awkward—especially when you were in a rush!

I could sense Jamie staring at me with a curious, pitying expression on his face. Then I looked down. My right leg was firmly jammed into my left sleeve, with the rubber cuff seal tightly clamped round my ankle. I was mortified. Help!

He grinned, and quickly grabbed and released the proffered ankle. Further embarrassment was to come as I struggled in vain to draw the neck seal over my head, and once more had to ask for his help. What a stupid dick! What must he be thinking? This clumsy quack can't even get dressed properly. God knows how incompetent he'll be on the bloody aircraft.

I couldn't fathom it out, till it dawned on me that I was just too damned fat for the goon suit, with the luxury of all these extra layers I'd put on for warmth, two layers too many. And I still didn't know what the hell I was doing all this for. As I shot through the door, I bumped into Sub Lt Paul Hunter, the OOD. 'Can you tell me what this SAR is about—and where we are going?'

'You're going to Skye, Doc. RCC says it's a three-year-old boy suffering from a… para-, para-… something,' he stuttered to pronounce the term, '…ehmm, a para-… phimosis, I think they said it was. And they want a doctor.'

'A whit!?' I exclaimed incredulously. ' A paraphimosis!?'

'Yeah, I think that's what they said.'

'Do you know what a paraphimosis is?'

'No, Doc.'

'It's a strangulated willie! They can't seriously want a doctor for a swollen tickie!'

They must have got it wrong, I told myself as I rushed to the aircraft. RCC can't be getting me out for something as trivial as this—after failing to call on me recently for heart attacks, asthma, and severe head injuries. I shuddered to think of some of the potential medical disasters at times encountered by my medics in my absence, due to inadequate information and guidance being given to the poor controllers at Pitreavie, who, unlike ambulance controllers, had no medical knowledge. There must be some way of improving communications. Two years ago, I had tried to promote the idea of a standard questionnaire, with a number of simple questions that any lay controller could use to elicit vital medical details from doctors, ship's captains, or men from the mountains. But the idea had never been followed up or implemented by the authorities, and here we were again—still playing 'three-and-fourpence'.

I could well imagine how non-medical air traffic controllers might get into a tizzy when presented with the medical evacuation of a 'para-something'. After all, 'para' has something to do with paralysis, or paraplegics—so must be very serious—call a Doc! The fact that the message had come via Ambulance Control in Inverness, as we later discovered, did nothing to improve my confidence in the system.

The aircrew were preoccupied with radio frequency problems, and it was well into the flight before I was able to confirm the diagnosis. Never mind, what the hell, I hadn't been to Skye since my first SAR. I might as well enjoy the trip.

I went up front to discover that not only were we bound for the wilderness of Knoydart and not Skye as promised, but in addition, we had weather as well as radio problems to contend with. Freezing fog was covering most of the country, forcing Jeff Ainsworth to switch on his de-icing and climb through the cloud to a height of 4500 feet. We emerged just in time to witness a wonderful view of the setting sun immersing itself in a fleecy, white, cloud sea—a gigantic, heavenly bubble-bath.

'This is typical of the weather you like to drag me out in!' I chaffed Ainsworth, recalling the midsummer trip from Arran to Glasgow with a severe head injury, which lasted six hours instead of one and a half, due to dense fog. 'I hope it won't be as long as the last one.'

A tiny gap in the clouds revealed Rothesay Bay below.

'Yeah! That was the day Charlie's Wessex was flying down to Bute, wasn't it?' Rothesay vanished as we overflew the misted and masked hills above Dunoon, where the crew had picked up a dead hill-walker earlier that afternoon.

Darkness began to set in from the east as we glimpsed Seil Island and then Oban, through further small breaks. Over to the west, the silver-gold cloud crests were turning a cold grey as dusk wrapped the hills of Mull in a freezing overblanket.

'You almost get an outline of the topography of Mull just looking at these clouds,' Jeff commented. 'Look at that big hump in the clouds just there. I bet Ben More is just underneath it… and that long dip is probably Glen Forsa.' Jeff was a stockily-built, open-faced, friendly fellow Scot from Perth, whose easy-going, relaxed attitude, and the casual but clear manner in which he outlined step-by-step flying procedures to his co-pilot and crew, inspired confidence—the hallmark of years of experience as an instructor.

He was a keen hill-walker, and his knowledge of the Western Isles and Highlands was most impressive—in fact, quite encyclopaedic—compared with that of some of his Sassenach colleagues.

Shaun Quinn, the observer, kept us on course above the cloud ceiling till we were over Muck and he got Eigg on his nose, then Clark Broad, our co-pilot, gently descended and emerged through the cloud, with the dark outline of the east coast of Rum showing five miles to port. Here, Jeff took over for a low flight up the Sound of Sleat towards the twinkling lights of a tiny clachan on the Knoydart shore. Carefully avoiding a stand of Scots pines, he gently put the aircraft down on a rock-free stretch of foreshore, lit by the headlights of an old Ferguson tractor and a pick-up truck. There was no obvious road to be seen, and in the gathering darkness, the fabled remoteness of wild Knoydart was only too real, with access only by boat—or helicopter .

Shielding our night-adjusted eyes from the glare of their headlights, we jumped out and walked towards the vehicles. A worried young woman sheltering in the pick-up handed over a wee bundle in a blanket to a tall man who had jumped from the driver's seat. He introduced himself as Simon's father.

'What's wrong with the wee fellow?' I shouted over the roar of the engines, half hoping that Pitreavie had misheard, and that I was really there to be of genuine assistance. 'Is there a doctor in Knoydart?'

'No. The nearest doctor's in Mallaig… Eh, I'll tell you about Simon on the helicopter.' His southern English voice dropped to a conspiratorial whisper, as he glanced back at the onlookers. 'It's… his privates!'

'Better tell me now, where I can hear you! I believe he's got what we call a paraphimosis.'

He nodded, and smiled apologetically. 'Yes. He had a bath last night, and when his foreskin was pulled back to be washed it got stuck tight. We couldn't pull it forward, and overnight it swelled up and turned almost black… We phoned the doctor in Mallaig this afternoon, and he organised the flight out.'

'Do you want me to have a go at reducing it here?' I asked, a bit concerned at the 'black' description. It was a genuine emergency.

He shook his head. 'He's settled now, and almost asleep. I don't think you'd achieve anything.'

I was secretly in agreement, having had several failed experiences with some of my own young patients, in much more relaxed surroundings than this one—standing on the seashore, in pitch blackness, on a remote west Highland peninsula, on a cold December night, being half blown over by helicopter rotor-blades whirling a few yards away! And anyway, it was only thirty minutes flying time to Belford Hospital and proper surgical care. A simple wee snip would release the stricture.

Jeff chose to fly at five hundred feet, under the cloud, and hedgehop over the Ardnamurchan peninsula into the Sound of Mull, rather than risk a flight over the cloud-veiled Ardgour mountains, with no guarantee of a sighting of Fort William on the other side—and the prospect of flying into the Ben.

Jamie Paterson, who had been listening in to RCC, suddenly exclaimed, 'Bloody hell, they're all out tonight! That's the Coastguard chopper… and one-three-one from Lossie… and there's something on at Culdrose as well!'

'Shit!' hissed Shaun Quinn. 'The radar's packed in.'

'God, that's all we need in the middle of fog in the Sound of Mull, a bloody duff radar.'

'Wait. It's OK now. I switched it off, then on again, and it's working!' A sigh of relief all round.

Simon and his Dad were plugged into the courtesy earphones, and while it was not obvious that the implications of loss of radar were alarming to his Dad, it certainly didn't faze young Simon.

'Moon!' A clear, sleepy voice broke the radio silence, as a crescent moon and attendant Venus suddenly appeared through a hole in the cloud and were framed for a few seconds in the cargo door window.

'This will be an exciting time for him. First time in a helicopter?'

'No. He's flown in one before.' rejoined his father.

'Seasoned flier, then? He'll qualify for a log-book!'

'Make a damn good aircrewman, too,' opined Jamie Paterson. 'He's fast asleep again in the back of the aircraft.'

An exciting trip, noisy engines and a sore willie had finally given in to a three-year-old's wonderful gift of being able to sleep through anything.

Shaun Quinn carefully guided us up Loch Linnhe and through the narrows at Corran Ferry, before Clark Broad was able to relax, circle the broad expanse of loch opposite Fort William, and come in to land on the esplanade car park.

Young Simon and his Dad were escorted to the waiting ambulance and waved us goodbye as we returned to the aircraft—to find our observer missing—presumably doing an aircraft inspection. I strapped myself in, as PO Paterson, standing by the door, burst out laughing.

'What's he doing?' I asked curiously.

'His flies up!' was the quick rejoinder.

The observer nimbly leapt aboard. 'There's a major leak by the starboard landing wheel,' he reported. 'I've checked it… tastes like beer.'

'How long till Glasgow, Shaun?'

'Forty five minutes—direct line.'

'We'll go for it. Straight down the loch and we'll miss Ben Nevis.'

The skies above were clear as we quickly rose to five thousand feet, and within minutes we were overflying Ballachulish Bridge. Like giant slumbering tigers, the massive, awesome shoulders and black and white snow-striped gullies of the Glencoe peaks drifted silently beneath us. 'We're right over Bidean nam Bian, the highest peak in Argyll,' came the authoritative voice of our driver/courier. It was a shortlived spectacle, obscured thereafter by cloud seas rolling southwards from Glen Etive as far as the distant glow of the Central Belt.

As we flew over Dunoon to avoid encroaching on Scottish Air Traffic Control air-space, the unseen Clyde coast was delineated by an eerie glow through the clouds from the port towns of Gourock, Greenock and Port Glasgow. Far to the east, we could see the navigation lights of aircraft doing a left-hand circuit prior to plunging through the fog on their automatic landing approach to Glasgow Airport's narrow runway.

'Must be quite a twitchy time for these fixed-wing pilots going down through that cloud, hands off, relying on auto-landing systems,' I observed, recalling the shared experience with Jeff of being talked down on to the wrong runway during our fogbound landing there five years ago.

'Yeah. I like to be in complete control myself… Yes, lads?' They laughed.

4

12th January 1993

BARRA: STORM FORCE ELEVEN

'Lashed during the night by the worst storms to hit Shetland for a hundred years, the Tanker *Braer* has finally sunk. At first light this morning, observers on the clifftops reported that the ship had broken into four sections, spilling the remainder of its 85,000 tonnes of light crude oil into the seas around Sumburgh. Salvage experts have given up hope of retrieving what was left of her cargo, and environmentalists are predicting a major wildlife catastrophe from the oil slicks now extending forty miles northwards along the west coast of Shetland, threatening many salmon fish farms, seabird and seal colonies.'

I listened with mounting despair to the eight o'clock news. I had been to Shetland as a student in 1963, long before the oil boom, and had stayed at Sumburgh en route to Fair Isle, where I had spent three memorable September weeks camping and birdwatching. It had been an unforgettable experience, made more so by the awesome spectacle of a ninety-miles-an-hour Atlantic storm thundering giant waves onto the rocks by the South Light. I had stood in the lee of the lighthouse wall for three hours, transfixed and mesmerised by the majestic, primeval power of the elements, and the amazing sight of grey seals sporting themselves nonchalantly among the roaring breakers.

By all accounts, this present storm, generated by a record low pressure area of 916 millibars which had passed to the north of Shetland the previous day, was the daddy of them all!

I had no time to listen to further details. I had a full surgery to attend to at eight-thirty, and a full bladder to attend to now. From the loo, I could just hear Helen shout something from the kitchen. I opened the door. 'What is it?'

'Jimmy!' She shouted again. '…It's *Gannet*!'

'Hello, Boss.' It was Fiona. 'Sorry, but we've got a job on… to Barra, and they want you in. It's a medevac, but I don't have any more details.'

My heart sank. I could hear the gale outside—and, what was worse—so could Helen! There were reports of blizzard conditions and blocked roads all over Scotland—and it had to be Barra!

Helen was desperately anxious. 'Do you have to go! Can't they send someone else? I'm sick fed up with this!'

'Yes, love. I'm sorry.' There was a longer hug than usual at the door as I left.

Traffic was nose to tail along the bypass, as cars slowed sensibly to cope with violent cross-winds, and at the same time, many slipped quietly to one side to let me through.

I had no trouble on this occasion with my goon suit. The Cab was up at the hangar, where it had been sheltered overnight from the gales, and I was glad of a lift up the hill in the OOD's car.

On board the aircraft, I was momentarily surprised to find Trevor Scott, my LMA; till he informed me he had just taken over as duty medic from Fiona, who apparently had been out to Islay in appalling blizzard conditions during the night, to pick up a ten-year-old girl with appendicitis.

We took off in fairly spectacular fashion, lifting up over the hangars and swinging across the windswept runways into the teeth of a south-westerly gale. As we made painfully slow progress across the Firth of Clyde, the crew volubly cursed SPLOT—the Senior Pilot—for his decision to send them round the west coast of Islay rather than take the shorter route through the Crinan Gap.

'Ted should have kept his bloody nose out of it, telling us not to go for Crinan… because of turbulence in Loch Fyne! How the hell does he know it's any more turbulent up there than crossing this shitty stretch of water? He's probably converted a one-and-three-quarter hour flight into a three hour one, sending us round the south of Islay!'

'Chrissakes, we're big boys now. It's not as if we're green behind the ears... been flying for yonks. Surely we can suss out for ourselves if something is dangerous—and take avoiding action!'

Meantime, the Sea King was playing three-dimensional havoc with my equilibrium as we lurched to windward over huge spume-crested grey rollers, sweeping menacingly and relentlessly up the Firth only two hundred feet below.

'Look at these. I've never seen the Clyde like this—ever!' exclaimed Steve Dow the pilot.

'Yeah. I reckon we're getting as much turbulence from these sea mountains as we would have got from the Kintyre peninsula, going through Crinan.'

'What's the groundspeed, Tim?'

'Sixty knots.'

'And wind speed?'

'Two-twenty degrees... Forty-two knots.' Tim Bishop went on, '...and I've a large land mass on radar direct ahead.'

'Yeah. Visual... Have Davaar Island on the nose.'

As we overflew Campbeltown, increased turbulence shook the aircraft as we were hit by strengthening winds funnelled through the Machrihanish Gap. Four geese, off to starboard, seemed to be flying only marginally slower than we were.

'Christ! Out of the corner of my eye, I thought for a second that was a formation of fighters!' chuckled Steve.

To port, Machrihanish Airfield, grey, desolate and deserted, looked almost welcoming, as we left behind the safety of land and headed seawards over a white maelstrom of surf pounding the broad beaches and breaking high on the black cliffs of the Mull of Kintyre.

The gale strengthened as we approached Islay, whipping up high angry seas, confused and turbulent, in the tidal race off the Mull of Oa. Far to the south, a huge unladen tanker pitched heavily as she battled westwards, prompting wry comments on the reliability of her engines. Shades of the *Braer*.

Safely beyond the Rhinns, Tim Bishop ordered a heading of 330 degrees, which now brought the wind abeam, and allowed us a few extra knots of ground-speed. With tar in my veins from titanic battles against Force Three breezes in my Mirror dinghy, I was curious to know how this tack would affect our speed.

'Do you benefit from winds from this quarter, Tim, and pick up speed like a yacht on a broad reach—the fastest point in sailing?'

'Not really, Doc. You can go a bit faster 'cos the wind is not directly opposing you, but the only time we get wind assistance is when it is directly behind us...' He suddenly broke off. 'Got a small object on radar... twelve miles dead ahead... might be a ship.'

Standing behind the two pilots, I could see nothing but mountainous seas merging with snow squalls, as the observer guided his pilots warily through gaps in the procession of ugly, menacing CBs thundering up from the south west. The sea state was worsening, as spindrift ripped from the crests of forty-foot waves. The windspeed was now Storm Force Ten—fifty-two knots -and rising.

God help anybody on a small coaster down there in this weather, I thought. Then my eye was drawn to a long line of white foaming surf just discernible on the horizon several miles off at ten o'clock. A tiny slim pencil with waves breaking half-way up it, rose from the centre. It was not a ship—it was Skerryvore lighthouse!

'Jeez! Look at those waves. Is Skerryvore still manned?'

'Yeah, I think so. Only two or three of them left now. It's planned to make them all automatic in the near future.'

'My partner had a casevac from Skerryvore... the summer of eighty-eight... brilliant, flat calm day. The Keeper had broken his leg and they had to manhandle him down all those stairs. I was on holiday—jealous as hell I didn't get that one!'

'Would have had a job landing you on today, Doc. Probably not for the next fortnight!'

The great skerries from which Skerryvore gets its name were totally hidden in a seething, boiling mass of heaving water, out of which great white geysers exploded high into the air, as wave upon wave impacted on submerged rock shelves. The helipad on which

Paul had landed—if it could survive such a dreadful hammering—must have been under twenty feet of water.

'Old Alan Stevenson must have been quite an engineer! Every granite stone was cut exactly to size, to within one-thirtieth of an inch before being shipped out to the skerries from Mull via Tiree. Each block weighed between two and six tons and had to be hauled onto the rocks from lighters. It took them five years to build—and there it is—still standing a hundred and fifty years on.'

A few miles beyond Skerryvore, the seas became even more horrendous, and the aircraft heaved and yawed badly in the storm. 'What's the windspeed now, Tim?' queried Steve Dow anxiously.

A mouthful of expletives emanated from aft. 'Sixty-two knots!... Force Eleven! That's about seventy-two miles an hour.'

'Well, we can't go back now—we've only twenty miles to run.'

'Shit! I don't think this Doppler's working... Light's going on and off.'

'God, that's all we need—a duff Doppler!'

'Wait. OK, Steve. Seems to have sorted itself out with a bit of switch twiddling... should get us there OK.' There was a big sigh of relief all round.

'I-spy with my little eye... Something beginning with 'W'.'

What's this, I thought... has somebody flipped?

'Waves?'

'No!'

'Windscreen?'

'No!'

'Water?'

'No!'

'Wot is it, then?'

'...White horses!'

'I-Spy something beginning with 'S'.'

'Sea?'

'No!'

'Storm?'

'No!'

'Shit in my goonsuit trousers?'

'No!'

'Speedometer?'

'Yes!'

Down below us, incongruously, flew a pair of Gannets—birds which should, by rights, have been feeding in the warm waters off the coast of Portugal at this time of year. They had probably been swept hundreds of miles northwards yesterday by the storm, and were now battling southwards against the gale, seeking shelter by gliding in the troughs between the giant waves. I hoped they would make it, as I pointed them out to the lads.

'Maybe they'd heard the price of fish has gone rock bottom off Shetland since the *Braer* sank,' came the unfeeling reply.

Tim Bishop meantime was steering us clear of some nasty CBs rushing up from the south west. 'We're alright for a while.' he reported, 'That CB seems to have passed away.'

'That's not an appropriate phrase for a SAR helo on a day like this,' he was rebuked. 'God! Look at these seas.'

Mountainous waves foamed and heaved viciously below as we shuddered in yet another squall.

'Yeah. HMS Inflatable wouldn't be much bloody use to us down there today if the gearbox went.'

'You wouldn't have far to jump though—about a hundred feet.'

'Depends whether you landed on a crest or in a trough.'

'On a day like this you wonder why they didn't send a back-up cab. If you did survive, you could be in the water for hours before anyone arrived—too late.'

'We're making better time, chaps,' the observer reported. 'ETA now down from two hours forty flying time to two hours ten.' That was encouraging.

'Imagine what it must be like on Jan Mayen Island in weather like this,' mused Tim Bishop.

'Where?' came the chorus.

'Jan Mayen Island,' repeated Tim. 'D'you mean to say you guys don't know where that is?'

'You're just a bloody spotter, Bishop. Bet you sat on a railway bridge in your short trousers, clocking trains.'

'Bet he still does.'

'For your information...' the observer continued in a superior tone of voice, ignoring the insults, 'Jan Mayen Island is four hundred miles north east of Iceland—twenty miles long by seven miles wide. I'm trying to raise an expedition to go up there. The mountains rise to seven-and-a-half thousand feet. There's a volcano, supposed to be extinct, blew in nineteen-seventy-one and reduced a five-mile long glacier to nothing in twenty-four hours. You should have Barra visual now.'

I gazed ahead to our own Jan Mayen Island. Barra lay low on the horizon beyond the mini-archipelago of Berneray, Mingulay, Pabbay and Vatersay. It was snow-covered from sea level to the twelve-hundred-foot summit of Heaval, a most exceptional occurrence, but a most welcome sight. Skimming in low over Kishmul's Castle, we circled over Castlebay and landed on the football field. Dr Heaton, a young English GP, met us by the ambulance with details of our patient Donald Manford, a middle-aged man, who had been in severe abdominal pain since 5 AM. He had been given morphine, then pethidine, and was on i/v fluids and quite comfortable when I spoke to him and apologised in advance for the rough trip he was about to experience.

'Och, but I'm used to it,' he replied. 'I'm crossing the Minch every week on the *Queen of the Hebrides*. It's no bother!'

Back on board and running short of juice, we had to detour forty miles north to Benbecula to refuel. Flying up the west coast of South Uist, the gale-lashed beaches and sodden, puddled machair were so depressingly different from the sun-drenched, sparkling silver sands and lively carpet of spring machair flowers over which Helen and I had strolled during a marvellous May holiday eighteen months previously... Memories!

At Balivanich airfield, a duff Harrier jet, rain dripping from its nose, lay disconsolately beyond the Loganair Bowser which refuelled us. With half its engine cowlings missing, it gave a distinct Hebridean impression, like the old abandoned cars lying behind every croft, of having been there a very long time. On the Uists, so the old cliché goes, there is no Gaelic word as urgent as *manyana*.

I reckoned that the combination of such a laid-back philosophy of life, coupled with traditional MoD bureaucratic inertia, would inevitably subvert even the most enthusiastic serviceman posted to Balivanich (considered an overseas posting by the RAF!), to produce, eventually, a red alert state just short of torpor.

It was a pleasant surprise, therefore, when Steve Chambers, the winchman, reappeared at the aircraft doorway carrying bag meals efficiently prepared by the Crab mess, for which he had apparently radioed ahead on our way out.

He signed a fuel chit for the Bowser driver, drew the back door shut, and we were off. Initially the flight was surprisingly stable as we headed south along the lee coast of the islands. Only the tell-tale swirl of squalls scudding across an angry simmer of grey spume-streaked wavelets hinted at what was to come.

In the lee of Hecla and Beinn Mhor, the two highest hills on South Uist, we were hit by gusts of severe turbulence from the downdraught over their tops, which sent the aircraft pitching and yawing like a yo-yo. The lads were getting tucked into their bag meals by this time. 'How are you doing, Doc? You've been very quiet back there.'

'I'm quietly enjoying not eating!' I replied with some foreboding, looking down with envy at the contented face of our casualty who was obviously on another sort of trip—flying five miles ahead of the aircraft on his pethidine and morphine. Oblivion… Lucky bugger!

'Feeling a bit iffy, then, Doc?'

I was feeling much more than a 'bit iffy'—more 'icky' than 'iffy', in fact, as I groped and grabbed for BAG, AIR SICKNESS NATO STOCK No 8105-99-130-2180. A few dry 'Hughies' and I was fine again, or at least less miserable, as we lurched back across a sixty-mile, never-ending stretch of terrifying, heaving, cruel, open sea, with no lessening of the storm. There was no back-chat now, as minds concentrated on avoiding CBs, staying on course, and getting us safely home. Trevor looked decidedly unhappy, and steadfastly refused to look out of the window at the weather. He later confessed—he doesn't like heights!

Steve Dow was trying for the short route through Crinan, but a huge build-up of black snow clouds over Mull and the Argyll hills forced him to abandon the idea. Despite all that had been said about him on the way out, wee Ted had obviously got it right after all.

'Could you give us a heading for the south west of Islay, Tim? This bloody weather is getting worse, and we'll have to go the long way round again!'

There was a sense of momentary relief when our course took us in through the narrow sound between Coll and Tiree, and the sight of land—even rocky shores pounded by huge breakers—provided at least an illusion of safety, something to cling to.

Then we were over the sea again, buffeted relentlessly on our starboard quarter by the ferocious wind for the next sixty-mile leg to the south tip of the Rhinns of Islay. Raging seas breaking over the Claddach and Portnahaven rocks, where Helen and the kids would sunbathe and watch seals on summer days, brought gasps of amazement from the two pilots and observer. Sadly, Trev and I had no window from which to share this spectacle.

'Jeez. Look at the power of those breakers! What a source of untapped energy.'

'Funny you should say that.' I broke in. 'For just north of Portnahaven, they've built an experimental wave power turbine to generate electricity for the village.'

'Is there, Doc? They should be building dozens of 'em.'

We shuddered across the mouth of Loch Indaal to the Oa, where Tim Bishop, giving his eyes a rest from his radar screen, latched on to its towering seacliffs as a future rock-climbing venue. Then we were over open sea again, but with a difference. For the first time, we seemed to be making progress; the wind was swinging behind us, and we were now rapidly picking up speed.

As we zoomed in low over Machrihanish, it was a tremendous relief to be over dry land again. The observer must have felt it too, having endured the same back-seat purgatory as Trevor and myself—bent over his radar for hours on end—just like we were, bent over our patient. He quit his seat and went forard for a breather. Pilots, like car drivers, are in total control of their element, and always have the best of it. It's the poor back-seat sods like ourselves who always get car-sick, whether on bumpy undulating roads, or in bumpy undulating helicopters.

Lucky for Tim, Trev and I were still stuck in the back, but with the wind now astern and the turbulence gone, it was quite comfortable, as was our patient, his pain banished and still sound asleep in the arms of Morpheus. Subsequently, Donald's symptoms settled completely in hospital, and following investigations, he went back home to Barra four days later.

I glanced out of the starboard window. The sea below was flashing past at a rate of knots as Steve Dow put the foot down for home with great gusto. 'What a flying machine!' he crowed. 'Look at this bird go! We must be doing a hundred and fifty K!' I looked over to the dials above the abandoned radar console.

'A hundred and sixty two, actually!' I confirmed.

'Well done, Doc. He knows where the GSI speedo is.'

Fiona was in sick bay next morning when Trevor and I related our experiences, and mentioned that Steve Dow the pilot had said it had been the worst weather he'd ever flown in. She was unimpressed, and coolly put us down with the quiet observation that in her SAR to Islay during the night, just prior to ours, they had flown out to Campbeltown at forty knots—and came back at one hundred and seventy. Trust a woman!

5

22nd January 1993

COLL AGAIN

En route back to Cathcart Street after visits, I dropped in at the house to pick up some casenotes from my study, reckoning I would have a spare half-hour in which to finish off dictating a back-log of referral letters before the start of my afternoon surgery at half-past two. Inevitably, as I put the key in the door, the bleep sounded—and I cursed both the timing and the inconvenience.

Only this morning I had been discussing the SAR callout rate with the POMA and staff at *Gannet*. Although it was still only the 22nd of January, they'd had an unbelievable thirteen callouts since the New Year, and this was my fourth one in a month—after six months of feeling totally ignored and neglected.

Despite getting the Ops Officer, Lt Cdr Bob Faulks, himself, on the telephone, it was, as usual, only the bare minimum of info which had been supplied by RCC. 'All we've got, Jimmy, is that a very ill patient on Coll has to be transferred to Glasgow. How long will it take you to get in?'

'About ten minutes, Bob.' I replied unthinkingly, then spent an apprehensive ten minutes racing up the bypass, wondering all the time if the engine would seize—and should I really be pushing ninety miles an hour in a new Cavalier, with only 200 miles on the clock.

The tall gangling figure of Gerry Flannery loomed in the locker room doorway as I rapidly changed. 'How's it goin' then, Doc?' His friendly Cumbrian voice greeted me above the roar of the waiting Sea

King. 'Can I do owt for ye?' Gerry was a reassuring bloke to have around on the end of a winch—never rushed, never flustered.

'Aye, could you fetch me a lifejacket from the line, Gerry?' He duly obliged, as I slipped the rubber neck seal of the goon suit over my head, pulling out a few more precious hairs in the process. 'At this rate I'll soon be as bald as you, Gerry, and you twenty years younger than me!'

'Ah, but in my case it's the virility does it, Doc! Sorry to get you out. We tried RCC to see if we could go with the MA alone, but they wanted a doc. They didn't have much info on the patient, except it's a seriously ill elderly male needing medevaced to Glasgow.'

'Thanks. I got as much from the OPSO. Not much to go on.'

It was the same crew as on the Barra trip, with Steve Dow as Captain, co-pilot Chris Reece, now left the Navy and flying commercially with Air UK, doing his annual three-weeks flying stint as a Royal Navy Reserve officer, Tim Bishop as observer, Gerry replacing Steve Chambers, and Trevor as duty MA.

As we flew up the Clyde, it wasn't difficult to see why we had been tasked for this job. A weather front was moving in from Ireland, preceded by sea fog and low stratus cloud with a ceiling of two hundred feet. Under these conditions it would have been impossible for the fixed-wing air ambulance to fly into Coll—and no doubt we'd find the airstrip waterlogged and unserviceable as well, after all the rain there had been in January.

In any case, as from the first of April, we had been led to understand from certain quarters, it would all be academic. There would be no fixed-wing Islander air ambulance; for Loganair had lost the contract to Bond Helicopters, who would be flying a Bolkow 105 helicopter, based across the runway from us at Prestwick Airport, as part of a nationwide integrated air ambulance service being set up by the Scottish Ambulance Service. It seemed SAR aircraft would no longer be required.

The scheme had been widely publicised in the national press by the Scottish Ambulance Service's general manager Andrew Freemantle, as being 'about to provide a high quality medical service for emergency cases on islands such as Arran, where in the past, there has been no emergency helicopter service'! In addition, he had brashly announced that 'for islands like Barra, where fixed-wing aircraft were dependent on tides, the new service could mean several hours being saved in taking a patient to hospital.' And also that, 'if one aircraft is deployed elsewhere, then the Ambulance Air Desk based in Aberdeen will be able to identify a back-up aircraft to be deployed or, *if absolutely necessary*, alert the MoD or Coastguard aircraft if we cannot provide one of our own.'

What had stuck in the craws of the SAR crews and the command at *Gannet*, was the fact that for twenty years, Navy Sea Kings *had* been providing a vital emergency helicopter service to Arran, Barra—and every island in between—and this had been patently and politically ignored by the ambulance hierarchy in the interests of promoting their own new service to maximum advantage. We well knew that only half the story was being told to the press.

At £2500 an hour for a Sea King, compared with £250 an hour for the small Bolkow 105, it was perfectly natural for the Ambulance Service to try and maximise the savings they might make using their own smaller and more economical aircraft. They had apparently calculated a saving of £500,000 or more on their budget, if they could do away with using MoD aircraft on medevacs.

However, what they had failed to do, for all their in depth consultations with various aviation experts, was simply to speak to RCC, RAF Lossie, or HMS *Gannet*, and find out just what kind of medevacs SAR crews had been in the habit of doing over the past twelve months; how many they had done, whether by day or by night, and in what weather conditions. It was unbelievable that they failed to carry out such basic market research—or simply convenient—if they already knew the likely outcome! For if they had done this research, they would inevitably have found their prospective savings slashed to the extent of the project not being deemed financially viable by the Scottish Office, and seen their proposals for an integrated air ambulance service well and truly scuppered. Furthermore, it had not been mentioned, in the initial fanfare of publicity, that the little Bolkow would only be flying Monday to Friday, eight to four—and that it had no radar and could only fly visual—i.e. in daylight, in good weather conditions, and not in foul weather, icy conditions or fog!

Initially we had all felt a bit threatened by this out-of-the-blue announcement, but when John Gregg and myself sat down and analysed our last forty medevacs, it only confirmed what we already knew—that *no more than ten out of the forty* could have been undertaken by a Bolkow 105! The vast majority of medevacs had been after dark, or in foul weather or fog. We would still be needed, a lot more often than *'if absolutely necessary'*—and this might come as an unwelcome surprise to the general manager of the Scottish Ambulance Service!

'There was absolutely no chance of a Bolkow getting off the ground, far less getting anywhere near Barra last week... but do you think they could have done this one, Steve?' I asked the pilot as we climbed through the fog and cloud to level out at 4500 feet. Beneath us lay an immense quilt of fleecy white cloud, tucked into the rim of the horizon in all directions.

'No chance! You need radar both for the heading, and for getting back down below this cloud without hitting a mountain.'

As if to emphasise the point, Tim Bishop informed us we were just passing over the Paps of Jura. But shortly afterwards, a bit of luck proved Steve wrong on the second count. A strange dark patch, far ahead, standing out like a crow in a snowdrift, turned out to be a small hole in the cloud just over the Ross of Mull. 'This is too good to miss, lads! I'm going down the shaft. Ears OK?'

We spiralled down in a rapid descent to a beautiful sight. Below us lay the scattered white crofts of Bunessan, and away to our left—Iona, fringed by silver sands edging into an aquamarine sea which sparkled the length of Loch Scridain.

As we flew north west over Staffa and the Dutchman's Cap, Tiree and Coll were clearly visible; and just beyond them, the northernmost edge of the weather front gave way to clear blue skies. Maybe because blue skies are such a rare occurrence on SARs, the crew began to wax lyrical on the magnificence of the view. Beyond the hills of Rum, low on the horizon, lay the jagged Cuillins of Skye, extending south-eastwards in an unbroken crescent of gleaming snow-dusted mountains, linked over a hidden Sound of Sleat, to the hills of Knoydart, Morar and Moidart.

It was a pity we had work to do! I had been annoyed about the dearth of information regarding our casualty, and had asked Gerry to contact RCC for an update. To my amazement, the reply came back—'Sorry, we've no update'—end of story! Not even an offer to try and get some more details. In frustration, Gerry called up Oban Coastguard. In seconds, they had contacted the Coll Auxiliary Coastguard, who was with the patient at the landing site, and who was able to tell us direct that we were about to take on board a very frail, elderly man with severe vomiting and dehydration. Why couldn't we have had this information an hour ago? And why could this patient not go to the West Highland Hospital in Oban? With his dehydration, and bad weather to the south, this might be a better option.

On putting this suggestion to RCC, the controller got a bit snotty with Gerry and informed him that Oban Coastguard were not supposed to be participating in this operation, and that 'your task is to take this patient to Glasgow.' Full stop! No reason given why it had to be Glasgow.

We said we would make our own medical assessment on the ground.

'The quicker we land the better!' moaned Gerry. 'I'm desperate for a pee!'

'Tough luck, Gerry! You've no chance with all these douce Presbyterian, decent-living, middle-aged ladies watching your every move out of their car windows!' Gerry swore and crossed his legs.

There were two cars by the landing strip, one with the old man in it, being attended to by the district nurse in her blue uniform. An elderly man and woman stood by the other—probably relatives, I thought, as I quizzed the nurse for details.

Yes, the old chap was being sick... he had a chronic bowel problem... he was also badly dehydrated, and had to go the Western, where he had previously been treated. There were two letters to go with him. No, he is not dripped, but is very weak.

'Maybe we'd better put a saline drip up on him, if he's as weak and dehydrated as you say.' I tentatively offered. 'We've come through some foul weather, and it's a long way to Glasgow.'

Then I looked at his veins—threadlike in the bitter cold wind. I backtracked rapidly. It would be too difficult, and I would probably ruin the chances of the young hospital JHO getting a line in. Despite his pallor, his pulse was still quite strong and fairly slow, so the obvious course would be to simply wrap him up snug and warm in an insulation blanket for the duration of the journey, and forget the drip.

Gently manhandling him out of the car, we made sure he was well cocooned before stretchering him on to the aircraft. Once on board I propped him up to help his breathing, and for good measure gave him some oxygen via a jury-rigged Venturi mask, after discovering to my annoyance that certain connectors were incompatible, and that one of the face masks was missing from the small oxygen cylinder carried in the backpack for mountain rescues.

Meanwhile, the weather had improved considerably, and after passing through Corrievreckan, we were able to climb to 1500 feet and fly directly over Crinan, Loch Fyne and Loch Striven to Glasgow.

At the debrief, I had a few pointed remarks to make (again!) on trying to improve this all-too-frequent poor communication between island doctors and RCC, and between RCC and the SAR aircraft. I also spelt out to my medics, in no uncertain terms, the importance of being more thorough with their weekly equipment checks; to make sure that, as far as humanly possible, we would always have the proper gear, in the proper order, to deal properly with any casualty. After all, just as we relied on meticulous aircraft checks by Flight Maintainers for our safe passage—likewise our patients depended on our thoroughness for theirs.

6

12th/19th February 1993

TO ARRAN... AND BACK

Sod's Law again! The raging tracheitis just starting to roast the back of my throat the night before I was due to deliver the Immortal Memory at Ayr Burns Club, had fortunately simmered long enough to let me complete that particular engagement without losing my voice. Which would have been fine... if I hadn't had still another brace of Immortal Memories to deliver on consecutive evenings... if we hadn't just reached a critical stage in the redevelopment of our surgery, which meant me going in to supervise structural work for several hours every Saturday and Sunday... and if Faither hadn't arranged—at the end of all that lot—to have his hip-joint replacement done this very morning in Ayr Hospital.

It takes a lot to keep me off a curling rink, but on Monday night past, after struggling through the previous week, I had felt so physically knackered that I called off my Gangrels Club game, with the aim of conserving what little energy I had left for today's big competition, curling for Ayr Rotary Club in the area playdowns for Scottish Rotary's National Ramshead Trophy. We had played two hard, keen games, made all the harder for me, having to sweep the ice myself for the first time this year—after a cushy season as a Skip standing all night at the head of the rink yelling at my sweepers to brush till their arms dropped off. Worried about Faither, I telephoned the hospital between games for news of his operation.

After curling, I went up to visit him. The operation had been a success, but he was still deeply sedated, and out like a light. I sat with him for a while, then gave his hand a wee squeeze and left him, snoring peacefully. There was a public meeting I had promised to attend at Alloway School, about proposals to establish a Burns National Heritage Park linking Burns's Cottage to the Visitor Centre and Burns Monument. As past President of Alloway Burns Club, and heavily involved in a campaign to preserve the adjacent seventeen acres of open agricultural ground from housing speculators, I had an obligation to be there.

Typically, the meeting dragged on till ten o'clock, by which time I was half asleep and wishing I was home, snug in bed, and snoring like Faither. Consoled by the knowledge that Scott had taken the bleep for the day, I lost no time in sliding between the sheets.

Totally zonked out when the phone went at 0130, I awoke disorientated, trying to unscramble a dozey brain to fathom out whether or not I was on call for the practice. I groped for the phone.

'John Gregg here, Doc… We've got a job on. I don't know where it is… Can you come in?'

Helen awoke, tired, angry and swearing. 'Oh shit! Not again!' she screamed. 'It's not bloody fair.' She beat her fists on the pillow in despair. 'It'll be another bloody waste of time. What rubbish is it this time? You're not bloody Superman! You're dead tired. Why can't someone else go?'

I secretly agreed with every word she said, but it would have been a bit off to ring Scott now and ask him to go, while I snuggled down again in my warm bed. If only John Gregg had followed the bloody protocol and used the bleep first! But my throat had settled, and I knew my ears would clear easily and cause no problems in flight, so I quietly mollified Helen, gently observing that it was a lovely still night, not a Force Eleven, and promised to phone from *Gannet* if it was going to be a long trip.

The roads were clear, and visibility was heightened by the town lights reflected off low stratus cloud. Chief POACMN David 'Wally' Wallace was still in the locker room when I arrived. A bit of a legend in Fleet Air Arm Circles, he had recently arrived at *Gannet* after many years as a SAR aircrewman at Culdrose, where he had collected numerous commendations—plus a George Medal, awarded after a remarkable exploit in a Force Ten gale, when he and a colleague winched forty crewmen to safety from a crippled Pakistani freighter, then jumped ninety feet from its stern as it sank under them. He had a formidable reputation, and I made damn sure this time that my legs didn't end up in the arms of my flying suit!

John Gregg popped his head round the door, and listened with a smug grin on his face, as the Chief gave me a heads-up on the SAR. 'It's just a short one to Arran, Doc, for a woman with abdominal pain… but RCC want a doctor. We've dropped the POMA. There's no need for him if you are going, and there will probably be a nurse travelling at the other end. We've got a weight problem as well… two observers on board. It's Lt Ronson's first SAR, and he's not familiar with the routine. 'Kiwi'—Lt Stephenson—is the pilot. Are you ready?' With that, he led me at a brisk trot out to the aircraft! After my two curling games, I was surprised to find I still had enough strength left to jump in the back!

Flight-wise, it was a straightforward trip across to Arran—till I went to look for the key for the controlled drugs, the satchel containing them, and the insulated box containing the i/v fluids. Chief Wallace hadn't seen them. Had John forgotten to stow them onboard? No panic. At least we still had enough i/v fluids in the grab bag, if needed.

Guided in by the new observer, we landed on safely at Knockenkelly, only to have to hang around for fifteen minutes for the ambulance to arrive. In the back was a young-looking fair-haired lass attending to an elderly lady in her early seventies, beside whom sat her husband holding her hand. Clutching X-rays and a referral envelope, the young nurse leaned forward and gave me a superbly efficient and professional briefing. The lady had a high bowel obstruction and had been vomiting frequently in the ambulance. She was on her third unit of saline, and had just had 75mg of pethidine plus 25mg of sparine intramuscularly.

When Wally poked his head round the door and presumptuously asked if she was coming too, she smiled, shook her head, and said she was on call. Only then did it click with both of us that this was no wee nurse, but the young Consultant Surgeon, Wendy Buswell, from Arran War Memorial Hospital! A sign of age when… !

There was an awkward delay after we lifted the patient from the ambulance stretcher onto the litter, as the new observer struggled with the safety straps, which were too tight and wouldn't connect up. Wally had gone back to the aircraft for something, and because I was holding the drip set, I could not give him a hand to adjust the buckles.

A small voice, barely heard above the roar of the Sea King, rose from the depths of the blankets, 'I'm bleeding!' In the darkness, I looked down aghast, to see fresh blood around her face as she moved an equally bloody hand. Shit! I thought. I hope she's not going to have a major haematemesis in the middle of this football field. Then I looked closer and sighed with relief. Her drip had come adrift, and blood was flowing out of the open end of the cannula at her wrist, which she had obviously, and unknowingly, wiped across her mouth. The giving set had been poorly secured at the hospital, and I quickly re-inserted it and bound it with tape. The observer was still 'fouterin aboot' with the strapping, and I was becoming increasingly concerned about hypothermia and the effect of a bitterly cold night on such an ill patient. 'Get her on board quick, and we'll sort it out there!' I shouted above the din, just as Wally arrived back with a survival suit for her husband, and deftly sorted out the strap problem.

Rather than use our cold Hartmann's solution, I borrowed a warmer unit of saline from the ambulancemen, and put it up once we had her onboard, tying it to the roof frame with a long boot lace which I always carry. Fortunately her drip was none the worse of its mishap, and ran quite freely during the ten minute trip across to Crosshouse. Mrs Moncrieff's symptoms settled after a week in hospital, and happily without any need for surgery.

Over a coffee at the debriefing, I quietly and diplomatically outlined to Chief Wallace my preference—and the benefits to the patient of better access and blood pressure control—of having her loaded with her head towards the body of the aircraft, not towards the tail as in this instance.

'I take the point, Doc. That was a good idea having a cord in your pocket to tie up the drip fluids.'

'Aye. But it's an awful bother sometimes trying to find a place to tie it on to.'

'I think I could rig up a small hook to slip over one of these tubular roof supports. Then it would be easy just to loop the cord over it, and save fumbling with knots.'

Every little improvement helps, I thought. At least we both seemed to be on the same wavelength, which was always a good start for a working relationship.

'Well, that's another job the Bolkow couldn't have done!' Kiwi remarked. 'I wonder how it will affect our long term SAR callouts?'

'If it's anything like the Cornwall Air Ambulance,' chipped in Wally, 'we'll have an increased workload. For when I was at Culdrose, folk got so used to phoning for the air ambulance, that we finished up doing more SARs than less.'

With that ominous prophecy ringing in my ears, I retired to bed. A SAR in the 'wee sma oors' of a Friday morning is hardly the best way to herald in a weekend on call!

Winter weekends are invariably busy. Babies get snuffly colds, mothers get panicky. Toddlers get sore ears, mothers get panicky. Alcoholics get drunk, depressed and need dried out; schizophrenics get paranoid and need help; and old folk simply die. Teenage daughters, with teenage friends running up teenage bills on their parents' phones, and octogerarian cronies of an octogenerian Faither in hospital, combined forces to generate a veritable phone-in. In short, the bloody thing never stopped ringing.

Early Sunday evening, it rang yet again. I cursed.

'It's LMA Scott here, sir… in sick bay. Has your bleep gone off?'

'No!'—I replied, then looked down at my belt with some embarrassment as I discovered the switch had been knocked to the OFF position. 'No, ehm…' a shade defensively, 'why?'

'There just seems to be a problem with some of them not working today. Mine didn't go off a couple of hours ago, and I was left behind when they went off on a SAR.'

Trevor was a solemn-faced, serious, methodical Welsh lad with deep soulful eyes, who always did everything by the book. With

Trevor, big problems would frequently materialise where only small ones were apparent to everyone else.

'If you ask me,' he intoned darkly, 'they are going to have problems! I've made inquiries. They've been tasked to pick up two climbers, one with serious head injuries... and I don't think they'll manage!' I was inclined to agree with him. Going off without the MA was a bit foolhardy, and was an event which had not occurred for a couple of years—since the time, after a similar incident, we had made pointed representations to the SARO about the dangers of aircrew being confronted with medical emergencies outwith their capabilities.

'And they're not short of problems here at *Gannet* either!' he confided, his toneless voice tailing off expectantly, a mannerism which I knew was meant to extract from me the question, 'Why?' I duly obliged.

'Because the SAR shack is burned out!' he triumphed. Trevor also had a sense of humour.

'What!' I exclaimed incredulously.

'The SAR shack is gutted! The fire brigade have been here for hours. The place is still full of smoke and running with water.'

'What happened?'

'Some silly bugger left a chip-pan on the stove when they went off on the SAR!'

'Oh, not the old chip-pan fire scenario,' I groaned in despair.

'Yeah, and I've lost all my kit—bergen, goon suit, flying helmet—the lot.'

'That's over a thousand quid's worth down the drain, just for your stuff—and there must be several other guys' kits as well... and the control console, and the computer, and video!'

'Yeah... and our defibrillator has probably gone as well.'

'You're joking!' We had just recently purchased a brand new HeartStart 3000 defibrillator for monitoring patients' condition inflight, and for treating cardiac arrests which might occur at a locus, or on the base itself. If the SAR crew had only waited for Trevor, the defib would have gone with him on the flight—and saved us six and a half grand. And by the same token, during those few minutes spent waiting for him, they would have remembered to switch off the bloody chip-pan—and saved the cost of the portacabin into the bargain!

'What's happening to the SAR crew?' I asked, trying hard to force a serious concern for their operational role to suppress that darker side of the human persona, that gloating, wicked sense of humour which tends to surface in us all, on hearing that someone else has landed neck-deep in the shit. 'Is *Gannet* still operational? And what about your own kit? Do you want me to cover?'

'Dunno, sir. The SAR crew hasn't come back yet.'

'They're probably heading for political asylum in Libya right now.'

After Trevor rang off, I contacted *Gannet* to check if the SAR flight was still operational, and was asking the duty rating to do a bleep check, when Jim Fergusson, the XO, came on the phone.

'Heard what's happened, Jimmy? The SAR shack's a bloody shambles... a right bourach. Chip-pan! I'll bloody chip-pan 'em!'

I could sense shit about to hit the rotors!

'What's going to happen SAR-wise?' I asked. 'I believe my kit in the locker room below the SAR shack is still OK, though it's probably stinking of smoke. Will they want me to stand in for the LMA?'

'No. That's all been taken care of. LMA Scott is up at the SE section just now, being kitted out with a spare rig.'

I relaxed. There was enough to contend with over the weekend without being first on call for *Gannet* as well.

About eight-thirty, the bleep went off. 'They've taken long enough to get round to testing this!' I remarked jocularly to Helen as I lifted the phone, while at the same time dreading her response if it was a callout.

'PO Wren here, Doc.' It was Nia Jones, who was in charge of ops room. 'Can you come in? There's a job on.'

'What is it this time... and where?' I groaned audibly.

'It's a climber with a bad head injury, in the Grampians.'

'The Grampians!' I exclaimed incredulously. 'That's well off our patch... what's happened to the Lossie Crabs?'

'Can't tell you any more, Doc. Shall I tell them you'll be in?'

Burdening poor Helen with the thankless task of phoning round for someone to cover the practice, I set off. It was a typically hellish night, with low stratus cloud and gale-driven rain from the north west, as I drew up outside the SAR shack. The portacabin was in a real sorry state, smoke blackened, its windows shattered and blown out by the scorching heat. Although the locker room portacabin was stacked directly underneath, being totally self-contained it had escaped fire and water damage, and luckily my goonsuit was not even tainted by the smoke.

Hurrying over to the line cabin to pick up my life-jacket, I noticed something strange. Instead of revving furiously to make me get a jildi on, the Sea King, for once, was sitting silently on the tarmac. I crossed the apron and was signalled out to the aircraft by a wave from the marshall's fluorescent baton. At first I thought there was no one else on board. Then, as my eyes grew accustomed to the gloom, the silhouette of the co-pilot materialised in the left-hand seat as he prepared to flash up the aircraft. Trevor was there too, sitting motionless in the corner behind the right-hand seat, almost hidden in the darkness. I plugged into the winchman's extended intercom cable, and sat down beside him. It was duff. I could hear nothing.

I motioned to Trevor, and he handed me his extension cable. I plugged in again—just in time to hear a burst of expletives from the co-pilot as he turned round and muttered, 'Cancelled!'

Back in OPs Room we got more details. Nia Jones's Welsh grasp of Scottish geography was well wide of the mark. The SAR had been to a climber on Ben Lui, south west of Tyndrum in Argyll, not the far Grampians. It was only an hour's flying time to the locus, but the mountain rescue team were apparently now well down the hillside, and reckoned it would be just as quick taking him to hospital by ambulance.

Thwarted again! I had now done over thirty SARs, and had yet to be involved in a mountain job. Ah well, back to the weekend on-call grind.

The following week was just as bad—a Monday afternoon site meeting with the builder, and then my first night off after a weekend on-call was commandeered by a practice meeting on the intricacies of fundholding, which dragged on till after eleven o'clock. Tuesday was its usual horrendous test of stamina and self control. Ten hours of unremitting pressure with only a quarter-hour break for a quick lunchtime sandwich. Home at six-thirty for an equally quick tea; then up to Ayr Hospital to visit Faither who, happily, was making great progress despite being subjected to the whims and vagaries of modern, improved, 'personal named nurse' care. For six days no one had bothered to ask if his bowels had moved! He made even greater progress after I took him to the loo myself.

Wednesday was my half-day, but any chance I might have had of resting up was stymied by a longstanding engagement to give a SAR talk to the ladies of Castlehill Church Guild. One of the doubtful spin-offs of being involved in great deeds of derring-do, was to be inundated with speaking invitations by club secretaries desperate to fill their winter syllabuses. While I enjoyed it, I had to limit myself—on Helen's orders—to five or six each winter, to preserve some of our precious free time. The Guild ladies enjoyed the talk, but their questions left me in no doubt where their sympathies lay—very much with Helen!

By Thursday night, a carbon copy of Tuesday's hassle, my stress level was rising as quickly as the barometric pressure outside was dropping. I was exhausted when I crawled into bed, almost oblivious to the sound of a rising gale blasting against the windows.

Almost to the minute, as if in a nightmare re-run of last Thursday's episode, at one o'clock, the bleep went. Helen was in tears of despair. 'You can't go!' she sobbed, and clung to me. 'You can't go in this weather! Listen to that gale. Don't go! Please! Get somebody else!' And then as I rose to get dressed, she got more and more angry 'It's time you gave this bloody nonsense up! It's not fair!'

I felt hellish, very guilty, and more than a little conscience-stricken, as I mouthed the usual platitudes… sorry, love, but I have to go—it's only a short trip—the wind is not so bad now… and left the bedroom.

For the first time ever, Helen didn't follow me downstairs. I pulled my bunny suit over my pyjamas, just as if I was going out on a night visit, donned my flying overalls, and closed the storm door quietly behind me.

Trevor met me at the gate, and handed me the drug satchel.

'It's a ten day-old baby with a hernia, on Arran. RCC wanted a doctor, and there is a spare observer on the Sea King, so I'm not going.'

On our approach to Knockenkelly, I had just finished checking the suction equipment, when we hit severe turbulence from the down-draught of a fierce north westerly sweeping over the heights of Mullach Mor on Holy Isle. Below us, in its lee, flickered the swaying riding lights of a small ship sheltering from the gale.

A young curly-haired girl was sitting in the ambulance, holding a peaceful wee bundle in her arms. There seemed little or nothing for me to do. Dr Malcolm Kerr, the local GP, was with her. I probed diplomatically to see if it was he who had requested a doctor.

'Yes. I know there is probably not much you can do, but the baby has an incarcerated scrotal hernia, and although he's not vomiting yet, I was worried about the risk of inhalation of vomitus during the flight. I was prepared to come across myself, but didn't want to get stranded on the mainland tomorrow by the gale. I spoke to the duty surgeon, and he suggested calling in the Navy doctor.' At least I knew it wasn't RCC this time!

We had flown out at fifty knots against a forty-two knot wind, and had the advantage of fifty-five knot gusts to blow us back to Crosshouse in ten minutes.

In my arms, the baby was sleeping soundly. What a nice short uneventful trip, I thought—just as Wally heaved the back door wide open and Bruce Morrison put the Sea King into a tight right-hand turn prior to landing. Strapped in my seat, aghast, I was looking straight down at ground rushing past two hundred feet below—and holding someone else's precious, but unstrapped baby!

I clung on to him like grim death. Macabre newspaper headlines flashed through my mind. Doctors have been known to drop babies—but never from two hundred feet! I shuddered as I recalled several 'near misses' as a medical student. The dreadful panic passed in seconds as the pilot trimmed the aircraft and we floated in to land as gentle as thistledown. I've never been more relieved than I was at that moment—handing back one blissfully unaware baby, to its blissfully unaware Mum!

7

18th/24th June 1993

SUNSHINE SARS

I have to confess it—SARs can be a wee bit addictive. The sudden gulp of anticipation as the bleep goes... the initial surge of excitement... the doubts, the apprehension... what's the job? Will I cope? The inflight buzz as the adrenalin flows—sometimes brown! Followed by the quiet relaxed pleasure and satisfaction of a safe patient transfer... And the final let-down of returning to base.

Then, after a while come the withdrawal symptoms—and cravings... everyone else is having SARs! Why can't I have one? Wee huffy feelings of being sidelined and neglected.

That's how it was around mid-June. It seemed a long, long time since the bustle and excitement of January and February, but things had been hotting up—for some! Craig had been to Arran; and during the following week, on the night before I was due to fly down to Portsmouth on an Aviation Medicine course—I had passed the bleep over to Scott, since I was on call for two practices. I don't know who got the worst of the bargain, for I had five night visits plus another three middle-of-the-night phone calls—and Scott landed another SAR to Arran.

A few days after my return from Pompey, Arran featured yet again—this time on a bright sunny Friday afternoon. It was only 1530 when Trevor phoned the surgery. Could I come in? There was an elderly man on Arran with a heart attack and appendicitis, and a doctor had been requested to escort him to Crosshouse.

A sunshine SAR! I'd never done one. And I'd as far back as I could remember, I had never been on Arran on a sunny day, even on holiday, so the chance was too good to miss. The eight-to-five air ambulance had obviously been tasked to another job.

As we flew in to Knockenkelly, Arran was at its most beautiful. Gleaming in the brilliant afternoon sunshine, small whitewashed cottages advertised their presence—some neatly lined along village streets, others sprinkled casually over green hillsides, or secluded in far, lonely glens. A prolonged north-westerly airstream had been pushing down pure Arctic air of such clarity that almost every boulder could be picked out on Goatfell and the distant jagged spine of the A Chir ridge. Brilliant!

Our patient was a cheerful, fresh-faced, seventy-year-old English holiday-maker, who had taken ill during the night in his camper van with severe stomach pains. He had stoically endured overnight before seeking medical help, and had been just as surprised as the doctors who admitted him to the cottage hospital, when they diagnosed a myocardial infarct as well as his appendicitis. This combination of illnesses was just too risky for the Arran War Memorial to handle with safety, hence the transfer to Crosshouse—which was smooth and uneventful—as was his subsequent appendicectomy.

That's more than could be said for the next seven days in the run-up to our long awaited 'holiday' to Norway and Denmark, with myself as 'team doctor' and Helen as 'team nurse' to the talented youngsters of the Ayrshire Fiddle Orchestra on their Viking Tour.

Hunched over a study floor littered with antibiotics, antihistamines, aspirins, elastoplasts, and even a portable nebuliser, the prospects of a quiet holiday were looking bleaker by the minute, as I spent Sunday morning busily assembling a medical kit for all eventualities—based on a check list sent in by the parents. Out of fifty-four kids, twenty (including our Fiona) had asthma or hay fever; another ten had various allergies, and six were 'veggies'! And here we were, Denmark-bound, in the middle of the silage season.

A call from Ambulance Control to attend a three car pile-up on the coast road at Dunure, disrupted my preparations. Luckily most of the casualties were only slightly injured, but the female driver of one of the cars was trapped by the foot, and had an open tibial fracture. The added complication of her being thirty weeks pregnant made extrication a wee bit tricky, but with the use of Entonox and a spinal board, we eventually managed.

That was the start of a week of typical pre-holiday clear-the-desk pressure, culminating on Thursday morning with an eight-thirty start at *Gannet* where, on top of a heap of fresh cases, the MAs had booked in three aircrew medicals. And to add insult to injury, John Gregg popped his head round the door mid-morning to tell me that the leading Reggie had given him a heads-up that the Jossman was looking for an urgent release medical on a pathetic, immature young deserter, who had just surrendered to the Master-at-Arms office after three months AWOL, and who was due to appear after lunch at the Captain's Table, prior to being drummed out of the Brownies—SNLR—Services No Longer Required.

'Could I have a word with you later, Sir?' he added ominously. 'We've got some problems!'

'Problems! You think you've got problems! Look at this bloody list of medicals I've got to get through… and all the bloody practice problems waiting for me this afternoon!' I checked my ranting and moaning. 'Better let me have it just now, John, I probably won't have time later… what's the problem?'

'Trevor has had a lot of bad SARs recently, Sir, and he's getting a bit twitched… like that bleeding ulcer last week, when he wasn't given enough information to call in a doctor, and had to cope himself… and you know there have been other cases.'

I knew only too well. 'I think it's time for a letter to the Medical Director of the Ambulance Service. Most of these medevac calls are now coming via the Scottish Ambuluance Air Desk in Aberdeen, and by the time they've passed through RCC, the SAR Cell, and then on to the medics, we're back to the old "Send three-and-fourpence" nonsense. I reckon if they could just fax the original Air Desk form, the problem would be solved.'

'And we've another problem, Sir.' John was sounding more like Trevor and the chip pan fire with every utterance, but with less to laugh about. 'We are not getting the Propaq monitor.'

'What!'

'That's right. I spoke to WO Kelly. He said it's not a standard piece of Navy kit and FONAC won't allow it!'

I couldn't believe my ears. The Propaq monitor was a first-class electronic monitor. Rugged and compact, it could measure pulse, BP, ECG, respiratory rate, and capillary oxygen. It was widely used in hospitals, had been used on the Sea King during a number of recent inter-hospital transfers, and was in fact, standard equipment on board the air ambulance Bolkow 105s.

For the past seven years my sole means of monitoring a patient had been to find a pulse, hold one finger on it for the duration of the flight, and keep the others crossed! Now, when we had the chance of a proven, purpose-built piece of kit to accurately monitor vital signs, Navy bureaucracy said we couldn't have it. I was furious.

Late or not for my practice work, I had to get a letter off to the Surgeon Captain at FONAC. I pointed out that we had a unique SAR role at *Gannet*, with so many of our medevacs from remote islands, and just how difficult it was to supervise these patients with inadequate equipment. The air ambulances, for whom we had to stand in so frequently, had a HeartStart 3000 defibrillator and Propaq as standard kit, and I felt we should have the same equipment. And on his point regarding 'standard Navy equipment'—most of the medical gear that I had begged, borrowed, purloined, and scraped together over the past six years to upgrade the *Gannet* Sea King had not been standard Navy equipment either—otherwise we would still be back in the Dark Ages, relying on their old, primitive, bog-standard ship's doctor's white box and one oxygen cylinder!

By the time I had these two letters written, I was away behind schedule. There was no chance of getting home for lunch, so to save time, I popped up to the wardroom for a quick omelette.

'How's it going, then, Jimmy? Keeping you busy?' Behind me, defiant fag in hand, grinned Jim Fergusson the XO.

'Too bloody right!' I grumbled. 'Four bloody medicals this morning—thanks to the Captain's Table.'

'Never mind, think of all the extra money!'

'Extra money! The way you lot pay me, the last two I did for nothing. Not only that, but FONAC have turned down our request for a Propaq.'

His grin went. 'Can't have! They spoke to me yesterday and gave me the go-ahead.'

'Check with the POMA.' I looked at my watch and left to cram in four visits before the afternoon surgery, which was fully booked. At four o'clock, I was interrupted by an urgent phone call from *Gannet*. It was Fiona to tell me that I was needed on a medevac from Tiree to Glasgow.

Anticipating problems on the bypass, which was suffering from severe cone disease, I green-lighted it through Prestwick. Gerry Flannery was in the locker room to help me into my flying suit. 'What is it this time, Gerry?'

'Heart attack on Tiree, Doc.'

'Male or female?'

'Dunno, Doc.'

Gerry wasn't flying. The aircrewman was a new lad by the name of Rowlinson, who used our flight up the Clyde, in beautiful clear visibility, as a navex to get his bearings. The rest of us just enjoyed the view of Loch Fyne, and the sight of red deer and a flock of wild goats on a rocky hillside above the impressive ruins of Castle Sween.

From the back came a curse, as Steve Barclay, the observer, who had been enthusiastically taking photographs through the port window, discovered he had no spool in his camera!

'And you passed his aircrew medical, Doc? Can't trust bloody observers!'

'And is that why you had all the maps out coming up the Clyde? Do you lot not even trust his radar on a clear day?'

Visual flying on a clear day in the Western Isles is an absolute delight. As we passed over the long island of Luing, then Bunessan on Mull, Niall 'Kiwi' Stephenson turned round in his pilot's seat and grinned. 'Ever been to Staffa, Doc?'

'Only in the passing,' I replied ruefully, 'and in foul weather. There was a POACMN—McDougall I think his name was—who had visited it once, and he pointed out to us where the caves were.'

'We'll do better than that. What do you say we fly right into the big cave, boys… and out the other side?'

'Better watch your tail rotor, Kiwi!'

'Och, we'll be OK. Staffa isn't connected to the National Grid yet.'

'Would you be referring to something, Doc?' Kiwi reproached in a mock-hurt voice.

Last winter, he and his SAR crew had a miraculous escape from catastrophe while on a night search of the fast-flowing River Awe in Argyll for a missing canoeist. They had been hovering with searchlights over the river in the course of a sweep, lulled by their Doppler readings into thinking they were stationary, when in reality the signals—pinging off the water surface and not solid ground—were registering the aircraft as stationary in relation to the water flow, but not the land itself. It was pitch dark, and they had no visual reference points to tell them that they were, in fact, reversing rapidly downstream at the same rate as the current. Suddenly there was a blinding flash as their tail rotor hit high tension cables spanning the river, and all the lights in the village of Taynuilt went out. What could well have been a terrible tragedy was averted, when Niall skilfully and safely brought his aircraft down to an emergency landing in a nearby field.

Staffa was approaching fast, as Kiwi dropped altitude and flew at a hundred feet, allowing us to peer into Fingal's Cave and gaze at the marvellous basalt columns as we sped past. Tiree was a short hop ahead, and five minutes later we were circling over squat, tarred-roofed houses, whose thick, whitewashed walls, more accustomed to deflecting grey Atlantic gales, now reflected brilliant sunshine. Guided in by an orange smoke flare, we landed on a flower-strewn machair meadow at the north end of the island, close to where the ambulance was parked on a sandy track.

Fiona and I jumped out to be met by the island GP, Dr John Holliday, who looked a bit fraught, and very relieved to see us.

'Have you a defibrillator or a monitor?' he asked anxiously.

'No. But I can always pump his chest for an hour!' I replied half-jokingly. 'Why do you ask?'

'Because he arrested half-an-hour ago at home while we were awaiting your arrival. I managed to defibrillate him with my own machine, and fortunately he has stabilised in sinus rhythm, and his blood pressure is one-fifty-ninety. He had diamorph forty-five minutes ago, and his pain is a bit better. His name's Ian McArthur, and this is his second coronary in three years.'

Bugger you, Steely-Pee, I cursed to myself, how would you and your bloody FONAC standard Navy equipment handle this scenario? Wouldn't it have been nice to have had our recently cremated defib, and a Propaq on board for this one? Just my bloody luck! I knelt down beside him, and was reassured to feel a strong regular radial pulse—at least my third left finger would have something to monitor on the way back to Glasgow. He was a solidly-built man of about fifty, and his ruddy-faced alertness, so soon after his cardiac arrest, gave me a lot of encouragement for the journey.

The flight back was pleasantly smooth, allowing Fiona and I to concentrate on Ian's problems, which started soon after take off, when his i/v drip blocked and had to be cleared a couple of times. To maximise the blood supply to his damaged heart muscle, we gave him supplementary oxygen at ten litres a minute, but despite this he began to get restless again. I hand-signed to him—had he pain in his chest?—and he nodded. The analgesic effect of a further injection of intravenous morphine was almost instant, and he settled into a relaxed doze for the rest of the trip.

I exchanged a look of relief with Fiona as we handed him over into the safe hands of waiting paramedics at Glasgow Airport for the short trip to the ICU at the Southern General.

'Remind me to add a postscript to that letter to FONAC when we get back to *Gannet*, and maybe we'll get our Propaq monitor after all!'

It was very gratifying recently to learn that Ian did make a full recovery from his heart attack, and nine years later was still on the island, and going to sea on fishing boats.

8

25th August 1993

DINNER FOR TWO?

Sat conspicuously on a bar stool in the corner of the wardroom, I recoiled as the steward approached and planked down in front of me a huge cheese and mushroom pizza—with chips! Sneaking a furtive glance across the room, I delved in, hoping none of my overweight customers would witness this sinful deviation from the straight and narrow path of 'healthy eating'. Well, I was hungry.

'Been on any SARs lately, Doc?' I jumped, ambushed from behind, as a fresh-faced, sandy-haired young Lieutenant came across to join me. I recognised his face as a new joiner, but couldn't recall his name.

'A couple of short trips to Arran in June, but none recently, I'm afraid.'

'Any down the wire?'

'No. Not since the Ardtornish Ferrex in 1991.'

'I did one with you last tour... I think it was a Spanish or Portugese trawler. You went down the wire on that one, didn't you?'

'No. As far as I remember that was a Spanish boat, and the guy had a bad eye injury. He was winched up by the aircrewman.'

The mention of that incident gave me the tag I needed. His name was Tribe, Dave Tribe.

'Are you busy, Doc?' he kindly enquired, and probably regretted it, for allowing me the opportunity to give vent to my current catalogue of moans!

'Too damn busy this week! I haven't stopped since Sunday, when I had a four hundred-mile round trip delivering my daughter to a curling coaching week at Aviemore. I was on call Monday night, late home Tuesday night, and now I'm missing my bloody Wednesday half-day because two partners have taken the day off and the others are on holiday. I'll be the only one of six working this afternoon. I'm going to be late… sorry to leave you—must go!'

I glanced quickly at my watch, conceded defeat to the big soggy lump of pusser's pizza left on my plate, crunched the last lump of ice in my fresh orange drink, and left.

To cover his absence, Craig Simpson had engaged a young lady locum namesake for the afternoon, but I never saw her for the next three hours' solidly booked surgery. I was under pressure to get finished early. Helen had been busy all day, doing floral arrangements and baking for the Ayrshire Hospice Summer Buffet Dinner, and I crossed my fingers there would be no late house-calls. I was looking forward to a pleasant night out in pleasant company.

At twenty-past five, my last patient left. I stuffed the ophthalmoscope into my case and snapped it shut. The dictation and letter writing could wait—I was off.

As if on cue, as my backside lifted off the chair, the bleep went. All that ops room could tell me was that it was yet another medevac from Arran, this time to the Southern General—a man with a cerebral haemorrhage.

I crashed through the door of the back office to tell the girls—to be met with 'Oh, before you go, Doctor Begg…'

'What!' I glared at poor Irene, our loyal, long-serving, long-suffering Practice Manager, who consistently bore the brunt of her employers' collective medical crabbitness with good-humoured resilience. An attractive young woman stood smiling by her side.

'This is Dr Simpson…' Irene continued, unperturbed.

'Hello. Sorry I've to leave like this.' I turned to go.

Irene stepped smartly in front of me with a grin, and held out her right hand: 'And this is her cheque needing signed!'

'Oh. Sorry!' I grabbed a proffered pen, scrawled my signature, and bolted for the door, mindful of the rush-hour traffic. Then I remembered—Helen was going to kill me for this! I skidded to a halt, and slunk meekly back in the door.

'Oh, Irene,' I grovelled. 'Could someone please phone my wife and tell her that I'll be late for the Hospice Dinner!'

Despite the heavy traffic, I was kitted up and out at the aircraft in only seventeen minutes. On board, I was almost taken aback to find John Gregg sitting beside me. He had been my POMA for over a year, and this was the first SAR we'd done together. From him, I got the alarming and disconcerting piece of information that our patient had indeed suffered a brain haemorrhage—and was on a ventilator. All sorts of potential problems then rushed through my mind—what kind of ventilator was it? Would we know how to work it? etc.

However, with Arran such a short distance away, there was precious little time to fret over hypothetical complications in the few minutes it took us to get there. Our usual landing site at Knockenkelly had recently been closed to allow for some improvements to the playing fields, and a new temporary site had been established on a point of land at the north end of Lamlash Bay—identified by a waiting police car. There was no sign of the ambulance.

It was a warm sunny day. Arran in sunshine—again! Definitely the greenhouse effect. Leaving poor Andy Birt lobster-faced in the cockpit to suffer his own greenhouse effect—Captain's privilege—the rats abandoned their s(t)inking ship to enjoy a bit of fresh sea air and sunshine.

Several sightseers' cars faltered slowly by, hoping for some drama, and were waved on by the local policeman. Then a large BMW sidled importantly up and stopped. Instead of the expected important personage, a tanned, fit-looking bloke in a scruffy tee-shirt and shorts jumped out and approached with a grinning air of familiarity.

A cry of recognition greeted him. It was 'Jock' Alexander, lately Lieutenant of *Gannet*, and now a Lt Cdr on *Invincible,* with whom I had last flown memorably in a Force Eight gale west of Islay, when he had skilfully unfankled our winch wire from the mast of the trawler *Voracious*. From his summer holiday cottage only a few hundred yards along the beach, he had seen us make our landing approach, and had come by to pass the time of day.

Pass the time it did, for it was nearly half-an-hour before the ambulance finally arrived from the cottage hospital. In the back, lying on a stretcher, was a deeply unconscious middle-aged man on i/v fluids, with a small middle-aged lady in a print frock sitting by his head. His wife, I supposed, till she spoke, and I belatedly noticed an ambu bag in her right hand.

'Are you an anaesthetist?' she demanded.

Momentarily gobsmacked by this unexpected query, I simply stuttered, 'No—just a GP!'

'Oh! I asked for an anaesthetist. I got one the last time from Crosshouse.'

'But that patient was probably going back to Crosshouse.' I explained. 'This one is for the Southern, and Crosshouse don't usually have spare anaesthetists hanging around for Southern General transfers.'

'Do you know anything about anaesthetics?' she pursued, checking the man's pupils, and leaning forward to inject a small measure of a milky fluid into his i/v drip, 'because this is not one of your usual CVAs. He's only unconscious because of the Diprivan. He's had a subarachnoid haemorrhage, and was very restless with severe headaches, so I had to anaesthetise and intubate him. His name is McFedries, Thomas McFedries, and he is sixty-three.' She continued to squeeze the ambu bag as she spoke, and glanced at a pulse oximeter which was registering a very satisfactory 96 per cent oxygen saturation.

She became quite agitated at my negative response. 'This man will need qualified anaesthetic supervision during his transfer, but I'm the only anaesthetist on the island! It looks as if I'll have to travel with you. Could have done without this. I've got a big dinner engagement with the Health Board in Brodick tonight! Can you bring me back?'

'Snap! I've got a big dinner engagement as well, with the Ayrshire Hospice tonight. Yes, we should both get back in time. Here, let me bag him while you change into something elegant!'

Sheila MacLeod was tiny, and looked like a punctured Michelin man as she disappeared into the depths of our one-size (six-foot-six) red survival suit. I continued to ventilate Mr McFedries while Richard Fox, the LACMN, took up as much of the slack as possible with velcro fastenings, thus allowing her to waddle over to the aircraft holding one end of the drip.

I jumped on board first and continued to squeeze the bag as the stretcher was slid into place. Dr MacLeod followed, 'airlifted' on board by Foxy and Dave 'Sumo' Simpson, the observer. Unruffled by her undignified boarding, Sheila took her place kneeling at the head of the stretcher.

'I'll bag him for you on the journey,' I offered, knowing that my grip and squeeze on the ambu bag during a forty-minute trip would be much stronger than hers. She gratefuly agreed.

What a boon it was to have the pulse oximeter on board; to be able to witness the efficacy of one's ventilatory technique, or the dip in oxygenation which would occur with a slackening of effort—and the immediate improvement brought about by a few extra compensatory squeezes of the bag. If anything more was needed to highlight the need for having our own monitoring equipment, it was this poor chap's predicament. While I rhythmically pumped air into his lungs, Sheila periodically checked his pupils for dilatation, and, as required, would administer a wee top-up of anaesthetic.

We flew smoothly at a thousand feet to maximise airspeed and minimise any oxygen deficit, and fortunately encountered no inflight problems. In next to no time, Andy Birt was bringing us gently down onto the Southern General landing pad, where a hospital team was assembled. At its head was a young officiously efficient lady doctor in a red 'I-am-a-Doctor' coat. Taking immediate charge, she got off on the wrong foot with Sheila by firstly almost ignoring her—I didn't count anyway—and then being somewhat pass-remarkable about 'why was this patient not being oxygenated on a ventilator?'

Sheila asserted herself as the anaesthetist in charge, and pointed out it was perfectly possible to adequately ventilate someone with air via a bag and mask, and that we had kept the patient around 97 per cent saturated all the way from Arran!

'That's the trouble with these young hospital doctors nowadays,' she muttered to me as we left the crowded lift and accompanied the procession into the neuro-surgical ward, 'They are so tuned into their flashing lights and high technology, that they have no idea that simple procedures can sometimes be just as effective!'

By the time we had carefully manouevred Mr McFedries safely onto a bed, seen him linked up to lifesaving high technology, and retrieved the Arran Ambulance Service's pulse oximeter, the young lady doctor had flushed through her surge of adrenalin, and thanked us affably for our assistance as we left for the helicopter.

Up front on the way back, Sheila was able to enjoy a wonderful panorama of the Firth of Clyde as we cruised at four thousand feet towards Arran. Away ahead of us, I spied a tiny long shape hugging the coastline and steaming northwards from Brodick. 'Is that the *Waverley*?' I asked, as I pointed it out to the pilots.

'No. Looks too small. More like a fishing boat, Doc.' came the confident reply.

'Fishing boats don't have two funnels!' I casually observed.

'Gee! You're right, Doc. Well spotted! It is the *Waverley*!'

'I didn't spend my summer holidays at the end of Fairlie Pier for nothing!' I crowed triumphantly. 'She's probably doing one of her last cruises of the summer. Looks as if she is heading for Tarbert or the Kyles of Bute.'

Leaving the *Waverley* to paddle her historic way up the Clyde, we banked left and descended towards Lamlash Bay, where a car was waiting to pick up Sheila MacLeod and take her to her Health Board reception.

Dreading my own reception as I drove home late, I was surprised to find Helen still waiting for me, and, what's more, in a benign and forgiving mood. She had been busy on her feet all day, preparing the floral arrangements for the Hospice Dinner, and had been quite content for once to sit back for a wee while, and await my return.

And for displaying such marvellous magnanimity, she received her due and just reward after the dinner when her fiver came out of the prize draw and she won a lovely £200 water-colour painting of roses by a well-known local artist. And I won yet another reprieve!

9

6th November 1993

'WE'VE LOST AN AIRCRAFT...'

As I double-checked the last few paragraphs of the Lockerbie Crash story, and began typing 'SAR Thirteen' into my Amstrad Word Processor, I could not have guessed what cruel, ironic twist the hand of fate was about to play when the phone rang at a quarter to midnight.

'Doctor Begg? This is Lt Mike Swales from *Gannet*. I'm sorry to phone you so late, but I'm afraid we have just lost an aircraft... between Northern Ireland and Islay.' A shiver of fear swept over me—Fiona, Mags, Trevor, wee Karen. John was on leave.

'Was it SAR or an exercise?' I asked, dreading his answer.

'No! It's not an exercise... it's the real thing!' he replied in an exasperated tone, then realising he had misheard me, continued 'It's not the SAR aircraft. We had two aircraft out playing with a submarine, when one suddenly ditched. The other aircraft has picked up three crew members and they are searching for the fourth. The SAR cab is on its way and should be there about now.'

Helen by this time was hovering anxiously in the background. Fiona was not due home till around one-thirty from a first showing of the Fiddle Orchestra's video of their Viking Tour—which was the main reason for my staying up late.

'What is it this time? Not another SAR I hope!' I covered the mouthpiece of the phone and shook my head reassuringly.

'How long will it take to get back?' I asked.

'About forty-five minutes flying-time. If the crew are uninjured, or just badly shaken, they'll be brought straight back to *Gannet*. Can you come in now, or do you want a call later?'

With things to tidy up at home, we agreed the latter option, but within a few minutes of putting the phone down, I was restless, twitched, and couldn't settle. There would be a hundred-and-one things to get organised—sick bay, FMed 4s, examinations, and—I shuddered at the prospect—four FMed 154s to complete. Recently revised up from six pages to twenty-one sections, some of them four pages long, this was the Air Accident Investigation Form which had to be completed by a station MO, whether Army, RAF, or Navy, following a crash. It was supposed to be user-friendly, but many sections dealt with technical aspects of flying, with questions which merely duplicated information that the aircrew would have already given the CO or the Air Engineering Officer during their debrief.

It was a bugger of a form, all the more so as I had just completed a set of four only a few months back, following a crash on the airfield when the tail rotor drive-shaft had failed on a Sea King coming into land, about twenty feet above the ground. By great good luck, it had crumped down on its side without catching fire, and the crew had walked out, completely unscathed, through the port personnel door.

This time, 819 Squadron's luck had run out. Two Sea King crashes in three months was, to say the least of it, devastating. We did not yet know what had happened this time, but it sounded like a catastrophic mechanical failure—and one man was still missing.

'Helen, I'll have to go out to *Gannet* now, to get things organised.' There was just no way I could hang around at home, waiting for that second phonecall. It had just gone midnight, and outside there wasn't much of a wind to shift the orange-lit stratus clouds which hung low over the town. At least the weather is fairly calm for a sea search, I reassured myself, as I turned into the base.

The ops room was crowded, the atmosphere sombre. Anxiety and strain showed on all the faces crammed round the radio operator. Commander Peter Galloway, the new Captain of *Gannet*, and Lt Cdr Bob Faulks, the OPSO, both looked up with a quiet nod of acknowledgment. Peter was having a hellish start to his captaincy, losing two aircraft like that, in quick succession. Mike Swales, the

Lt Cdr Flying, strode quickly across the room. 'Glad you're here, Doc. We were just going to phone you. The rescue aircraft is taking the crew straight to Ayr Hospital. We've had word that two are OK, but they are worried about the third, the observer. He's got a head injury, a possible broken leg, and has been vomiting and lapsing in and out of consciousness.'

'I'd better go and meet them at the hospital, then,' I suggested, knowing that, in addition to their own welfare, their survival suits and other gear would also have to be carefully checked and quarantined for the Accident Investigators.

'Yes. We were hoping you would do that.'

'Who are the crew… and who are they still searching for?' I asked hesitantly. Mike Swales gestured towards the flight board. 'The aircrewman is unaccounted for.' I scanned the crew list—Goodenough, Gamble, Mailes… and Scott! My heart sank with a dreadful foreboding. 'Oh, no! Not Jim Scott!'

A terrible, gutted, empty feeling swept over me. It couldn't be Jim. But no amount of wishing, or hoping, or denying, could alter the grim fact of that name chalked up on the board. If it had been anybody else, a callous and unreasoning little voice kept telling me, it might not have been so bad… But that was stupid! Any lad lost out there in that black night should deserve equal concern, I pointedly reminded myself. But at the same time, this was personal. I knew Jim Scott well. He had been our aircrewman on that terrible night of the Lockerbie disaster; he had flown SAR with me one December night to a fishing boat south of the Isle of Man; and had fished me out of the sea during sea drills off the Cumbrae.

I had done Jim's release medical examination in June 1991, and had been sorry to see him go—only to be delighted when he breezed into sick bay several months later with a cheery 'I'm back, Doc!' Unable to get a job outside, he had been 'lucky' enough, due to a shortage of experienced aircrewmen, to be allowed to re-engage at a time when other Branches were pushing redundancies. A quiet, dependable Scots lad with a wee curl of a smile always at the corner of his mouth and in his eyes, he was unflappable, and exuded a steady competence and confidence which I always found reassuring, especially on SARs. He was a dedicated SAR aircrewman, and had been one of the first in the squadron to undertake and complete the new, specially designed, three-week, Advanced First Aid course run by the RAF and Ambulance Service. I could only hope that his experience and survival training would stand him in good stead this night, and that he would be quickly located and uplifted by a helicopter or one of the searching vessels.

It had all the air of a typical Saturday night, when I walked through the A & E doors of Ayr Hospital at half-past midnight. The waiting room was still stuffed with the lumpen relatives and hangers-on of maimed, mauled and maudlin members of the local pub-club, boozer-bruiser brigade, mingling unfortunately, and unavoidably, with the douce kin of those poor honest citizens who were seriously ill through no fault of their own.

Leo Murray, the A&E consultant, emerged dishevelled from a cubicle, his receding hairline more than amply compensated for by his huge Old Testament beard, his wire-rimmed glasses balanced half-way down his nose. Leo was always dishevelled. By nature a workaholic, his dedication and enthusiasm had transformed sleepy old Ayr County Hospital Casualty practices into a slick, highly-trained and professional resuscitation team at the new hospital. The beads of sweat glistening on his brow bore witness to a hectic evening's work, and I almost felt guilty having to tell him there was more trouble on its way. I started to brief him, but needn't have bothered.

'We know! We know!' he interrupted with a smile. 'Sky Television were on the phone over twenty minutes ago, asking for an update on the condition of the casualties... and they haven't even arrived here yet. You'd hardly believe it!'

'That's incredible,' I rejoined. 'They must have somebody permanently tuned into the channel sixteen distress frequency. What chance do these old Reuters correspondents have nowadays?'

A quarter of an hour later, the familiar throb of a Sea King could be heard in the night sky, and soon materialised, as a set of powerful landing lights approached over the treetops to the north east of the hospital, to make a pinpoint landing on the new helipad.

Standing apprehensively alongside the ambulancemen, I waited till the personnel door opened before approaching. Three aircrewmen climbed out and walked up the path to the waiting ambulance. As the ambulancemen ushered them aboard, there was some resistance, gesticulation towards the aircraft, and a shout of 'There's a man on board a lot worse than us!'

By this time I was already up the steps and squeezing my way past the sonar to the rear section, where the third survivor, Sub Lt Ian Mailes sat slumped against the bulkhead—a sorry sight. He looked ghastly pale, both eyes puffed and closed, with some blood trickling from his left eye. The front of his inflated lifejacket and his sodden goon suit were covered in vomit. He reeked of aircraft fuel.

At first glance, I thought he was unconscious, and was relieved when he responded lucidly to my questions. Sitting propped up well away from the open rear door during the search, he had initially been able to breath better in this position, having been badly affected by the aircraft fuel he had swallowed and probably inhaled during his struggle to escape from the torn and sinking fuselage. But the combination of being violently sick and shocked, while remaining semi-upright, must inevitably have dropped his blood pressure and reduced the oxygen supply to his brain, and this was the most likely cause of his reported lapsing in and out of consciousness on the journey back.

Aided by Greg Carnell and Tim Olivey, the observer and aircrewman of the rescue aircraft, I unbuttoned his lifejacket and used it to support his head as we carefully lowered him to the recovery position. Two ambulancemen appeared at the door with their stretcher trolley, but the first problem was to extricate our casualty. 'Could you bring me a spinal board!' I shouted above the din. One was quickly produced and slid under Ian's body as I held his head steady. Thereafter, it was simplicity itself to lift him on to the trolley stretcher.

In the midst of all the turmoil, I hoped the aircrew would take note of how easy it was to extricate a casualty using the 'coffin lid', as it was known to rescue workers. We'd used it for years at road accidents and, recognising its value, I had had three made for use at *Gannet*, but it had taken six months before I finally persuaded the

SAR crews to accept one, placed permanently under the Stokes Litter mattress on board Rescue 177.

Minutes later, I discovered that my powers of persuasion regarding another SAR issue must also have—by some perverse natural law—been following the same protracted timescale, for when we attempted to wheel the loaded trolley round the nose of the aircraft, we found that the hospital management had not yet laid the tarmac pavement border for the under-sized landing circle, which they'd promised me last spring! As a result we had to bodily lift the heavy trolley across soggy, slippy, yielding grass to reach the ambulance.

In the Recovery Room, Leo Murray and his team speedily got to work with practised efficiency. I grimaced as heavy shears ripped open Mailes's goon suit from stem to stern, from wrist to oxter, and ankles to crutch—four hundred quids-worth of flying suit in shreds! I lent a hand with the long johns.

Expecting to find him bone-dry and warm underneath his many layers of woollens and long johns—fully protected as per the Survival Equipment manual by his 'dry suit'—I was shocked to find him soaking wet, shivering, and hypothermic. Several pints of sea water slopped on to the floor as the nurses turned him, removed all his clothing and simultaneously dried and wrapped him in blankets and foil.

Wired up to the monitor, and with an i/v infusion running, he still looked bloody awful, but all his vital signs readings were reassuringly normal. There was still some breathing difficulty due to fuel inhalation, and a chest x-ray showed some patchy inflammation of his lungs. Supplementary oxygen was administered and the head of his bed raised to ease his breathing, while waiting for the Ophthalmologist to come down and check his eye injury.

Happy with his stable condition, I turned my attention to the other two lads, lying stripped and blanket-wrapped in adjacent cubicles. Both were mildly hypothermic, but apart from grazed shins, and some small lacerations on Donnie Gamble's forehead, they were unscathed—and very, very lucky to be alive.

I was checking Donnie over, when a policeman stuck his head round the curtain and asked if he could have a statement. This interruption flashed up memories of Saturday night Casualty at the Western Infirmary in the distant sixties, when, as brash young residents—God's gifts to medicine—we would have cursed this unwarranted interference by officialdom in our 'lifesaving' work. But now, mellowed by years of close teamwork with the police at many tragic incidents, I fully understood and accepted that there were important forensic and statutory reasons for such intrusions, however inconvenient—and there were also spin-offs. Standing back and quietly listening to Lt Gamble's account, I was able to gain an early insight into exactly what had happened, out there, in the pitch dark, in the driving rain, in the icy sea, six miles south west of Islay.

They had been submarine-chasing with a 'playmate' Sea King, and had been two minutes into a protracted hover at forty feet with their sonar dipped, when there had been a sudden loss of control. They had tried to execute a 'freestream' manoeuvre to pull themselves up and away from danger, but the aircraft's nose went up, there was a sudden bang, and they hit the water and turned upside down—all in twenty seconds. Donnie had escaped through the left hand pilot's window, using the new Short Term Air Supply System (STASS) oxygen bottle to breathe as he fought to reach the surface. Neil Goodenough had surfaced beside him and they had buddied up. Then they had seen Ian Mailes's lifejacket sea-light, but couldn't reach him. There may have been a fourth light, but he wasn't sure.

The playmate Sea King had come over them pretty smartly, but because of the heavy swell, it had taken forty-five minutes before all three had been winched safely onboard. Shortly afterwards, the aircraft's search for the fourth crew member had to be abandoned because of lack of fuel, forcing them reluctantly to head for home.

Next door, Neil Goodenough seemed a bit more shaken than his co-pilot, and with good reason. When the aircraft inverted and started to sink, he had tried to escape through the right hand window wearing his Personal Survival Pack. The PSP is a bright yellow, flat, square plastic box containing a liferaft and other survival gear, on which the pilot sits during flight as an integral part of his seat, and which is optionally connected to his lifejacket by a couple of strap clips. Some pilots don't use them. Neil got half-way out of the window and no further, when the PSP jammed in the narrow opening. Struggling frantically, and almost out of air, he had activated his STASS bottle, giving himself a vital extra minute's oxygen in which to disconnect his PSP, break free, and shoot to the surface.

'It saved my life, Doc. It was brilliant!'

Both lads were obviously desperately tired and ready to be shifted to the short stay ward. I left them in peace and went into the consultant's office to phone and update *Gannet* on the state of the survivors and on their initial account of what had happened. Graeme Abernethy, the co-pilot of the rescue Sea King, was already there. 'Hello, Doc. How are the boys... and Nursie?'

'Nursie?' I queried, thinking it a queer time for him to be eyeing up the nursing talent.

'Yeah, "Nursie"—Ian Mailes—it's his nickname. He used to be a nurse before he joined up.'

'Apart from hypothermia, Neil and Donnie are both fine. I've just seen Ian's leg x-ray and there's no fracture... and the Eye Specialist thinks he's just got a tear inside his eyelid, and there's no damage to his sight... so he should hopefully settle with a few days in hospital.'

'Well, we're Downbird now ourselves. We've lost our UHF aerial, and have very little fuel left. I've just rung for the Maintainers to come out and give the Cab a check before we risk flying back to *Gannet*.'

'Where's Paul Hunter?' The other pilot had been around earlier, but was now nowhere to be seen.

'He's gone back down to the Cab to do some checks. Why?'

'Well, I've located all the lads' gear. The nurses have put all their kit into separate yellow bin bags and they are lying in the storeroom. Could you or Paul take charge of it and make sure it gets back to *Gannet* safely? It will all have to be examined by the Accident Investigators. I'm off home now, I'm whacked!'

I left just as an old man, in acute heart failure, was being wheeled in, and the A&E team—with one job well done—geared up smoothly for their next one.

By the time I crawled into bed it was two-thirty. Helen was still awake. A Sea King passed through the night overhead as we switched off the light. The boys were going home.

I couldn't sleep. I was thinking of Jim.

Sunday broke grey, wet, cold and depressing. I was up early. The crash and search was first item on the 8.15 BBC TV Breakfast News, with Bob Faulks trying to put on a brave face for the media. The missing man was well-equipped with life-jacket, survival suit, and personal locator beacon. They were hopeful he would be found soon by the two helicopters, the three lifeboats and the fishing boats at the scene. The search would go on all day.

Half-an-hour later, in the ops room, the haggard faces and hushed knowing atmosphere told the real story. Jim had been in the water overnight, in worsening weather conditions. His PLB was not transmitting, which meant only one thing. Though no one said it, we all knew deep down it was hopeless—but the search would go on. An aircraft roared overhead, arriving back to refuel, change crews, and go back out again. All available personnel had been recalled for a normal working day.

The Naval Air Accident Investigation Branch personnel were due to arrive shortly, and the RMAS salvage vessel *Salmoor* was already on station over the wreckage which had been located by signals from the aircraft's transponder. It was lying in two hundred and sixty feet of water, six miles south west of Orsay Lighthouse and the village of Portnahaven, on the southern tip of the Rhinns of Islay. I knew the area well, with its hidden reefs, fearsome currents and tidal races—where the full might of the Atlantic Ocean surged round Islay, to be compressed into the narrow North Channel between Scotland and Northern Ireland. An aircraft disintegrating on impact would be scattered by the currents over a wide area. Jim could be anywhere.

I headed for the sick bay. There was a lot to do, and I baulked at the prospect of the work in store filling in those FMed 154s. This would entail interviews with the surviving crew members, and a detailed examination of both themselves and their survival gear.

Eventually, after much rummaging, I found a supply of forms in the POMA's drawer—after asking the telephonist to ring for Fiona, who was duty MA, to come up and help me. The poor lass arrived, ashen-white, blear-eyed and exhausted. I had dragged her out of bed! Unbeknown to me, it had been Fiona, and not Trevor as I had been told, who had been out all night searching. She had arrived back at eight o'clock, and had just crawled into her scratcher for a couple of hours, while Trevor departed for the crash locus with the relief crew. She was obviously deeply distressed, though trying hard to hide it. I let her talk.

'It was horrible out there... looking for someone you knew. Not like a normal search... and in piss-awful conditions! We had to search at forty feet, and could see nothing for the spray from the downdraught. If we rose any higher, we were into low cloud and the searchlights were lost in the mist and driving rain. It was hopeless!'

On looking through the FMed 154s, I decided that to save time until I saw the lads again—and Goodenough and Gamble were not due to be released from hospital till late morning—my best plan would be to check over their survival gear down at the squadron.

Up at the SE Section in the main hangar, the POSE, 'Jacko' Jackson, and his killick Willie Carr, made safe the pyrotechnics—flares carried in the lifejackets—and helped me empty the yellow bags one by one and lay out each crewman's gear. Every item was sodden, and reasons were not too difficult to find. Donnie Gamble's left flying boot had a ragged tear through its leather tongue, and a corresponding rip directly underneath in the rubber 'sock' of his goon suit. He'd had no chance of staying dry. Neil Goodenough's neck seal had several small nicks around the rim—enough, Willie Carr assured me, to allow water to seep—or in this case—pour in. Ian Mailes's suit, not surprisingly, was too shredded to make much sense of, but the deep puncture wound on his right shin meant that his suit must have been punctured at the same time.

Examination of their mark 25 life preservers was equally illuminating. They had all inflated properly, and their PLBs had functioned—unlike poor Jim's. Despite his eye injuries, Nursie had managed to fire off a couple of flares—one of which, we heard later, had nearly shot down the rescue helicopter when it passed up through the whirling rotorblades! The other two lads had used their STASS bottles, but not much of their other survival gear, which was not surprising with a helo just overhead. Fortunately, they had all been sensibly wearing multi-layers of clothing, and this had effectively minimised their hypothermia, even though they were soaked to the skin.

All these details were carefully documented, and no doubt would be later duplicated and enlarged upon by the Air Accident Investigators. I glanced at my watch as my stomach rumbled—twelve noon.

In the wardroom, 'brunch' was a solemn affair, with just enough half-hearted banter to keep spirits up. The conversation ranged over the rescue efforts, the comforting of LACMN Scott's wife, herself a serving CPO Wren, the prospects of salvaging the aircraft, and the arrival of the investigating team who would be around for the better part of a week, gathering all available evidence and statements. Goodenough and Gamble had been released from hospital in midmorning, and were having an hour or two at home before coming back for a squadron debrief—following which they would be free to come up to sick bay to complete the FMed 154s.

About Jim Scott there was no news, and the increasing pessimism about finding him alive was underlined by the sombre, guarded nature of the statement by Phil Avery, *Gannet*'s PRO, on lunchtime TV News.

I felt bad about having to ask the two pilots to drag themselves up for yet another interview less than fifteen hours after they'd stared death in the face—police interviews, Hospital histories, squadron debriefs, FMed 154 completion, then the first of several searching interviews by the Air Accident people!

When Neil and Donnie did arrive around three o'clock, I was surprised how bright they were. Almost too bright, I thought—something is going to give later. Physically, too, they seemed none the worse for their ordeal, apart from some developing muscle aches and stiffness. I took them individually over sections on crew numbers, weather conditions, sea state, mechanics of ditching, escape from aircraft, physical examination and psychological factors. 'Are you married? Is this your first, second or third wife? How much have you had to drink in the past seventy-two hours? What did you have to eat for lunch? How many hours uninterrupted sleep, hours on duty, in the past twenty-four hours', etc. Then there was a section on their self-assessment of lifejacket function and other survival equipment.

It took almost an hour for each man, made more uncomfortable for me by the knowledge that Neil Goodenough had then to go straight back down to the squadron for his first interview with the Board, possibly lasting two hours, and Donnie Gamble might well have to hang around till about seven o'clock before his turn came. While appreciating that it was essential to have a debrief as soon as possible while details were still fresh in their minds, I felt that the lads had had enough for one day, and phoned their CO, to see if these interviews could be compressed. Fortunately this was achieved, and they were stood down just after six, and allowed home to their desperately anxious wives and families—with whom they had so far spent less than an hour of what must have been the longest, most terrifying day of their lives.

For Jim Scott's wife Bridget, herself no stranger to the harrowing signals and the sympathetic and supportive procedures involved in dealing with compassionate cases, through her work as a CPO Wren at Faslane, the ordeal would not be over for many weeks. By nightfall, all prospects of finding Jim alive had vanished, and everyone's thoughts were with his wife and parents.

Over the next few days, high hopes of at least finding him in the wreckage were dashed when the fuselage was located by divers and brought eventually to the surface.

It was empty.

10

10th November 1993

THE AFTERMATH

In the days following the crash off Islay and Jim Scott's death, the atmosphere at *Gannet* was an understandable mix of emotions; a strange brooding emptiness, an unspoken sense of loss, and, for many, a deep, personal grief. There was a lot of soul-searching too, as young pilots, observers and aircrewmen, and their wives and girlfriends, were forced to think the unthinkable, and voice unspoken fears and doubts about their future flying careers, and the possible effects on their families.

Among the surviving aircrew and their rescuers, the initial show of bright and brave faces in the aftermath of the tragedy, and that natural self-effacing tendency of servicemen to understate their feelings, quickly disappeared over the next few days, to be replaced by confessed nights of disturbed sleep, days of self-doubt, and unwarranted feelings of guilt.

Anticipating this would happen, I had seen all the lads for long individual chats on the Monday morning and again on Wednesday. As a result of these consultations, I had a feeling that a more professional post-trauma counselling approach might be worthwhile, and was glad of the advice of Surg Cdr Richard Hadden from Yeovilton, the medical expert on the Accident Board, when he dropped into sick bay late on Wednesday morning for an update on the FMed 154s. Our discussion ranged widely over the lack of progress of salvage attempts due to wild weather, their hopes of locating Jim

Scott's body when the Sea King fuselage was raised; and an outline of the procedures for initiating formal post-traumatic stress counselling for those immediately involved in the tragedy.

Inevitably, by the time I finally completed the FMed 154s for the Board, and arranged group counselling, it was almost two o'clock, and my half-day was slipping far astern. More so when I got home to find that Betty had phoned. I had been due to pay her a routine revisit before lunchtime, but with all the hassle at *Gannet*, I had sneakily hoped I might just be able to put her off till the next day. However, she was in tears when I rang back, acutely depressed and distressed with the added burden of some major domestic crisis, on top of her multiple medical problems. From her agitated tone, I realised there was no chance of postponing a visit. She needed her urgent call, regardless of its effect on my own urgent plans for what was left of the afternoon—like getting the last load of winter logs carted home and under cover, and taking Islay for a walk.

Due to a prolonged autumn drought, the River Doon had yielded up a bounty of stranded, easily accessible tree trunks and boughs; and for the past six weeks, my fishing half-days had been more profitably spent landing logs rather than salmon (season's grand total—zero!). This was to be the last load, and I was anxious to get it in before the weather broke. Frontal systems nudging in from the Atlantic last weekend, had already skirmished with a huge high pressure area centred over northern Scandinavia, which was now beginning to weaken.

I finally arrived at Doonholm at three-thirty—it would be dark by five. The logs were lying where I had barrowed them up from the water-side, beside a narrow, grassy cart track which rose in a gentle gradient from the Doonholm walled garden to the big house stables. Hurriedly I loaded the trailer, inverted the barrow on top, and lashed it down securely. Islay was desperate for her walk and, in the gathering gloom of a November dusk, I let her roam free to rustle and sniff through the drifts of fallen leaves carpeting the river path. A wee seatrout splashed mockingly in the tail of the Orchard Pool, safe in the knowledge that the fishing season was now over.

It was almost dark when we got back to the car. A heavy dew silvered the grey grass, and gathering mist over the holm silhouetted the still figures of four blanket-clad ponies. It was going to be a foggy night somewhere. I started the engine, slipped into second gear, and slowly pulled away up the slope. After thirty yards, the wheels began to spin on the wet grass, and we slithered to a halt. I reversed and tried again—only to gain ten yards, then slip helplessly backwards as the gradient increased. It was no use. In grudging desperation, I partly, then fully unloaded all the logs. Even at that, the car couldn't take the brae. As a last resort, I uncoupled the trailer, hoping that the car would make it unladen—otherwise I was in big trouble. With a wee bit of coaxing, and great relief, we gained the level road by the stables—leaving a four hundredweight cart and eight hundredweights of logs stranded a hundred yards back down the lane.

It annoyed me. I was buggered if I was going to be beaten! The exercise would do me good! Just what I needed to improve my aerobic fitness if I was going down to do the Dunker at Yeovilton. Pulling a four hundredweight trailer is child's play on the level—but on a gradient? By the time I had hauled it up the brae, hitched and reloaded it with six barrowloads of heavy logs—buggered I most certainly was! I looked at my watch. Twenty-to-six!

Helen had beef olives and a frosty look ready for me when I got home, having just seen Fiona off to her violin lesson at Maybole. 'Look at the state of you! At your age! Will you never learn to stop bashing your pan out till you are exhausted? You'll have to go down to Maybole for Fiona at a quarter-to-seven. I'm going out at seven with Christine and Anne to the Floral Art Christmas Demo at Auchincruive.'

I finished off the beef olives by a roaring fire, and dozed off—better a doze now by the fireside than later, on the winding bends of the nine-mile back-road to Maybole. A faint peep-peep at my waist woke me with a start. It was six-thirty. My heart sank as I groped for the phone and dialled *Gannet*. Young Karen Burnett was duty MA.

'We've a job on, Boss, and you're needed… a severe head injury on Islay.'

Helen came downstairs, half-dressed and wholly enraged. My heart sank even further.

'You can't go! What about Fiona? I'm meant to be picking up the girls at seven o'clock!... This is just bloody not on!'

'Can't you phone Will or Eileen?' I lamely suggested.

'No!' she screamed. 'They're going out! I'll just have to cancel my night out!'

She was at the same time, very angry and very distressed. I knew she was thinking about Jim Scott, still missing off Islay since last Sunday, and I felt shit-awful. A real crap-creep. But I had to go.

POACMN Jamie Patterson was waiting for me at the main gate. I was pleased to see him. It would be our last SAR together, as he was due to leave on Friday on a two year posting to a full-time RAF Search and Rescue job—something he had set his heart on—and something he had almost lost on account of a twelve month grounding for dubious medical reasons, which I had challenged, fought his corner, and won the day. The good news had just come through last week. He grinned. 'I've looked out all your gear, Doc.'

'Thanks, Jamie. I hate rummaging about in my locker for kit when that bloody machine is revving up outside.'

'Did you get the details, Doc? It's an unconscious woman, with a bad head injury. And just to complicate things, Glasgow is closed due to fog right now, and we're thinking of taking her to Ayr Hospital...'

'No, you're not,' I interjected. 'This is one where you will have to use Crosshouse, despite their bloody, muddy, landing site. They have a proper Intensive Treatment Unit for severe cases like this... and it is twenty minutes nearer to the Southern General Neurosurgical Unit, if she has to be transferred later by ambulance.'

Once on board, I confirmed this plan change with Greg Carnell, the observer. I was somewhat surprised and quite impressed to find Greg back flying SAR, so soon after hauling his three colleagues to safety from the sea last Sunday. I knew he had been badly shaken by the experience, and it took a lot of guts to get back into action so quickly. Especially as this was a night job, and back to Islay. While he was advising RCC of the possible destination change to Crosshouse, his high frequency radio packed in, and for the rest of the flight, all signals had to be relayed to RCC through Clyde Coastguard.

'It might be as well to get them to ask the police to check visibility at Crosshouse as well,' I suggested, 'for there was some fog building up at the Monkton roundabout when I drove in to *Gannet*.'

Busying myself in the back, I checked the oxygen cylinder. It was half-full, and there was a bad kink in the plastic tubing which could obstruct the oxygen flow. I cut off the twisted segment, reconnected it to the cylinder, and checked the suction apparatus. Karen brought down the spare cylinder from the front of the aircraft.

We had cleared Machrihanish and were heading out over the Sound of Jura when Greg got a relayed message from RCC bearing the glad tidings. Glasgow was still closed—and so now was Islay Airport!

'Bloody brilliant! That's all we need. What are we going to do now!'

'Try and contact the local police to organise some blue flashing lights to mark the landing site.' suggested Greg Lawrence, the pilot. By this time we were closing rapidly on Port Ellen, with only ten miles to run. The radio crackled. It was the Islay police. Yes, they would try to have blue lights for us at the airport.

'What is your position at present?' the observer asked.

'Just north of Port Charlotte.'

'Thank you. Do your best.'

'That's on the other side of Loch Indaal—about twenty miles away!' Jamie Patterson laughed. 'We've only five miles to run ourselves.'

'I've got the airport visual,' came a voice from the cockpit. 'and it's all lit up! What the hell was RCC talking about, saying it was closed?'

'Mebbe they meant it was closed for the night after the last Loganair flight left… but it always opens for SAR flights!'

'Well, it's bloody misleading info that has caused us and the local police a lot of hassle. I'd better stand them down.'

Having left a foggy, frosty Prestwick, we were quite unprepared for the driving rain which lashed the aircraft as we landed and taxied up to the airport terminal. As if on cue, the ambulance arrived just as we drew to a halt. It was some distance away, and the relentless downpour looked like making the patient transfer a miserable experience—till the airport staff showed some real initiative. The door of what looked like a mini hangar was swung open and the ambulance reversed right inside, so that the change-over to our lightweight stretcher could take place in comfort.

Dr David Hardie, the Bowmore GP, stepped down from the ambulance, smiled, and shook my hand. 'Glad to see you again. This poor woman has been causing us some concern. She lives alone, and was found unconscious in her back garden this afternoon. There wasn't much sign of an obvious head injury, but we admitted her to the cottage hospital for observation. Unfortunately she did not regain consciousness, but has just got deeper and deeper, and has now developed a fixed dilated right pupil. Looks like a subdural haematoma, so we phoned the Southern for her immediate admission.'

Catriona was a huge woman, probably in her mid-fifties, and took a lot of lifting—with care. She was not wearing a cervical collar—her neck was too short and thick—but was on oxygen and was being monitored on the ambulance HeartStart 3000.

'Well, it won't be the Southern, I'm afraid.' I replied, as we stabilised her on the stretcher. 'Glasgow Airport is closed due to fog, and we are taking her to Crosshouse.'

'You should be able to get into Glasgow now. We've just heard it's open again.'

That was news to us, but very welcome news at that. The airport Sherpa van was reversed up to the hangar door and Catriona, on the lightweight stretcher—now a misnomer if ever there was one—was slid gently into the back and driven across to within a few yards of the Sea King. A smooth, dry and effortless transfer.

Once airborne, Jamie let the others know that Glasgow was now open, and that our casualty was in urgent need of neurosurgical treatment. RCC were similarly advised, confirmed that the airport was indeed operational, and undertook to inform the Southern General of our intentions. Our ETA was sixty minutes.

Not long into the flight, we hit heavy turbulence as Greg Carnell tried to avoid some big CBs by directing us down round the Mull of Kintyre. CBs and beef olives don't mix, but I survived! Linked up now to our HeartStart 3000, the patient's heart rate was a worryingly slow 38-42 beats per minute. Her breathing was shallow, but at a normal respiratory rate, as we saturated her with eleven litres of oxygen per minute to maximise brain perfusion. It was not long before the first cylinder was exhausted, and I had to bag and mask her while Karen struggled with a difficult connector on the replacement one. The timing was going to be critical—with forty minutes of oxygen left—and forty minutes to run!

The weather improved as we flew up the Firth, allowing the pilots to take the aircraft up to eight hundred feet and make rapid progress—till we passed Greenock and hit thick fog over the Clyde opposite Dumbarton. Conditions deteriorated rapidly. There was a fog bank right up the middle of the river, and to crown it all, Glasgow Air Traffic Control reported an oil rig parked in the river somewhere upstream of Erskine Bridge!

'A fine bloody time to tell us now!' cursed Greg Lawrence. 'I can hardly see a bloody thing up front. I'll take her over to the right bank, and we'll follow the road… I can see street lights and cars.' By this time we were down to forty knots, and flying just fifty feet above the water as we moved cautiously forward to pass underneath the Erskine Bridge.

'Shit! There's another fog bank directly under the bridge!' He lifted the aircraft's nose and climbed rapidly to five hundred feet—up and over the bridge, up and over the red warning lights of the adjacent high tension cross-river pylons, and up and over the fog itself. It was as if large areas of Glasgow had suffered an electricity blackout, with wide swathes of nothingness interspersed with islands of bright light. Glasgow Airport, built on an ancient swamp, was smothered in fog. It would be impossible to land there. We could see nothing. There was only one thing to do—make directly for the Southern General itself, which luckily was centred in one of the pockets of light.

We landed just as the oxygen gave out.

Jamie Patterson left the aircraft and came back shortly, fuming. 'We'll have to lug the stretcher over to the ambulance, because the guy in charge won't allow it to be driven nearer the aircraft in case it damages their running track!'

Unloading the stretcher with the help of a couple of firemen, we had to half-walk, half-run with our heavy load about seventy yards to the ambulance—only to discover there was a trolley stretcher on board which would have made life very much easier if it had been allowed to come to the aircraft! I briefed the young lady doctor in the ambulance, as another, taciturn, individual took position at Catriona's head without as much as looking in my direction or saying hello. As we unloaded the stretcher, he snapped 'Any X-rays?' and muttered something about these incompetent island hospitals as he swept past, leaving me feeling as if it was all my fault!

In the rescusitation room, the ambulancemen wheeled the trolley alongside the examination couch, and suggested pumping it up a foot to the same height as the couch. They were ignored as Bossman took charge from the head of the patient. 'No. We'll just do a four man lift.'

'There's an eight-handled canvas underneath her if that will help.' I suggested.

'That won't protect her spine.' he replied abruptly.

'Well, she's lying on a spinal board, and that will protect her if we lift her on that.' I pointed out helpfully, well aware from the history given by the Islay GP that there was unlikely to have been any spinal injury.

He ignored me. 'I'll stabilise her neck, somebody get the chest, pelvis, and legs, and when I say 'lift'—lift!'

Leaning over someone's body, especially someone as obese as Catriona, lifting her up a foot and holding her steady without sagging, while nurses drew the trolley out from under her; and then having to move her forward three feet to land safely on the examination couch; seemed to me to be a classic way of putting nursing staff's backs at risk—if not the patient's! So, mindful of my own bad back, and the prospect of others suffering the same problem, I made one last plea: 'This lady weighs sixteen stones!' I protested.

Instead of putting my back out, I put Bossman's back up.

'Look! If you don't want to do it, just step back and let us do it our way!' he barked, looking daggers.

I gave up. He had the easy job, holding the head. Pride wouldn't allow me to let a wee nurse take my place. I only just managed to grip Catriona round the chest, and when Bossman called 'lift', I lifted with the others, praying that my back would survive the experience. Like a sack of potatoes, she was carried forward and laid on the couch, fortunately without mishap to either of us.

With the help of the ambulancemen, I retrieved our stretcher, blankets, picked up my helmet and left—acutely aware of being totally ignored by Bossman. It was as if I had never existed. Not a word of acknowledgment, thanks, support or encouragement, for what had been for all the aircrew, a pretty harrowing transit. The guy's arrogance and discourtesy towards a colleague got right up my nose. I was furious—and so were the ambulancemen. 'Thinks he knows everything, that bugger!' one of them grumped as we left the building.

'Who is he?' I asked.

'Dunno. Some consultant, likely, who thinks he's God's bloody gift to A and E. You would think we were numpties who had never handled a head injury patient before—and not bloody using a spinal board, when it would have made the lift so much easier and safer!'

Pointedly, I asked the sick bay staff next day what their reception was usually like when delivering casualties to the Southern. 'I don't even bother going in with the patient now.' said Magz. 'Any time I tried to explain things I was just ignored. They never listened, so I gave up!'

A wee injection of some of the quiet thoughtfulness and gentle humanity shown by the staff at Islay Airport would work wonders in certain parts of Glasgow!

After immediate neurosurgery to remove a large brain clot, Catriona happily survived to make a good recovery.

11

6th January 1994

MULL MISSION

The headlines on the front page of *The Herald* leapt out at me—'Fishing Boat Tragedy in the Firth of Clyde'. Two crewmen aboard the Ayr boat *Sea Harvester* had been found lying unconscious in their bunks by their skipper, possibly overcome by fumes. A Sea King from HMS *Gannet* had been scrambled, and, according to the newspaper report, one of the men had been resuscitated by an aircrewman winched down from the helicopter. The men had been taken to Ayr Hospital, where one had been pronounced dead. The other had been flown later to Faslane for hyperbaric oxygen therapy.

What I read worried me. I felt a sinking feeling of guilt, though I had no reason to do so. Shortly after the Sea King crash, a bit of soul-searching had taken place at the surgery as well as among the aircrew at *Gannet*, with my partners patently unhappy about flying SAR ever again. As Scott summed it up:

'I think we've all enjoyed the excitement of doing SARs in the past, for we all thought it was safe. But two crashes in four months puts a different slant on things. It's all very well being a hero when the thing goes down with us in it... there would be something in the papers, lots of nice words said, and that would be it—final!'

I had always been acutely aware of the imposition my contract at *Gannet* had placed on the boys, with its insistence that, in my absence, I would arrange for a locum from among my partners to provide medical cover for base personnel—and to be available for emergencies, including SARs.

As a result, I had consciously held on to the bleeper most of the time over the past seven years, especially in winter, and in foul weather, to minimise the risks to them. In winter, this had seldom caused Helen or myself much inconvenience as far as our social life was concerned—whatever other strife it might have caused in our family life! But on fine spring and summer weekends, we had often begrudged the personal loss of freedom to get up and away on family outings, picnics, country walks or sailing—especially when the partners frequently swapped their on-duty weekends with members of another practice, and consequently left me without anyone to take the bleep,even for a few hours if I wanted away fishing. Despite this modest involvement, over the years, predominantly during my summer holidays, the lads had still managed to clock up a dozen, mainly fairweather, SARs.

The situation had to be resolved one way or the other. The income which *Gannet* brought to the practice could not be lightly ignored, and might possibly be jeopardised if SAR cover was withdrawn. I arranged a meeting with the Captain.

Peter Galloway was very understanding. 'I don't blame them, Jimmy. If I was a casual flier, I wouldn't want to fly in foul weather off the West of Scotland either.' He made enquiries, and established that the MoD's commitment to the Health Service was simply to supply a helicopter, for emergency transport of patients—and they were not necessarily obliged to provide a doctor, or even an MA.

'So by providing the expertise of yourself and the MAs, we are throwing in a bit extra, and giving them a superior service.' he concluded with a grin. 'I'll have another look at your contract, and we will amend it accordingly.'

That let the boys off the hook, for which they were truly grateful! And the upshot was, that I would continue to cover SAR as before, but if I wanted to get away for a day, a weekend, or on annual leave, I would simply notify the POMA, and he and the others would just have to cope to the best of their ability with whatever medical emergency they came across—which was what they were in the habit of doing anyway. To help maintain and improve their skills, I would continue to hold debriefings on the SARs they had done, and keep them abreast of any new protocols, or changes in the management of acutely ill patients in transit.

But true to form, here I was, only four days into 1994, and being assailed yet again by the Law of Sod. I had been on call for the practice over Christmas, and had looked forward to skipping a rink in the Ayr Curling Club's annual Ne'erday Bonspiel. *Gannet* had been notified I would not be around for a couple of days.

On the second day's curling, blissfully ignorant of the drama unfolding on the Firth of Clyde just a few miles from the ice rink, I had skipped my rink to an ignominious exit from the tournament. Next morning—those headlines! And I hadn't been available.

I was upset. Young Karen had been on duty, all five-foot-two of her—a skelf of a lass handling two unconscious casualties. How had she coped? Could I have done anything more myself?

Anxiously, I spoke to her on Wednesday morning. 'Oh, I had no time to think, Boss… It was such a rush. I just got on board and went to do what I could.'

'Were you winched down?'

'No, thank goodness. It was very rough so they sent Foxie down… and he was as sick as a pig!' She giggled. 'I'm glad it wasn't me, for I'm not a good sailor. I always chew a seasick pill on my way down to the aircraft when we've got a job on.'

'Did Foxie have to resuscitate either of them?'

'Not really. One of them was already dead, probably for several hours, and the other one was rousable. We just gave him full oxygen all the way to Ayr Hospital.'

The following morning, by sheer coincidence, LACMN Richard Fox breezed in the door for his annual aircrew/diving medical.

He was his usual, cocky, confident, grinning self. I put him through his paces on the Harvard Step Test, which he just survived. 'Time you gave up these fags!' I rebuked him and, just to rub it in, added mischievously, 'Sorry to hear you were honking all over some poor guy's fishing boat the other day!'

'Who told you that?' he demanded, laughing.

'Oh, just a wee fairy. Anyway, it makes me feel a lot better knowing that big heroes like you can throw up just the same as me.' Foxie had recently received a Queen's Commendation for a difficult and hazardous mountain rescue on Ben Lui.

'Well, the weather was pretty shitty, and the boat was cork-screwing about a lot... I think that's what did it.' Having made his excuses, he retaliated. 'Have you been out recently, Doc? I remember the last medical I had, you were called away on a SAR.'

'Not today, I hope. I'm taking a half-day's holiday this afternoon to curl for our Rotary Club in the Ramshead Trophy.'

I didn't add, for good measure, that Helen was taking the dog to the vet, running Colin to the train back to Glasgow, and offloading Fiona at Ayr Ice Rink for a final team practice in the afternoon, before I ran her team down to Lockerbie at five o'clock for the Scottish Junior Curling Championship playdowns. It was going to be a busy day.

Three-quarters of an hour later, Karen popped her head round the door. 'PO West would like to speak to you on two-two-three, Boss.'

Extension 223 was the emergency line. My heart dropped.

'Doc, we've got a severe head injury on a fishing boat, and the SARO would like you to go. Can you come down?'

It was eleven-thirty. I was due to curl at two o'clock!

'Where is it?' I asked, praying it was off Arran or the Cumbraes.

'Somewhere between Tiree and Mull... about an hour's flying time away.'

That was my curling buggered up. I thrust my Rotary Syllabus into Karen's hand, and asked her to telephone John Davidson—but forgot to tell her to phone Helen as well! I could only hope that Helen would put two and two together when I didn't turn up at lunchtime for my curling gear—and be gracious unto me!

Mindful of Foxie the Jinx's recent digestive disaster, I popped a Kwell on the dash down to the SAR locker room. And, equally mindful of Donnie Gamble's recent hypothermia, I donned as many layers as would squeeze into my goon suit. The aircraft could wait. Pete West fetched my lifejacket and helped me zip up.

Once again, Greg Carnell was the observer, but the aircrewman was new to the SAR flight—POACMN 'Smiler' Smiles, recently arrived with 826 Squadron from Culdrose. There was no more information on the state of the casualty, so I checked out all the gear I thought we'd need, then went forard. The co-pilot was Greg Lawrence, and the pilot, Andy Morell. As we passed over Knapdale in Kintyre, the distant Argyll hills covered by a white icing of snow down to the eight-hundred-foot contour, I couldn't help but comment on the stark contrast between this and the climatic conditions which Andy had just left—the steaming jungles of the Far East, where he had been on draft as an observer on the ground with the UN peace-keeping force in Cambodia.

Clyde Coastguard were playing some game or other with SAR Ex Two, and were unable to come up with any new info.

'Never mind. We'll soon be able to get Oban Coastguard.' Greg Carnell announced from the back, unaware he was being eavesdropped.

'Rescue 177. Oban Coastguard... We can hear you loud and clear. The present situation is that we are in contact with the fishing boat *Golden West*. The Skipper has a severe head injury. Position north west of Iona and the Ross of Mull. The *Lord of The Isles* is in attendance, with two doctors on board, and they are giving medical advice to the crew of the *Golden West* ,which is heading for Fionnphort with an ETA of thirty minutes.'

Before Greg could acknowledge this signal, a conversation between the *Lord of the Isles* and *Golden West* broke in on channel sixteen. Some dramatic proposals were being floated. They were discussing how it might be possible to transfer one of the doctors from the CalMac ferry on board the fishing boat, whose crew were a bit apprehensive about the outcome! It could only be done with a dinghy, and they felt it would be too risky due to the sea state. But the *Lord of the Isles*, obviously anxious to be of assistance, was still pursuing this course of action.

'Tell them we've got a doctor on board, and will be over them in thirty minutes.' Andy Morrell instructed. 'What do you want to do, Doc?'

'I'll probably go down first and assess him, taking the oxygen and Stiffneck collars... Smiler could then come down after me with the stretcher. Could you find out how he is at present?'

'*Golden West*. This is Rescue 177... rescue helicopter. We have a doctor on board, and will be with you in thirty minutes. Do you read me?'

Golden West acknowledged.

'How is the casualty? Is he conscious or unconscious?'

'He was unconscious for a while, but he is now thrashing about, and we are having to hold him still.'

I made some encouraging noises in the background.

'That is good! The doctor says that is a good sign.' Greg reassured the crewman on the far end of the line. 'When we arrive overhead, we will winch the doctor down to examine him.'

'Here, that's a funny high-pitched voice... sounds like a woman.'

'Or the cabin-boy!'

'Whoever they are, they seem to be keeping their cool anyway.'

Iona was now visual. *Golden West* gave her position and her ETA at Fionnphort as fifteen minutes—the same as ours. It wasn't worth while attempting a winching—quicker running for port. We radioed our intention to land by the pier, and meet the boat as it arrived. With that decision confirmed, *Lord of the Isles* signed off from her assisting escort duties, and resumed her voyage to Oban.

The flashing blue light of the local Coastguard van indicated a cleared landing site as we overflew Fionnphort car park—normally chock-a-block in summer with buses and cars of tourists visiting Iona, but on this bitter January day, desolate.

By now the pilots were in visual contact, and we overflew the *Golden West* as she approached from the north into the narrow Sound of Iona, escorted either side by two other local fishing boats. She was a small thirty foot creel boat with a forard deckhouse. From a fairly tall mast, two radio aerial wires trailed aft to the stern. A broad platform overhanging the stern was piled high with lobster creels.

'Thank God we didn't have to winch down on to that!' exclaimed Andy Morrell. 'We would have had a helluva job.'

The Coastguard Sherpa van was stuffed with rescue equipment, some of which had to be jettisoned to make room for the stretcher for the two-hundred-yard drive down to the slipway where the *Golden West* was making fast just as we arrived. The timing could not have been better.

Grabbing the cervical collars, I leapt aboard to find a young man lying in a crumpled heap on the open deck where he had fallen after being struck on the left side of his head by the swinging boom of the creel hoist. His head and yellow oilskin jacket were covered in blood which, together with rain and sea water, had saturated an old pillow brought up from below decks to make him more comfortable. An oilskin-clad fisherman knelt beside him, supporting his head. Behind me the wheel-house door opened, and I looked up in surprise to see a young woman dressed in a blue fleece jacket and jeans emerge, her face anxious and strained. So it *had* been a girl's voice controlling the rescue operation from *Golden West*!

The injured man was still unconscious, but restless, and thrashing one arm about. His left ear was in tatters where he had been struck by the hoist, and he had another deep gash on his forehead.

'How long has he been like this?' I asked.

She hesitated, her recollection obviously in disarray from the trauma she herself had endured. Then she gathered her thoughts and confirmed that he had been deeply unconscious for the first half-hour, and thereafter had become restless and agitated. They had been unable to move him into shelter from the awkward corner where he was jammed, and he had lain on the open deck for the past hour-and-a-half while she brought the boat back to port.

'He's obviously had a nasty skull fracture, and we will have to take him straight to the Southern General Hospital in Glasgow.' I informed her gently. 'What's his name?'

'Chris… Chris Poulton. Can I come too?' she immediately responded. I looked across at Greg Carnell, who had just arrived with the stretcher. He nodded.

Chris could hardly have fallen in a more awkward spot, jammed between the gunwales, the aft bulkhead of the deckhouse, and the fish hatches. I tried to fit a cervical collar, but it made him even more restless and agitated. After considerable thought and manoeuvring, we managed to align stretcher and patient sufficiently to allow a careful straight lift with head and neck protected, on to the stretcher.

Once on board, and on eleven litres oxygen per minute, he settled down and I was able to bind his ear wound with a large field dressing. Heavily wrapped in blankets, his hands were icy cold, and he was obviously hypothermic. Although his pupils reacted well and his respirations were normal, I could not get a wrist or neck pulse. I turned to PO Smiles and asked for the HeartStart monitor. He went forard, and returned without it, looking puzzled—and so was I—till I remembered that the MAs usually brought the HeartStart on board the aircraft themselves. It was still lying in sick bay!

So it was back to the old grope-a-pulse routine. I concentrated on trying to find his wrist pulse; but it was not until my third fifteen-minute systems check, when he had warmed up a bit, that his pulse re-emerged, strong and regular.

I had been oblivious to everything else during this time, except an all-pervading smell of sick, which worried me in case Chris had vomited silently under his mask. I checked, but there was nothing to see, and he continued to breathe normally.

By this time, we were over Glasgow and approaching the Southern General. Chris began to get restless again, possibly irritated by engine noise and vibrations. I was relieved when we landed, and the POACMN prepared to transfer him to the waiting ambulance—first surreptitiously sweeping a puddle of vomit out of the rear door with an old rag! So Smiler had been the culprit all along—the end result of wolfing down his meal in a hurry when the SAR call came. First Foxie and now Smiler. I'd never feel bad about being sick on a SAR again!

In the ambulance, we were joined by the same A&E doctor whose back I had put up last time. I was intrigued as to how he would react this time, and was agreeably surprised. He listened, and nodded empathetically as I briefed him en route to the recovery room.

The two ambulancewomen had their trolley already at couch height, and our only problem now was the patient transfer.

He quietly asked, 'Do you have a spinal board under the

stretcher?' I quietly replied yes, but in the event, we simply used the eight-handled stretcher canvas that had also been placed under Chris when we lifted him from the boat. No problems—lessons learned!

'Good evening, Doctor Begg!' Honour satisfied by the simple gesture of having my presence acknowledged, I was suddenly gob-smacked to think that someone here even knew my name. I turned my gaze to an attractive young anaesthetist busy attaching monitors to the patient's chest. She looked up and smiled. It was Dr Carol Murdoch, daughter of Ronald and Muriel Murdoch, close medical friends and near neighbours in Ayr. I'd known Carol since childhood, and had chatted to her at home just a few days before Christmas, when she had told me she was now working at the Southern General—but not that she was working at the sharp end, in the A&E Department.

Victim, herself, of a horrific road accident on the A74 a few years back—when she had almost lost her right arm and nearly ended a promising medical career—Carol had made a courageous and remarkable recovery. I watched in admiration as she deftly inserted an i/v cannula.

Chris was in a safe pair of hands. Subsequently it was found that his head injury was so severe that it required surgery to elevate the skull fracture and relieve pressure on his brain. Despite this, and probably due to his rugged occupation as a fisherman, he was fit enough to be discharged home less than two weeks later; and not long afterwards he was back at the fishing on *Golden West*.

12

24th January 1994

FINGER ON THE PULSE?

'Fiona! You nosey besom! You've spoiled my surprise!'

Fiona was sitting at John Gregg's desk, Pandora-like, with the open box in front of her. Her forefinger stuck in the sensor, and her head stuck in the manual, she looked up with a big-eyed disarming grin. 'Sorry, Boss. I met somebody from stores leaving the office just as I came in, and thought he'd left the box... Just a woman's curiosity!'

A few seconds previously, I had just put down the phone, having successfully persuaded David Dundas, the Health Board's Emergency Planning Officer, that this spare pulse oximeter—which had been bought originally for the Immediate Care Scheme doctors—would be much more useful monitoring seriously-ill patients on helicopter transfers to the Board's hospitals, than lying unused in the back of my car. That recent severe head injury transfer from Mull had once again spotlighted a long-recognised and major deficiency in our monitoring capability.

Our current request for a Propaq monitor had just been knocked back several months till helicopter trials were completed at the Boscombe Down Research Establishment—though we were quietly chuffed that this project had come about as a result of our initiative at *Gannet*—and rumour had it that the SAR unit at Culdrose was now jumping on the bandwagon and keen to order *three* for their Sea Kings.

Up until now the poor relation and country cousin, it was nice for *Gannet* to be setting the pace in SAR equipment, ahead of Culdrose who had always been the Navy's busiest Search and Rescue unit, with three designated, stripped-out Sea Kings, loads of gear—and kudos—and lots of public exposure from their often dramatic rescues off Land's End. And just to rub it in, the recently published Rescue Coordination Centre statistics for 1993 had shown *Gannet*'s SAR unit, with 232 missions, to be the second busiest in the UK, well ahead of Culdrose, and only just behind RAF Lossiemouth.

Possibly as a result of this dramatic increase in activity, and the squadron's persistent requests over the years for a designated SAR Sea King at *Gannet*, permission had at last been granted to strip all the sonar equipment out of one of 819 Squadron's aircraft. This would finally allow us to lay two stretchered casualties side by side in the back, where they both could easily be monitored, rather than jam one in the narrow passageway alongside the sonar, where it was almost impossible to treat a patient, or even move from one end of the aircraft to the other. Karen had experienced this problem recently with her two carbon monoxide poisoning cases, as had Trevor with two severe head injuries in transit from Fort William.

Things were looking up! All we needed now was permission to use the HeartStart defibrillator on board the Sea King—and I had the ammunition here in my hand.

'Right, Fiona. As a punishment for your noseyness, you can type out this report for FONAC... but check it for accuracy with Gill first.' I slapped a three-page report on her desk.

Gill Dorman was Magz Brodie's replacement. Magz had at last become a 'real Jack', having just got the sea draft she had been hankering after, and had left us at Christmas, en route for the Adriatic on *Illustrious*. Young Gill was another wee skelf of a lass, like Karen, and had just had a very traumatic experience on her first SAR duty. They had been tasked to search for a missing woman hill walker, Judith Leslie from Glamis, reported lost in a blizzard in the Grampians, and had found her at four o'clock in the morning in Glen Clova, lying in deep snow, frozen rigid, and pulseless. On board the aircraft, the backseat crew had initiated mouth to mouth respiration while Gill went forard for the HeartStart monitor, and had progressed to cardiac massage by the time she returned. She had assisted them for the half-hour flight to Ninewells Hospital at Dundee, where an ambulance paramedic team had come aboard, attached their HeartStart, and defibrillated the patient before any of the crew could stop them!

Judith's heartbeat had been restored to sinus rhythm, and although she had required several further defibrillations in the hospital, she had miraculously survived—and so had the aircraft. The Sea King had been burning and turning with all systems operational during the whole procedure, with the pilots blissfully unaware of what had been done, till well into the flight home.

This trial by error was too good an opportunity to miss, so I had written up the incident for the FONAC powers-that-be to assess along with any other experiences of on-board defibrillation. Hopefully it might bear fruit—and soon.

As I struggled to force down the last mouthful of an over-large portion of baked potatoes and tuna, which Helen had lovingly served me just before a big curling match at 7.15, I was thankful that I was Skip and did not have to sweep the ice for a couple of hours. This state of grace lasted all of thirty seconds—till a bleep sounded somewhere below my belly overhang.

Ops room was engaged, so the MoD policeman manning the gatehouse phone put me straight through to the SAR Cell. It was to be a short trip fortunately—to Arran, to medevac a man with a broken neck—but a doctor had been requested. Could I come in?

The night was typically miserable, with low stratus cloud and rain, and I carefully controlled my speed on the wet bypass. On arrival, there was no noise of revving engines—they'd either not yet flashed up the aircraft, or had gone without me. And there was no one at hand to fetch my lifejacket, so, struggling to close the last zip on my goon suit as I ran, I crashed into the line cabin to find it stripped bare and unoccupied. Bloody hell! What was going on? The whole place seemed deserted. Cursing, I ran over to the ops room, but the wee Duty Wren hadn't a clue where the lifejackets were now kept. In desperation I rushed through to the new SAR Ready Room, and luckily was able to grab a spare one there.

Head down to protect my glasses from the rain, and fumbling with lifejacket buttons as I went lumbering through the darkness in my heavy flying suit, I found myself standing out on the apron—all alone—no ground crew—and no bloody helicopter!

Surely the buggers hadn't left without me again? Then, in the distance, from the direction of the hangar, I heard the sound of engines firing, and glimpsed flashing red navigation lights. They'd obviously decided to take off from the hangar precincts rather than bother getting the ground crew to tow the Sea King down to the apron. The 'bother' was now for me to run two hundred yards up the hill to the helicopter! I was knackered when I got there, and just had about enough puff left to heave myself into the back.

The low stratus dictated our flying altitude, and Greg Carnell took us across the Firth using SCAs, or Self Controlled Approach, a navigation system which locked the aircraft at a pre-determined height of 200 feet, on a heading of 280 degrees, and at a speed of 70 knots, to guide Kiwi Stephenson to within a quarter mile—and a visual sighting—of the temporary rough landing site still in use just north of Holy Isle, which was pinpointed as we approached by the blue lights of a police car.

The ambulance was not long in coming, and I was warmly greeted by Wendy Buswell the surgeon, fully aware this time that she was not a staff nurse! She briefed me. 'It's a Mr James Kirk, a man of sixty, with three fractured cervical vertebrae. No loss of consciousness, and fortunately no neurological deficit either. He is able to move his arms and legs.'

I clambered into the ambulance. On the stretcher, a middle-aged ruddy-faced man looked up, his rueful smile contorted into a grimace by the restrictive effect of a firmly applied stiff-neck collar. Opposite him sat Mrs Kirk with, understandably, a very worried expression on her face.

'How did this happen?' I enquired gently.

'He was up a ladder in the living room, and suddenly lost his balance. I think he hit the back of his head or neck on the furniture as he fell.'

It was raining heavily outside. I looked around the cramped interior of the ambulance. Getting him off the ambulance stretcher and on to our lightweight stretcher inside the vehicle without causing some spinal movement could pose problems.

'We've got him in a KED spinal splint, doctor.' volunteered the ambulanceman. That should give us enough support.'

'Yes, I see that. But it's such a tight awkward lift here inside the ambulance, that I'm worried we might not get a secure enough grip to steady him.' I turned to John Gregg. 'Could you bring me in the long spinal board?' As far as I was aware, our new spinal board had never been used in anger, and this was an ideal opportunity to demonstrate its simple effectiveness to the lads. It worked a treat! Slipped gently under Mr Kirk, in a few seconds we had him lifted, stiff, straight, and safe, on to the lightweight stretcher.

So far so good. Now to monitor him for the journey to Crosshouse with our other new bit of kit. Confidently I turned to John. 'Could you bring me the Pulse Oximeter?'

He looked distinctly sheepish. 'Sorry, Doc. I didn't have the chance to bring it. I was forty minutes into a training session in the gym when the bleep went, and had to rush straight down to the SAR Cell. I was knackered!'

That made two of us, I thought. And it's Sod's Law again. Here we are, just got a new toy this morning, now have an ideal patient to try it on, and the bloody thing is on the far side of the Firth of Clyde! In fairness to John, I wasn't all that worried about the need for monitoring, as our casualty was alert, comfortable, and totally stable. Still, it would have been nice to have trialled it.

On the trip back, Mr Kirk was, indeed, looking very relaxed and comfortable, but thanks to Smiler, it was his poor wife who caused me problems! Smiler had helped the good lady aboard and in his wisdom had plonked her in the seat immediately behind the observer, which is where I normally sat when supervising patients, handily plugged into the adjacent intercom cable. Unfortunately, she was a fairly ample lady, and the spiral cable was rather short, barely reaching as far as my helmet in the seat next to her. As a result, I had to sit cuddling her, my left arm curved awkwardly round her shoulders with my fingers straining to hold the intercom plug in its socket. At full stretch, I could hardly manage it, and as the poor soul looked increasingly uncomfortable and embarrassed, probably thinking she was being snogged by this total stranger, I cut my losses, pulled the plug, and sat incommunicado!

Out of the starboard window, I could see the lights of Troon slipping past beneath us. We were flying low, about three hundred feet. I signalled to Mr Kirk that we had only five minutes to run to Crosshouse, then sat back in my seat and relaxed. However, for some strange reason, the journey just seemed to go on, and on, and on! I couldn't fathom it at all. I peered out of the window, then looked at the altimeter. There was no sign of street lights, and we were now flying at less than two hundred feet and only making sixty knots—very low and slow. Through the amorphous greyness of the night I could make out strange, smudgy, white patches. Surely there couldn't still be snow lying in the fields near Kilmarnock! At that moment, sudden agitated movements from the stretcher caught my eye. I leaned over. Mr Kirk was trying to tell me something, gesticulating towards his face and chest. I put my head down close to his, and just caught his words above the roar of the engines, 'Oxygen!... have you got any oxygen?'

Then it dawned. He had been so well strapped into his spinal jacket that he could hardly move his chest enough to breathe! I quickly plugged in to the intercom again and asked John Gregg to fetch the oxygen cylinder. John swiftly connected him to the face mask, and within a few seconds he was comfortable again.

Air Traffic Control chat seemed to be clogging up the air channel, probably the flying school practising night flights. I glanced over John's shoulder as the aircraft suddenly banked, and gasped—below us was a runway! We were back at Prestwick. The 'snow' which had puzzled me must have been white breakers as we flew parallel to the shore after doing a big circuit around Troon.

While I had been 'snogging' Mrs Kirk with my headset unplugged, Kiwi had run into serious navigational problems as he flew inland towards Crosshouse, as the ground rose quickly to merge with the low stratus cloud. He was left with no visual references, and felt there were too many high-voltage cables and pylons to risk a helicopter with eight people on board. As a lucky pilot who had already collided with one high tension cable and survived, he was superbly qualified to make that decision.

More used to slagging off fog-bound Glasgow Airport for the bother caused during patient transfers to the Southern General, we had never before been stymied by a similar situation less than ten miles from our home base at Prestwick. With humble apologies to our passengers for this unforeseen diversion, they were both safely transferred to complete their short journey up to Crosshouse by ambulance.

As it turned out, I was very glad to have insisted on using the spinal board for our patient's ambulance transfer, for it was subsequently found that his vertebrae had been dislocated to such a degree that he was later transferred to the Neuro-surgical Unit at the Southern General for operative fixation of his cervical spine. He went on to make a full recovery.

13

15th March 1994
GOFFERED

I never like Tuesdays. Tuesdays mean an 0815 start. Tuesdays mean taking all the early morning house-calls—at least as many as can be crammed in between eight-thirty and eleven o'clock. Tuesdays mean the mobile phone ringing in the middle of every roundabout and heavy town traffic, with nowhere to draw to a stop. Tuesdays mean multiple telephone interruptions during the late morning surgery—clearing up all the rubbish when the rest have hopped it on visits or half-days. Tuesdays mean a ten minute lunch of tuna and turkey salad rolls snatched between the late morning and the early afternoon surgeries. Tuesdays usually mean late house calls—and late home for tea at six-thirty—after picking up my in-laws. I hate Tuesdays!

On Tuesday, the phone rang at 0730. It was John Gregg. 'Can you phone the SAR Cell, Sir? There's probably a job on, and they want to talk to you about it. It's a Navy job... on the *Superb*.' John tended to mumble a bit on the other end of a phone, and at seven-thirty, especially on a Tuesday, my brain was not at its sharpest. 'Oh, the *Superb*. Yes, OK,' I heard myself muttering before I put down the receiver. The *Superb*? What the hell is the *Superb*? I wasn't long in finding out.

'Hello, Doc. Thanks for ringing back. We've had a signal from one of our submarines, the *Superb*. They've a man on board with a bad head injury they want casevaced to hospital. We are at the briefing just now, and plan to take off at oh-eight-hundred hours. We'd like to take you with us, along with the MA... Can you come in?'

'How far out is she?' I asked, with some misgivings, thinking of the day ahead.

'Somewhere off the Mull of Kintyre... We should have an ETA around oh-eight-thirty.'

I breathed a sigh of relief. Could be there and back in an hour and a half. Shouldn't upset the practice applecart too much! Helen insisted on breakfast. Half a plate of Alpen and half a cup of tea. Still, it was better than nothing, and as the weather had sounded pretty rough outside during the night, and I had no idea on which side of the Mull we'd find our sub, I reckoned it was more than ample. Even so, I played it doubly safe and munched a Kwell en route to *Gannet*.

With a planned deadline, it was a pleasure to get dressed slowly and enjoy a leisurely walk out to the aircraft, instead of the usual limbo dance and sprint. Young Gill Dorman was duty MA, and was sitting surrounded by a clutter of rucsacs up front. I gave her a wave and strapped myself in behind Trev Steele the observer, and LACMN Paddy Green. Adrian Hands, the new SARO, known to all and sundry as 'Fingers', was left-hand pilot, and Lt 'Ratty' Roll was in the P1's seat. We lifted off at eight o'clock on the dot.

'Did you get the details, Doc?' Trev Steele enquired.

'Yes, but do you have an update?'

'Just hold on a jiff, and I'll see what's what.' He spoke to the submarine. 'He's had a bad head injury, and they are talking of lifting him in a Neil Robertson stretcher. Paddy will go down first, then yourself, to assess him. When were you last on the winch? Are you quite happy?'

'About a year ago. Yes. Fine.' I felt even finer when he gave a heading of 235 degrees and an ETA of twenty minutes, which meant our quarry was on the lee side of the Mull of Kintyre. There's not much to hold on to on the slippery deck of a submarine in a heavy sea—especially if I was trying to hold on to my breakfast at the same time!

Very soon we were in visual contact with a long black shape, steady in the water as she headed up the Firth in a light four-foot following swell, just east of Sanda. At least we would not be washed off her deck by a big sea, like in that famous scene from 'Sailor' when *Ark Royal* rendezvoused with a nuclear sub in mid-Atlantic!

Trev Steele made further contact with the *Superb*, and reported somewhat surprisingly that the casualty was now 'walking wounded' and would come on deck himself.

'Is it a fin transfer, then?' asked Ratty.

'No. They will bring him up through the deck hatch.'

'Forard or aft?' queried Fingers.

'Aft. Why?'

'Well, they'll need to turn the submarine right round into the wind to allow us to make an aft transfer.'

We had already made several circuits of the submarine. Low in the water, nosing through the waves, it looked small from the air—till our eyes measured the tiny figures on deck looking up at us. From the waterline to the top of the fin must have been over twenty feet.

'Do you want to use the video?'

'Yeah. Might get some good footage.'

'As long as the Glencoe Mountain Rescue Team don't get to hear of it!'

'Och, the waves aren't mountainous enough for them to get called out… so there's no problem!'

Both the RAF and Navy SAR helos had been loaned video cameras by STV to take footage of rescues on land or sea which might prove newsworthy, and the Glencoe MRT Secretary had recently been involved in some controversial letter-writing to the press, in which he complained that the RAF were trying to hog the scene and take all the credit for mountain rescues, with their publicity-seeking videos of incidents. We had been smugly happy to let Lossie take all the flak on this one, despite ouselves having a similar camcorder! In reality, it was seldom used, for on the big newsworthy jobs, which went largely unreported, the weather was either too foul, the action too hectic, or the circumstances too dangerous to permit anyone the luxury of playing about with a camcorder.

There was a small delay as the sub made the requested 180-degree turn, and Ratty brought the aircraft in to a low hover over the stern. I sat in the sonar operator's seat as the aircrewman was dropped on deck, and then the strop, retrieved by Trev, was slipped over my shoulders. I bum-shuffled to the door and swung out on the wire. The short drop was a pleasant change from some of the highline winches I'd previously experienced, and the deck was dry. The sea state was three-four, and the waves, riding along a rock-steady submerged hull towards the tail fin and vanes, were several feet below deck level. No problem.

A curious fishing boat hovered in the background, keeping her distance. Since the sinking of the Carradale boat *Antares* with the loss of four lives several years back, there had been bitter rows between the Clyde Fishermen's Association and the Royal Navy on the conduct of submarine exercises in the Firth of Clyde and up the west coast. Various procedures had been thrashed out to minimise the risk of such a tragedy happening again. But the mistrust persisted, fueled by several near misses and incidents, not necessarily involving Royal Navy subs, and further restrictions and bans were being called for by the fishermen's leaders.

Two ratings swung open a heavy steel hatch just aft of the fin, to reveal a narrow, circular, very deep shaft. I took a quick look, and gulped. My problem was that the top of the ladder leading to the bowels of the sub was about five feet below hatch level! Gingerly, I sat down on the rim of the shaft with my hands either side, and swung my legs into space. Bending my elbows, I cautiously lowered myself till my searching toes scraped the top step. I was safe.

Descending to the main deck, I wasn't really surprised to find that a nuclear sub was considerably larger and better appointed than the old diesel-powered *Odin,* on which I had done my second-ever SAR, seven years ago. Met by the Executive Officer, Paddy and I were taken forard to the wardroom where an ashen-faced young man, his cheek and nose bruised, and his right arm beautifully splinted, sat slumped against the side of his bunk. He was fully conscious, but could not speak because of a painful swollen jaw.

'What's the story?' I enquired in general to the group of men surrounding him.

'Lt Burnet was on deck watch last night, Sir, when he was hit by a big wave which swamped the fin and knocked him hard against the metal rim. He was knocked unconscious for about a minute, and was under water for part of that time. We managed to get him down safely, but he lapsed in and out of consciousness for half an hour, and was a bit confused for another hour and a half…' I looked up. This didn't sound like the *Odin*'s 'Cook with the Book'. This was a real POMA. And he continued with a first class history—probable broken jaw, injury to right shoulder, blood pressure, pupil sizes, 'all detailed in this letter for the hospital, sir.'

Superb had requested that we bring on board a survival suit, and our first problem was trying to dress the young Lieutenant. He was able to stand unaided and get his legs into the suit, but his injured arm prevented him getting fully dressed and we had to abandon the attempt. Although he had coped well with this manhandling, I was professionally unhappy about him trying to climb that ladder on his own, and suggested the Neil Robertson.

A voice behind me intervened, and the three rings on his shoulders informed me he was the Captain. 'It is very difficult using a stretcher… there's just no room for anyone to go up alongside the patient. He managed to climb down himself, so he should be able to get back up with a bit of support.'

That said, I was left in a terrible dilemma. The Captain's experience of the awkwardness of a Neil Robertson in submarines versus my total ignorance of this alien environment. My experience and training, relating to proper splinting and immobilisation of head and spinal injuries—against my making a big issue of it, insisting on its use, and then finding it impracticable. I had to make a quick decision. The lad was upright, walking, and fully alert, though a bit green about the gills. He did not complain of any neck pain. Against my better judgment, I agreed to the climb.

Helped along the passageway, young Burnet was sat on a stool by the control console amidships, while an extension to the ladder was rather awkwardly fixed in place to fill the five-foot gap we had struggled down! That was a big help, but I thought it strange that, in these days of high technology and wire guided torpedoes, no one had designed a simple sliding extension like the Ramsay ladder up to my loft! Or even a simple pulley system for a Neil Robertson stretcher.

'Paddy, could you go up first and signal down the stretcher. I'll follow you, and the casualty can be helped up when everything is ready.'

Paddy went up first, and I followed quickly, to find the Sea King standing off and just coming into the hover, prior to lowering the stretcher. It would take a few minutes. Something made me glance round, and my heart sank as I saw our casualty's head and shoulders appear through the hatchway straight behind me. The silly buggers had sent him up far too early! We couldn't send him back down again! He would just have to stand on deck till we got the stretcher down. He was swaying, pale, unprotected, and shivering with cold, as the edge of a rain squall swept past. There was nowhere to sit him down, and he had only one arm to hang on with. All I needed now was for him to faint and slip into the sea. The ship's diver was on standby, but that was small comfort! I hovered around him like a mother hen for interminable seconds till the stretcher arrived, and heaved a sigh of relief when he was hoisted safely on board.

Gill wrapped him quickly in an insulated flectron blanket, but he continued to shiver violently, and I had an anxious moment when he tried to retch and his eyes rolled. My God, I should have insisted on that Neil Robertson after all! Luckily, it just a fleeting wave of nausea, and he settled for the rest of the short trip back to Ayr Hospital.

Disconcertingly, there was no ambulance in attendance when we landed on, and we sat waiting for several minutes, till a resuscitation trolley, jet-propelled by a man with wild, waving hair and a white coat, came hurtling down the long track from the A and E Department—Leo Murray to the rescue! I appraised Leo of the casualty's state, as much as my peching and panting would allow, as we pushed him at a rapid rate of knots back up the hill to the resusc room. The ritual shredding of Navy issue garments revealed a swollen bruised shoulder but no other injuries, and happily, subsequent X-rays showed no fractures of arm, skull, or jaw.

After a night in the Observation Ward, Lt Burnet pitched up next day at *Gannet* just as I was about to leave, a bit battered and bruised, but none the worse of his ordeal. I apologised for the unnecessary stress we had put him through by asking him to climb the ladder.

'Don't worry about that, Doctor. I felt I could do it, and didn't fancy being hoisted on deck in one of these things anyway! I felt a bit groggy standing up there, but it was probably easier the way we did it. It is very difficult to get a Neil Robertson up through these hatches. I remember off Norway we had a casualty who could not walk, and we had a lot of trouble using the stretcher.'

'But is it something you practise regularly?' I asked curiously.

'No. Very seldom... probably we should do it more often.'

'What exactly happened to you the other night?'

'There were two of us on night watch on the fin about oh-one-thirty, when a big wave crashed over us. We turned our back to it, and then were goffered by an even bigger one which slammed me against the rim of the cockpit. I just remember a thump as my head hit the metal, and then being under water for a while... mebbe thirty seconds before it drained away. Then I was helped below, and felt very woozy for an hour or two, with a splitting headache, and couldn't move my jaw or shoulder.'

'Were you wearing a safety helmet?'

'No. We always wear a safety harness to stop us getting washed overboard, but not a helmet.'

'Why not?'

'I suppose it's the old macho thing... only wimps wear helmets. Probably no one has ever thought about it.'

'Mebbe it's time they did. Even the bootnecks and paras wear hard hats... and they are hardly wimps! You would think in this day and age, with the Navy preaching about "Health and Safety in the Workplace" on ships and shore stations like *Gannet*, that they would take similar safety measures on the exposed decks of submarines. I'd have a go at them when you fill in your accident report at *Neptune*.'

'Yes, I think I will. I was lucky. Another officer I know down south has been off duty for eighteen months following a similar head injury.'

'Is this fin night-watch a common duty then? I thought you would just go down into the cool, still deep at night, away from all the storms and gales.'

'Very common, at least in this part of the world. Because of the fishing boat problem, we are not allowed to steer a submerged course at night in the Clyde area or off the west coast of Scotland, so there have to be two lookouts on the fin all night, in all weathers... and accidents can happen.'

This was the other side of the *Antares* coin, about which nothing was ever publicised. Young lives were at risk on both sides. 'Those in peril on the sea'... I shook his hand as he left.

Over the weekend, it still rankled with me that there should be such a major problem of extricating a casualty from a submarine, and such a risk of making his condition worse by rough manhandling. OK—submarines don't have masts, pulleys and rigging, but submariners are sailors, and surely there must be some old salt on board who knows all his knots and wrinkles, and the principle of pulleys, and could rig even a one-to-one pulley system by throwing a rope over the topmost rung of the ladder to haul up the stretcher. Simple! I would write to the PMO at Faslane. And while I was at it, I would ask why fin lookouts don't wear hard hats!

With the letter duly composed, I breezed into sick bay to find Fiona looking glum. 'Hello, Fi. Could you send this off to the PMO at *Neptune*? Have you had your hundredth SAR yet?'

I should have kept my mouth shut! After two years at *Gannet*, she was sitting on ninety-nine SARs, a fantastic total, but had missed out on several recently due to being stood down or left behind. And yesterday, to crown it all, with only seven duties left till she went on draft, they had gone off to fish a reluctant windsurfer out of the Solway Firth, and hadn't bleeped her. The bloody ungallant lot! Typical male chauvinist pigs! Not wanting a poor lassie to reach the Ton—about twice as many as any of them had done! But she had duly gutted them all on their return and felt the better for it.

Postscript:

1. Fiona reached one hundred and two SARs before she left.
2. As a result of this incident, my letter to Faslane, and the pertinent points raised, it is now mandatory for all Royal Navy submariners on deck watch to wear hard hats!

14

10th June 1994
CHINOOK DOWN

Summer or winter, fair weather or foul, major or minor, comic or tragic, the one constant and invariable factor during eight years of SAR work, has been their total predictability. Without fail they always crop up at the most awkward bloody moments—leading one to the inevitable conclusion that Sod's Law must have been specifically promulgated with SARs in mind!

For six months, Roddy, my fishing buddy, and I had been looking eagerly forward to the last week in May and the prospect of a magic week's trout fishing on the famous machair lochs of South Uist. Sadly, what we hadn't appreciated was that Sod's Law also has a built-in sub-clause pertaining to such presumptious angling aspirations. The brilliant sunshine and cold east winds of previous weeks—the fishless curse of all knowledgeable anglers—had given way at long last to gentle south-westerlies, warm fronts, cloud and drizzle. Just what our knowledgeable angler prays for—near perfect conditions—but nobody told the machair trout!

Caught unawares on the first day, Loch Hallan yielded six beautiful brownies weighing six pounds—a modest bag by all accounts. Over a drink in the Lochboisdale Hotel bar that night, knowledgeable fellow anglers confidently predicted we'd double our bag on Loch Bornish on the morrow. It was, after all, the best loch on the Uists—and the trout there were as fat as pigs on the rich feeding. Fat as pigs they may well have been, but just like pigs, they had their snouts firmly in the swill trough of the loch bed all day, guzzling water snails, and we caught damn-all. Wee bits of feather tied on metal hooks just don't inspire *bon appetit* in gourmet trout when *les escargots* are on the menu. And no-one has yet invented the snail fly!

The following day, we were rudely blown off Loch Altnabrug by a half-gale, and on Thursday had the doubtful privilege of fishing Loch Ollay—a privilege made all the more dubious by whispered intelligence from old Ernie, a delightful retired Irishman and one of the hotel regulars, who confided to us that there were three Loch Ollays—West Ollay, North Ollay, and F*** Ollay! And guess which one we were fishing.

It was in this sad, fishless state of mind, on our last evening, that we drove the length of the Dark Island, past Benbecula's rocket range and Balivanich Airport, to North Uist, to have dinner with Roddie's cousin Katie and her husband Hamish. Roddie's mother had been a Uiseach. Hamish was now retired, but Katie still taught the one teacher school at Claddach. Their son Ruaridh, now back on the island after a spell working near Edinburgh, joined sporadically in our conversation as it ranged over the upsurge in Gaelic teaching in Hebridean schools, the awful prospects for the island of the loss of seven hundred jobs if the threatened closure of the Rocket Range took place—and the fishing.

As I threw in my own tuppenny connections with the Outer Isles—like that horrible winter SAR to Barra when we had to fly on up to Balivanich to refuel, young Ruaridh interrupted, 'There's been a military helicopter crash on Mull tonight… I've just heard it on the seven o'clock news.'

A horrible cold shiver ran through me, shades of last November… Jim Scott… Surely not again! This was my first holiday break away from *Gannet* since SAR cover had been withdrawn by the practice. Was it the SAR Sea King… with one of my MAs on board?

'Did you hear anything about it?' I demanded anxiously. 'Was anyone injured?'

'I only caught the tail-end of the news, but there were a lot of people on board… over twenty, I think, and there were some casualties.'

I immediately and selfishly breathed a sigh of relief—no Sea King could carry that number. 'Did they say what kind of helicopter it was? Was it a Chinook?'

'Yes, I think that was the name of it.'

In a matter of seconds my thoughts raced through the whole gamut of emotions—fear, relief, anxiety and guilt. Fear for my MAs' lives. Relief for their safety. Deep anxiety about how they would be coping, perhaps with many casualties, and no medical back-up. Guilt, because I was not there to help them, and because my own personal sense of relief was inevitably at the expense of someone else's personal grief and pain. I conjectured to myself on what might have happened. Probably an Army Chinook on some exercise. The weather had been foul all day while we were fishing, with low stratus cloud at 200 feet. Could have hit a hill, and Mull had plenty of them!

Sod's Bloody Law. It would have to happen while I was away. And last May's fishing trip with Roddie to Sutherland had been just the same, when an RAF Hercules had flown straight into the hills above Blair Atholl in good visibility, killing all eleven crew members and poor Fiona had had to cope with the grisly aftermath.

A pleasant dinner was all but ruined. Conversation flowed over my head. Roddie had a lot of family catching-up to do. I chipped in now and again out of politeness, but my mind was preoccupied. Ruaridh reappeared after the ten o'clock news. 'They've released more details on TV. The accident was on the Mull of Kintyre, not Mull, and there were twenty-nine people on board the Chinook... from Northern Ireland. Police and soldiers travelling to a security meeting at Inverness... and there have been casualties.'

Mull of Kintyre! Only twenty minutes flying time from Prestwick. *Gannet* must have been involved, and with that number on board, how would they have coped with multiple casualties? Yet, deep down inside, I feared the worst. If the big helicopter had hit a hillside hard, there might well be no survivors to treat. In a way, I was relieved when we said goodbye to Katie's wonderful hospitality, and set off back to Lochboisdale. Driving along the unlit, narrow winding roads, in inky blackness, my worst fears were confirmed on the midnight news, when it was announced that the search for survivors had been called off. There were none.

Back at work on Monday morning, I learned that Karen had been duty MA on the first helicopter to reach the scene, but even at that early stage, there had been no hope of finding anyone alive, and after flying around in appalling visibility caused by a combination of hill fog and burning moor, they had been stood down at Machrihanish, and then later tasked to fly officials to the scene. The five-hour delay in releasing the grim news had been a classic example of breaking official bad news gently to the British public. The cream of Ulster's anti-terrorist security forces had been on that Chinook—Police, Army, Air Force and Home Office specialists—a grievous loss of human life, and an incalculable loss of pooled intelligence in the fight against the IRA. The buzz around the base was—Why? Why? Why?

Why did they choose a Chinook which was not fitted with radar? Why did they authorise the flight when the weather forecast was atrocious, with fog-banks and low stratus cloud? Why did they choose a helicopter, when a fixed-wing aircraft, flying above the weather, would have been quicker and safer? Why were all these high-ranking people being flown in the one aircraft?

Only after all these questions had been answered could the secondary issues of pilot error be considered. Why were they navigating so close to the Mull of Kintyre, with miles of hill-free sea on either side? They knew it was there! Why did the pilot not climb to 3000ft to avoid the Kintyre, Jura or Arran hills? Was there any question of a young pilot Flight Lieutenant feeling pressurised not to be a wimp, and to continue on a flight he was unhappy with, simply because of the high-ranking passengers he was carrying, and the nature of his mission? Many of these questions would be answered at the various forthcoming inquiries, and no doubt heads would roll, but would they be the right ones? Only the future would tell.

Meanwhile, back at the surgery, it was business as usual—the usual first-week-after-a-holiday disaster scenario. Scott and Paul were both on leave, and Pauleen, of course, never works on a Monday. I was on call. Fiona was ill, and kept us up till two o'clock. I had four night calls, and two hours sleep.

Tuesday was no better. Pauleen had decided to take Tuesday off as well—presumably something to do with a golf ball—and I struggled on without lunch till six-thirty, when I steeled myself to stagger home for tea and conversation with both sets of in-laws.

On Wednesday the practice rota denied me even the solace of a half-day, and *Gannet* sick parade went like a bloody fair, with four aircrew medicals flung in for good measure. A couple of salad rolls for lunch, afternoon surgery, Fiona's hospital appointment, then a late visit. Net result—exhaustion.

The sick bay mob—and I thought they were my friends!—continued to put the boot in on Thursday morning with another batch of four medicals. A quick ploughman's lunch in the wardroom left me suffering from gherkins and pickles, and in no frame of mind to face another late surgery and quarter-to-seven homecoming.

I was so tense and exhausted the following morning that I felt quite weak and wobbly during my morning visits. Still, it was my half-day, and I could always look forward to a well-earned rest. But I was unhappy about the way I was feeling. Last week, I'd had some worrying runs of extrasystoles (irregular heartbeat) while trekking across the Uist moors in blinding rain, so I collared Craig and asked him to check my blood pressure—reassuringly normal. 'Och, Your extrasystoles were probably due to unaccustomed exercise.' he smugly reassured me from his superior place in the aerobic pecking order, as a macho, squash-playing, jogging-with-the-dog fitness freak.

'Come off it!' I retorted. 'I've just tried the Harvard five-minute Step Test I make the aircrew do as part of their flying medical, and passed it... and they're all half my age! But I wouldn't mind an ECG.'

Harassed as she was, Anne Cooper, our super-Sister, obligingly squeezed me in between smears, jabs and dressings, desperately resisting a retaliatory urge to shave great swathes off my hairy chest as she stuck on the cardiograph leads. Gratefully unmutilated, I was even more thankful to be presented with an extrasystole-free, normal ECG. Relieved and uplifted, I struggled through the late morning surgery dross with a wee bit more verve than I thought possible, grabbed my bag at the finish, and was for offski.

'Before you go, Doctor…' I turned. It was Janet. 'Could you make these return phonecalls?'

Averil—'The hot water is running scalding hot… Could you fix it?'

Irene—'The cleaner says the Hoover is not working… Can you have a look at it?'

Anne—'The patients' toilet is blocked…!'

'Oh, shit!' Sod's Law again. By the time I had phoned around, borrowed a plunger from the plumber and blasted the offending throne turdless, it was a quarter to two. Some bloody half-day. And I had still the bank, the building society and the accountant to visit… and still had to buy Karen's wedding present!

The first three tasks accomplished, I shot out to *Gannet* to pick up some new cardiopulmonary resuscitation charts which I wanted to miniaturise for a flip-card aid-memoire I was making. Then I would get the pressie and give it to Karen on Monday.

Young Gill was alone in sick bay. 'Where's Karen?' I asked.

'On three week's leave. She left yesterday afternoon for Aberdeen to get ready for the wedding. Calum and I are going.'

'Damn! I haven't got her present yet! Could one of you take it up when you go?'

'Sure, Boss. No problem.' The phone rang. Gill picked it up. 'Yes… yes, he's here just now.' I groaned. Not the Reggie's office with some bloody rating on a charge needing a 'Fit for cells' medical.

'It's the SAR cell on, Boss. They want you. There's a job on. Some old man suffering from a stroke. don't know where.' Quadruple Sod's Law!

Dave Tribe popped his head round the door of the SAR shack as I was about to struggle into my goon suit. 'You won't need that, Doc. It's overland all the way. Just take it with you, and wear your overalls. The info we've got is of a seventy-nine year old man collapsed with a stroke on Ben Lawers.'

An old man of seventy-nine with a stroke! What a first mountain job!

The scenery made up for the lack of drama. With the distant mountains beckoning, our route took us over my cousin Jim's house in Bearsden; over the Lake of Menteith, dotted with boats full of dotty anglers pursuing spotty rainbows; and over Roddy's wee stocked hill loch on the slopes above Loch Vennacher. I pointed them out to Kiwi who used to boast of fishing for rainbows—big ones, of course!—in his native New Zealand.

He turned round in his seat with a grin. 'Thought about you this time, Doc... Need to keep your flying hours up!'

'Thanks a bundle... This is meant to be my half-day.'

'Where were you going, Doc?' Foxie chipped in mischievously.

'To my bloody bed to sleep!'

'You wouldn't want to miss this historic SAR,' reproached Kiwi. 'It's my hundredth... the big One-Zero-Zero.'

'You'll be buying lunch and drinks all round, then?'

'And you've still to beat Fiona... one hundred and one, and her photo in the paper... and Karen has had hers in as well!'

'I get my photo in the paper!'

'Yeah... Only the front page of the *Daily Record*, with the headline: BUZZ OFF—WE DON'T WANT TO BE RESCUED!'

Away back in March, I had crossed swords in a four letter, vigorous correspondence with the editor of the *Daily Record*, before his paper finally apologised for their sensational misreporting and gross distortion of the part played by Kiwi and his crew in a mountain rescue in appalling circumstances on the north face of Ben Nevis earlier that month, and the lads had been very appreciative.

Steve Roberts in the back, who had just been in touch with Edinburgh Rescue and the Killin Mountain Rescue Team as we overflew Lochearnhead, passed the locus coordinates forward. Foxie, the death-or-glory boy, with already one Queen's Commendation to his credit, was bitterly disappointed.

'Shit. That's not very high up. I like my rescues above three-and-a-half-thousand feet at least! This one's only on the tourist path above the visitor centre.'

Crossing Loch Tay, Kiwi located the Scottish National Trust Centre on the hill road over to Glen Lyon, and followed the tourist path up the mountain. Below us, the Killin MRT boys were just starting off from the car park, lugging their stretcher and rescue gear. Within minutes we were on scene, about a mile above the centre, to discover, to our surprise, an ambulanceman and policeman already in attendance, tending an elderly lady—not a man—sitting slumped on a grassy bank by the path. She was being given oxygen, and her pulse and blood pressure were reported satisfactory. She was fully conscious, and fortunately did not seem to have any permanent paralysis.

Her husband was with her. They were a Dutch couple, and like most Dutch folk, had enough English to appreciate what we were doing, and to accept our reassurances about her satisfactory condition, and the short flight to hospital. If you happen to be a tourist in Scotland, and have to be flown to hospital, it would be difficult to find a better, or more romantic landing site, than the picturesque King's Meadows in the shadow of the historic ramparts of Stirling Castle!

RNAS Prestwick, home to HMS Gannet *and 819 Squadron from 1971 to 2002. HMS* Gannet *SAR Flight still occupies the airfield site beyond the road—two large hangars. Two SAR Sea Kings can be seen on the apron.*

1987. All geared up and nowhere to go! The author in goonsuit, PLP and bone-dome, with mark 6 ASW Sea King in background.

Atmospheric shot of Rescue 177 in the mountains. Rotorblade tips and rockfaces don't mix!

Sea drills in the Clyde off Cumbrae. The author about to be winched up from a one-man life raft. Note the spray from the downdraught.

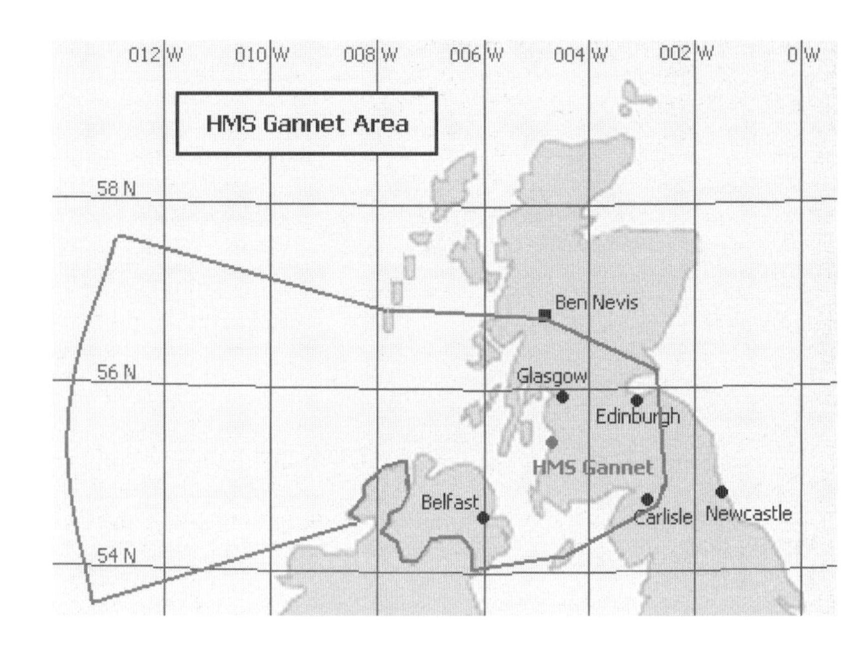

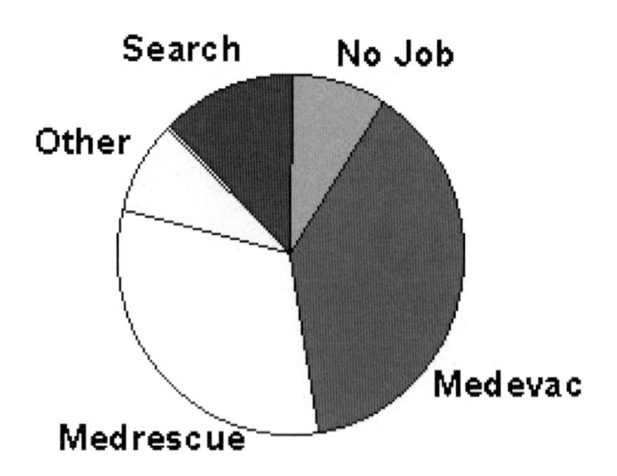

2001 call-out categories—the proportion of different jobs done by Rescue 177.

The 'Wee Team'—not just a game for macho men! MAQ Fiona McWilliam, MAQ Magz Brodie and LMA Karen Burnett with POMA John Gregg, 'Doc' and LMA Trevor Scott, 1993.

The 'Big Team'—newly formed HMS Gannet *SAR Flight, 2002.*

Hopefully not 'Downbird' in the West Highlands!

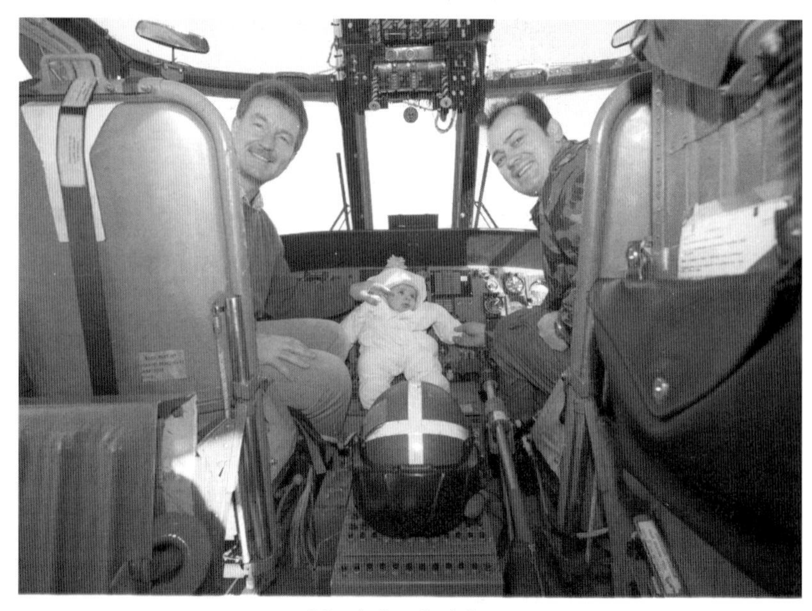

Newly hatched flier?

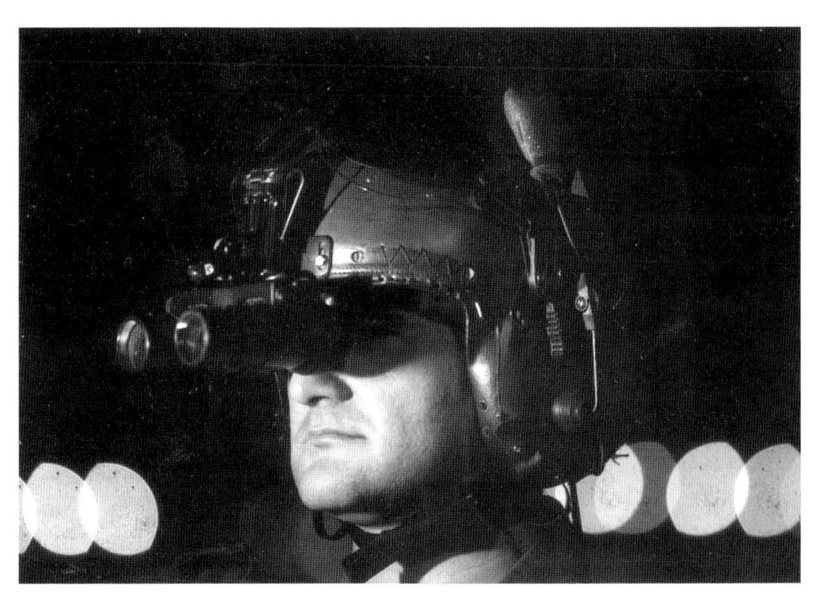

The new night-vision goggles—of immense importance to safety when night-flying in the mountains.

LWACMN Bernie Pope.

Russian Victor Three hunter-killer submarine 60 miles north west of Cape Wrath, February 1996.

POACMN Ian Copley directing the historic medevac.

15

3rd August 1994

FISHLESS

Just back from three unforgettable and wonderful weeks in Canada, traversing two thousand miles of forest, lake and prairie by train from Toronto to Edmonton; driving through the spectacular Rockies; white-water rafting—and casting a futile fly—on the Athabasca River; stern-wheeling on the Fraser River with its phenomenal annual run of five million salmon; comparing notes with a Cowichan Indian on Vancouver Island on the striking similarity between the poaching methods used on his river and on my River Doon (Was it the Patna poachers who taught the Indians—or vice-versa?)—the call of the wild tonight had been too strong to resist!

After stoically enduring another spell of glorious weather on our return home to Scotland, I had shouted for joy on learning that the river had risen overnight after a welcome burst of heavy rain, and the salmon were running. Standing beside the fishing hut at Doonholm after work, on a pleasant summer evening, it was great to be alive and fishing. Eagerly threading the line through the final few rings of my fly rod, I jumped suddenly, and missed the tip ring as the bleep went off from the depths of my chest waders. Shit! A thousand times shit!

I phoned *Gannet* from the Keeper's cottage. It was a short trip... to Arran. A boy of fifteen with severe abdominal pain, and RCC had requested a doctor. I had my doubts.

Karen was duty MA, and was already onboard when I pitched up. 'Paddy' Green, the pleasant young Irish LACMN, had stayed behind to see me alright.

'Got your overalls, Doc? The water temp's warm, higher than fourteen degrees, so you don't need to wear your goon suit.'

'Thanks. I'm wearing cotton anyway, so I'll just put my goon suit on top of my shirt and cords.' I couldn't be bothered transferring all my bits and pieces out of my goon-bag into my overalls, but soon regretted my laziness. It was a warm, humid night and by the time I had run out to the helo I was dripping wet inside.

The brief was an eighteen-year-old with severe abdominal pain for Crosshouse Hospital—and I still couldn't fathom why I had been called out for such a short transfer. With Greg Lawrence his P2 at the controls, 'Ratty' Roll turned round in his seat with a grin—'Sorry to hear we've buggered up your fishing, Doc!' He must have been telepathic. My sentiments exactly.

'Ee never catches anything anyway!' piped up Karen. 'Ee's been promising me a big trout for the past two years.'

I ignored her. It was a pleasant evening. The light rain had given way to beautiful evening sunlight and the sea below was calm. Even the throb of the Sea King sounded somehow less intrusive than usual. Peace. All was well with the world.

'The events of thirty-five or forty years ago seemed like yesterday… the searchlights, the whistle of the bombs, the sound of sirens, fire engines, ambulances… the musty stale odour of the underground shelters. The indomitable spirit of the Londoners. The singing, the crush of people—hot sweat, warm flesh… sweet perfumes… Yes, perfume. O Priscilla! Warm pressing flesh. The rustle of silk as her skirt slowly inched slowly up her thighs. His hand followed…' One of the backseat pair had obviously flipped his lid in the heat!

'Here. That's enough of that sexist shit! We've a lady on board.'

'Wot? Karen!'

'Yeah, she's blushing.'

'Not Karen! She's an old married woman now. She's done it all before.'

'Watch it you lot. Or she'll get you to pee into the neck of a broken bottle at your next aircrew medical! Anybody due an injection?'

'We're clear ahead to land at Knockenkelly.' Ratty brought us abruptly back into line as he skimmed in low over the newly turfed football pitch and landed carefully well clear of the playing surface. 'Don't see the ambulance yet.'

It was the middle of the holiday season, and the roadside fence was lined with dozens of rubbernecking holidaymakers as the ambulance arrived. The driver thoughtfully closed the door to give us some privacy. On board was a young teenage lad from London, who had somewhat overestimated his agility ability and come a cropper while vaulting a fence. He had landed heavily on his left side and sustained internal abdominal injuries—possibly a ruptured spleen. However he was very comfortable, and there was really not much for me to do apart from clear his drip during the flight. This concerned me, for my MAs were often being called out to severe head injuries and other problems which might have benefitted from a doctor's presence, while I was being called out for simple things like this—and missing a night's fishing! The Sister in charge of the ITU at Crosshouse was similarly perturbed when we dropped young James off at the hospital—from which he was discharged, none the worse, two days later.

'We didn't know you were coming. Nobody notified us officially... we only heard a rumour and we did not have time to provide fire brigade cover. Could you please sort out this lack of communication with your Rescue Control Centre so that we don't have this problem again?' I promised to relay her comments to the crew for action on our return to *Gannet*.

Karen was sitting behind the pilots, perched on the SAR gear like a wee garden gnome, when Ratty suddenly turned to her. 'I've a medical emergency here for you, Karen.'

'What?'

'It's this zit on my nose that needs squeezed!'

'Watch it, Karen! Squeeze that and it'll splatter the windscreen like a shitehawk!' Karen duly declined.

'Well, I'll do it myself.'

'Hats off if you do!' taunted Greg Lawrence, seconds before a triumphant forefinger was waggled under his nose as proof!

The boys were having fun as we overflew the patchwork of rolling fields and secluded woodlands, intersected by hedgerows and quiet minor roads, which bounded on Prestwick.

'Hey. There's a good lay-by down there for a bit of the other… Take a note of the map ref!'

'So that's why it's called a lay-by! I've often wondered.'

'Boss! I'm ashamed of you!'

'Sorry, Karen!'

Strapped in for landing, we rolled slowly to a halt as ops room called. 'Keep your rotors running. We may have another job for you.' Steve Roberts disappeared into the ops building.

A few moments later, Ratty twisted round in his seat. 'Don't think you'll be needed, Doc. It's nothing that Karen can't cope with… a fifteen year old boy missing in a river near Tyndrum. We'll have to search. May be a while, but you can come along for the jaunt if you wish.'

Much as I would have liked to, it was not very politic… Helen didn't even know I'd even been to Arran. And anyway, I might still get a cast at a salmon if I hurried!

16

30th October 1994
DUTY CALLS

'I've had enough of this!' Helen gave an anguished cry as I put down the phone. 'I'm getting too old to have my night's sleep disturbed again and again and again. You'll have to give this up, I can't stand it!' I said little as I slunk out of bed and crept past Fiona's bedroom in my pyjamas to collect my flying kit from the boot of the car outside the front door. But I felt a right bastard!

There was little I could do about it under the circumstances. It was one-thirty. A superb night out had been ruined by a phonecall that should never have happened. After a hellish Thursday night on call when I had put five into hospital, Helen had slaved all Friday to produce one of her culinary masterpiece dinner parties for Peter and Denise Galloway and our friends Christine and Tom Bryson. Peter and I had been fishing together a lot during the summer, but had resisted the temptation to bore the arse off Tom—a fanatical golfer—with tales of the loch.

Instead Peter had modestly recalled some of his experiences and his inner feelings of turmoil and fear as Senior Observer on *Invincible* during the Falklands War, when he had to plan squadron operational sorties,and look after Prince Andrew's welfare and flight programme—usually in an opposite direction! And Denise gave a rare insight into how a newly-wed Navy bride had had to cope with her own fears and loneliness, and frustration, when her husband was abruptly torn from her side, on the very day he had just ripped out all the old kitchen furnishings in their new house. Unlike the rest of the country, she and her friends had not sat glued night after night to their television sets.

Tonight, it had been Helen's turn for a treat—a superb meal at Braidwoods, a newly opened haute cuisine restaurant in the north of the county—and we had arrived home about midnight, replete and ready for a good night's sleep. I had previously told sick bay I would not be available on Friday or Saturday night for SARs, but somehow Steve Roberts the duty observer had not been informed.

'Make some excuse you can't go.' Helen stood behind me on the stairs. 'You don't have to do it… it's voluntary now.' It was difficult to argue the finer points of professional duty while zipping up flying overalls on the doorstep. If I hadn't been at home, RCC would have had to find another doctor—probably using the same Campbeltown GP who had requested the doctor escort for his patient with breathing problems in the first place. But I had been at home, I had personally answered the phone, I was not drunk, ill, or otherwise incapable, so in all fairness I could hardly back off at this stage. What if the MAs couldn't cope and the man died in the helicopter, and at the Fiscal's Inquiry somebody asked where had the doctor been. 'Oh, in his bed, he refused to come out when we called him.'

I had faced similar dilemmas on many occasions over the years when requested by Ambulance Control to attend RTAs, and had always felt duty-bound to attend. This duty thing wasn't something that was easy to explain. It wasn't the blind obedience type of duty expected of the services. It was a professional duty, the old concept of which seems nowadays much less fashionable or acceptable among younger doctors and other professionals, than it was twenty-five years ago for those NHS idealists who graduated before the Swinging Sixties; those of us whose characters were formed in the still-disciplined post-war days of the early fifties, when some of the duty and obedience of our parents' generation—to which they had sacrificed so much during the Depression and the War years—rubbed off on us, and was still very much to the fore in our schools, bible classes, Scouts, Guides and Boys' Brigade.

At that time, a jingoistic 'We won the War!' mentality still prevailed. We would chant this slogan victoriously in the primary school playground after inter-class pitched battles. We worshipped the heroes of 'The Dambusters', 'The Colditz Story', 'The Cruel Sea', and 'Reach for the Sky'. Subconsciously we were influenced by the all-pervading sense of duty and tremendous self-sacrifice which flowed from the pages of these books, and the inevitable film versions. Our comics, *Adventure*, *Hotspur*, *Rover* and *Eagle*, were full of glamourised war fiction, football heroes, and fair play. In every school playground, the ring of eager spectators demanded, and got, a 'fair fight!'

Our parents all worked long hours. Doctors worked dedicated long hours. It was expected. We were privileged to become doctors. We were told by eminent consultants that ours was a vocation, a calling, not a nine-to-five job. It was glamorous at first to ponce around hospital in our pristine white coats, saving lives. We told—or kidded—ourselves, that it was great training to work ourselves into the ground on a one-in-two twenty-four hour rota. It had always been like this. We might well have been mugs. We probably were. Those who followed on in the seventies certainly thought so, and militantly fought for more pay, more humane working conditions, and more off duty. And good luck to them.

Changing attitudes in Maggie Thatcher's eighties—the twin pursuit of pound and pleasure—tipped the balance, and off-duty became increasingly more important than duty. And it rubs off. As the young ones demand fewer nights on, and longer holidays, so the auld yins, nearing 'burn-out' after twenty-seven years of grinding on-call, are quite happy to go along with it. Even more to the point, long-suffering GP wives, constantly and dutifully tied to the phone and the house for decades, have come to resent the personal freedom that deputising services, Cellnet and Vodaphone, have given their younger sisters and, like Helen, are screaming for release from their lifetime burden of sleepless nights and fagged-out days. Duty can get stuffed!

And so tonight—as far as Helen was concerned—could *Gannet*. But she knew how much I loved the work; how it was for me a haven of sanity, where I could recharge batteries exhausted from an uphill struggle with the ever-mounting irrelevancies which, in the name of progress, were being foisted on those of us who still believed in good old-fashioned patient care. I kissed her gently on the cheek and prayed for forgiveness soon—it usually took a couple of days! Anyway, Campbeltown was only twenty minutes flying time away, it was a nice night, and I shouldn't be too long. My last two quickie jobs to Arran had only taken an hour. I should have known better!

The duty crew were still in the SAR Cell when I arrived. Steve Roberts met me. 'Hi, Doc. Glad you could come in. Hope we didn't disturb anything! It's an elderly man in Campbeltown with severe breathing problems. We wanted to bring him to Crosshouse, but the doctor over there is insisting he goes to Oban.'

'You must be joking. That will add at least thirty minutes to the flight time… and I don't fancy that if he's desperately ill.'

'Well, they've asked for a heart monitor, oxygen, suction, i/v fluids, and a doctor to go with him, Sir,' interjected Fez Parker, my new LMA. Fez was an Oggie (i.e., from Cornwall), born with tar in his veins, whose old man was Chief POMA down at Culdrose. Tall, slim, good-looking, super-keen, efficient and wi' an awfy guid conceit o' himsel, he had had previous SAR experience at HMS *Osprey*. His enthusiastic words comforted me no end! 'I'll try and get the doctor for you on the phone, Sir.' He disappeared into the SARO's office. I waited a couple of minutes for the call, and when he didn't return I went through to find him busy in conversation and jotting down notes on his pad. He put his hand over the mouthpiece, looked up, and started to give me details.

'Is that the doctor you are speaking to?' I asked curtly.

'Yes.' he replied.

'Well, I think I had better speak to him myself.'

'Hello. Doctor Begg here from HMS *Gannet*. I believe you want us to take this patient up to Oban instead of over here to Crosshouse or Paisley…' I got no further. There was a muffled explosion at the other end of the phone.

'This is the fifth time I've had to explain myself! This man is for Oban… Oban is where our District Hospital is. There is a Chest

Unit there and the consultant visits Campbeltown every week.' I backed off, bloody annoyed that Fez had gone for details instead of putting me straight through myself.

'I'm sorry, Doctor. I've just arrived and wanted to speak to you myself as you had requested a doctor to accompany your patient… we'll do as you say as long as you are happy that he will stand an extra thirty minutes on the aircraft.'

Ratty Roll, the duty P1 pilot was still loitering in the SAR cell as I emerged. I confirmed our destination.

As we left the ops building, it crossed my mind that maybe I should let Helen know that we might be a wee bit later than anticipated, but decided that discretion was the better part of valour! Anyway, my most important concern at the moment was for the thirty pound gourmet dinner lolloping around in my stomach as I heaved myself on board the aircraft. Would it still be there when I got back?

Surprisingly enough, despite all my bending and shifting of gear en route while setting up the HeartStart monitor, and checking the pulse oximeter and oxygen cylinders, I did not suffer even the slightest heartburn—a compliment to both the gastronomic excellence of nouvelle cuisine—and a level flight. I looked up just as we overflew Campbeltown.

Ratty landed in a nearby park, and a waiting ambulance took us quickly up the brae to the hospital. A small, greying, middle-aged doctor in a white coat met us in the corridor. His face was strangely familiar, although I knew I had never met him. Then I remembered… on TV, being interviewed in the aftermath of the Chinook disaster on the Mull of Kintyre—a local GP who had been one of the first on the scene, Dr Horton. We shook hands and he ushered us into a side room, where a dreadfully frail elderly man lay propped up in bed, monitored, dripped and catheterised; his ash-white face hidden behind a green oxygen mask. His son and daughter were by his side.

'This is Duncan. He had an anterior myocardial infarct forty-eight hours ago, and has been in respiratory failure today. He's been nebulised, and has had i/v hydrocortisone and diuretics. He has stabilised a bit over the past hour or two, but is too ill to keep down here. He needs the services of Oban.'

Duncan just lay there, exhausted and past caring. He would need to be transported in a sitting position. 'Can I borrow five or six pillows?' I asked Sister. 'I'm sure Oban will give you them back.' Fez and Foxie laid the stretcher on the floor beside the bed, while Dr Horton unclipped the monitor, leaving in place the two defibrillation pads. I built a back-rest of pillows on top of the Flectron blanket, and Duncan was gently lowered into place. By a cunning use of blanket straps we were able to enclose the pillows inside the blanket and secure our patient in a comfortable, upright position. Simple but effective.

'I hope you have a quiet night,' I solaced Dr Horton on our way out. 'Not much chance of that!' he grimaced, 'with a hallucinating psychotic just along the corridor, and a drunk who hit his head on the road after he claimed a fox had jumped out at him!'

On board the aircraft, we had problems initially fastening our monitor leads to the defibrillation pad studs, and were quite relieved when a nice sinus rhythm trace appeared on the screen. The pulse oximeter was working well, however, and showed a gratifying 94 per cent oxygen saturation at a flow rate of six litres per minute. So far so good.

It was very dark in the back of the cab. For some reason, Steve Roberts was only allowing us the red nightlight, possibly because Ratty was flying low up the Sound of Jura, and he was having to concentrate on his radar to avoid hitting small island tops. Duncan lay quiet, insulated from all the noise by a pair of ear muffs, his breathing imperceptible and monitored only by the faint intermittent misting of his clear oxygen mask. I signalled Fez for the use of a torch. His drip had blocked, but only took seconds to clear.

We settled back to relax as much as we could in a tangle of wire leads and oxygen tubing. Suddenly, the oximeter figures began to tumble alarmingly—90, 85, 83, 80, 78 per cent saturation, and his pulse began to rise. Something was wrong. Fez looked over at me. I quickly checked Duncan's airway and got Fez to hold his head steady while I turned the oxygen supply up to ten litres. We both sighed with relief as the saturation levels rose quickly back to normal over the next two minutes. A handy piece of kit, that pulse oximeter.

Without it, Duncan would have become quietly anoxic without our being aware of it, lulled into a false sense of security by his oxygen mask. It could have had serious consequences.

'How far till Oban now, Ratty?' I inquired anxiously.

'About five minutes to North Connel. We've taken about forty-five minutes from Campbeltown.'

'Why North Connel?' I asked, for this landing site was about four miles out of Oban, and not ideal for someone as ill as our old lad. 'Why not the shinty pitch in the town?'

'It's too risky for a night approach, Doc. We could have problems.'

'Do you know there is a new hospital opening in Oban in the next few months? I hope it has a helipad on site.'

'Nobody has told us about it, but I'll check when we get back.'

The ambulance was waiting on the airstrip, and Duncan was transferred and wired up to their monitor and oxygen supply for the bumpy journey to the West Highland Hospital. We wished him well. Hopefully this type of risky transfer would soon be a thing of the past.

'Take us home, Ratty, it's past bedtime!'

It had been a task which had given us all a wee bit of job satisfaction, and we were quietly elated as we flew down Loch Fyne at four thousand feet, well above the patchy fog which filled the glens below. I was standing behind the pilots, admiring the view, when suddenly Ratty exclaimed, 'What the hell's that!' as a waving beam of light shot up through thin cloud partly veiling the orange streetlights of a small Argyll village, possibly Furnace. The powerful beam continued to wave.

Probably the local bobby with nothing better to do at half-three in the morning.'

'We'll soon sort that,' said Ratty, as he switched on the aircraft's swivel searchlights and trained them down the offending beam. 'That'll zap him. Teach him to meddle with us!'

'Yeah. There will probably be a report in next week's *Oban Times*—"Inverary Policeman Makes Contact with Extra-terrestrials"! Beam him up, Ratty!'

17

17th August 1995

CARDIAC ARREST

Eddie Welsh, the Ambulance Training Officer, poked his head round the door of the lecture room. 'Would you like a cup of tea?' I looked at Don Clark who nodded an affirmative.

Don had recently returned to *Gannet* for a second stint as my POMA after a sea draft on HMS *Edinburgh,* and we had just embarked on a long overdue reappraisal of our SAR equipment—which was why we were sitting in Ayr Ambulance HQ on a Thursday morning, picking the brains of Stewart Kane, the Assistant Training Officer, on the various types of grab-bag used by his paramedics.

The problem was that our big red bag was specially equipped for me to deal with medical emergencies, and was not very suitable for MAs or aircrewmen to hump on to mountain-sides or ships. Last week, on a visit to Troon Lifeboat Station, I had seen an excellent carrying case for a D-sized oxygen cylinder, standard issue to RNLI, which was rugged enough and ideal for our purposes—but too bloody expensive! What we really needed was a small rucsac just large enough to carry a D-sized cylinder, stiffneck collars, some i/v fluids and a variety of dressings. This morning, unfortunately, we had found that the ambulance paramedic bags were far too big—the latest model could almost have been used as a body bag! We would have to try one of the local climbing shops.

Through in Eddie's office, we chatted over our cuppas and exchanged ideas. Although Rescue 177 had done more than 160 SARs since the New Year, it had been a very lean spell for me personally over the past six months, with only one job. Yet it had been very satisfying in other respects. At *Gannet* a couple of months back, we had jointly trialled the new neonatal incubator mark two, a pig of a machine to lift into an ambulance, and even worse to lift four feet off the ground into a helicopter. But we had managed it, and the aircrew had devised a successful method of securing it to the bulkhead in flight. It had given us all a quiet glow of pleasure, a few weeks later, when it was used to transport a very premature baby safely from Campbeltown to Ayrshire Central.

Also, after two years of persistent letter writing, authorisation had at last come through from FONAC for our Propaq monitor—and even more important, after four years of pleading, the HeartStart 3000 had finally been approved for use as a defibrillator on board Navy Sea Kings, subject to various safety restrictions. Only last week I had drafted operational guidelines for the MAs and SAR crew.

Despite the daytime presence of Helimed 5, or 'Undercoat One', as the SAR boys had uncharitably christened the wee yellow Scottish Ambulance Bolkow 105, there had been a surge of medevacs, partly due to an industrial dispute between the Argyll and Bute Health Board and Calmac the ferry operators, which had resulted in *Gannet* being regularly tasked, during the night, to transport pregnant women and heart cases from the Island of Bute across the Clyde to Greenock only a few miles away.

This was generally felt to have been a dodgy use of the Search and Rescue Service, and had caused some senior rank irritation in the squadron, and frustration among the SAR crews, but it had also highlighted the need for a continuing update of our medical skills if we were being expected more and more to take on the role of the air ambulance paramedics. Don and several of the others had been down to Haslar for a defibrillator course, and I was now the odd man out—and felt it.

My last SAR had been to transfer an uncomplicated heart attack patient from Coll to Oban. With little to do apart from glance occasionally at the monitor, the trip had been memorable for the beautiful sunset above Coll on the way out; and on the way back, a magnificent full moon over Mull, with hill lochs glinting silver on the black flanks of Ben More. This idyllic scenario had contrasted very dramatically with a tragic situation in which Fez Parker found himself a few weeks later, on an evening when I was unavailable due to practice on-call duty.

They had been tasked to pick up an elderly man with a heart attack on a yacht less than a mile off the Arran coast, and because of the likely difficulties and delays in trying to winch him off the small craft, it seemed quicker and easier for the yacht to head for an anchorage, now less than half a mile away, where the transfer could be more easily accomplished.

Sadly he had suffered a cardiac arrest only a couple of hundred yards offshore, with no one on board competent enough to apply CPR to keep him alive till he got there. This tragic climax had generated a lot of 'If onlys' and 'What ifs' heart-searching back at *Gannet* among the aircrew and the medics. If only they had dropped the winchman or medic on board to accompany the patient to shore. If only they taken the defibrillator, they could have done CPR, monitored and defibrillated. What if I had not been on call for the practice... could I have been of any assistance? And so on.

Like so many previous SARs, it had made us all look again at our procedures. In future the crew would attempt to put someone on board, and now painfully aware of how quickly a coronary patient can go 'off', they might be just be a wee bit less reticent in calling me out for heart attacks or other serious medical emergencies. It was an 'auld sang', and one I had sung to successive SAROs and crews over the years, with mixed results. I could just as easily have been in Fez's place that day, hence the urgent desire to update my defib skills.

'Can I fix a definite date before we go, Eddie?'

'Sure. How about Monday morning about half-ten. We're doing a post-proficiency exam for some of the frontline crews, but you and the young medic Don mentioned... eh, Rob... can use the sideroom with resusc Annie, and I'll switch between rooms.'

'Thanks a lot. I've only had one job since last October, and I'm getting gey rusty and badly in need of a refresher. It's my own fault.

I've now got this bunch so highly trained that they just don't need me any more… like your paramedics have cornered the RTA market and left us BASICS doctors out of work.' I couldn't resist a wee backhanded compliment to the skills of the local ambulance paramedics, whose increased presence over the past few years had greatly reduced the demand for our services at road accidents.

At 3 o'clock, about halfway through my afternoon surgery, the bleep went. I got the shock of my life. 'Pete West here, Doc… ops room. We've got a heart attack on a yacht off Tarbert.' I had a distinct dose of the déja-vus. 'How long will you be?'

'About ten to twelve minutes.'

As good as my word, I rushed up to the locker room, put my left foot straight off into the right leg of my goon suit, sorted myself out, zipped up, then scrabbled for my flying boots on the floor of the locker. They had gone… some bastard had nicked them!

Stuffing my feet as best as I could into my working shoes, I grabbed my helmet and ran, muttering oaths about there being no such a thing as an officer and a bloody gentleman nowadays as I wrestled with the lifejacket buttons. An urgent voice snapped 'Hurry up! You can do that on board!' It was the duty observer.

I stumbled up to the front of the aircraft, strapped in as it shuddered into the air, and glanced over at Gill Dorman, my MAQ. She had a troubled look in her eyes, and a determined set to her wee pointed chin. She chinagraphed on her knee-pad, 'I'd like to speak to you when we get back.' I groaned inwardly and scribbled back, 'Why?' Was there more trouble between her and the crew? Gill had had a rough ride from the beginning, despite her Boyd Trophy award for that memorable first SAR. She was a slightly built, fair-haired, wee skelf of a lass with a quiet, unassertive personality, but good at her job. Being only a Junior Rating MA, female, alone on an aircraft with Officers and senior aircrewmen, her unenviable position was a bit like that of a houseman telling his consultant what to do—although she ultimately had clinical responsibility for her patient in flight. Unfortunately, her quiet manner was interpreted by some of the more macho, 'It's a Man's Navy' types among the aircrew as demonstrating a lack of confidence and unwillingness to fly—which was utter rubbish.

Halfway up the Clyde and clear of Air Traffic Control radio chaff, I was eventually briefed. A man with a heart attack on a catamaran off Tarbert, Loch Fyne—it would only be a short transit—about fifteen minutes. Scarcely enough time to get the defibrillator ready—and would I be able to use it effectively? Och, it was idiot proof! I'd manage… and Gill had been on the course!

As we approached Tarbert, Clyde Coastguard reported that the catamaran had reached the harbour and was moored at the fish quay. Neil Goodenough looked over to his co-pilot Lt Steve Bucklow, who was scrutinising the map. 'Where is that?' Standing just behind them, I pointed to the spot. 'There, on the south side of the harbour. I was in Tarbert just a couple of weeks ago—on the last day of my holidays.'

I had no sooner spoken, than the aircraft rounded the corner and we were hovering over the picturesque haven, packed with summering yachts and small craft, and overlooked on three sides by greystone hillside villas, and an L-shaped harbour frontage of shops, restaurants and hotels. With no landing site in view, Neil chose to winch Sgt Phil Hill, our pet Crab aircrewman and myself on to the fish quay itself. What a drama for the gawping holidaymakers lining the harbour rails—as fish boxes and creels were blown up into the air or down into the sea by the tremendous down-draught—and two medics stumbled and ran through the chaotic debris to the ramp leading down to the mooring pontoon, where a knot of anxious people was standing by a green-hulled catamaran.

At the hatch door stood a kent face, Dr Neil MacDonald, the Tarbert GP. He exchanged a wry 'Hello, again!' as his outstretched hand ushered me into the cramped cabin. Along the centre table lay a large, motionless man wired to a HeartStart defibrillator, on whom two hot and perspiring ambulancemen were frantically performing cardiac massage while the local Coastguard bag-and-masked him from the other side.

'How many shocks has he had?' I shouted.

'Three!'

'Is he still in VF?'

'No… Asystole… the defib is in a no-shock mode… can you intubate him?'

Asystole—a completely flat trace—meant it was a pretty hopeless situation, but out of the corner of my eye I could see a desperately worried-looking, fair-haired woman standing quietly in the galley behind the ambulance technicians—probably his wife. I would have to do something... at least try. Grabbing the airways box from my bag, I drew out an endotracheal tube and the laryngoscope, and clamberd over the Coastguard to jam myself into the tiny space between the patient's head and the forard end of the cabin. He had been sick in the final throes, which didn't help matters, but at the second attempt I got the tube down. His colour had gone. His pupils were fixed and dilated. There was no flicker on the monitor screen. It was a waste of effort—just prolonging a last hope which was beyond hope. I took a deep breath, and uttered those few words that even after twenty-nine years of saying them, still don't come any easier, 'I'm sorry. I think he's gone.'

Leaving the ambulance boys to deal with the formalities of removing the dead man, I joined his wife and two friends on the quay. Gently I enquired what had happened. Amazingly composed under the circumstances, she explained that they had been moored in Stonefield Castle Bay, just a couple of miles round the headland to the north. It was very hot, and her husband had been swimming off the boat. He had only gone about twenty yards from the cat when he suddenly turned, swam back, and instead of climbing up the ladder, had hauled himself up over the gunwales, gone inside and collapsed. She had started mouth to mouth respiration on him as her two friends made all speed back to Tarbert, alerting the emergency services en route.

'Would it have made any difference if we had stayed where we were and called an ambulance?' she asked anxiously.

'No.' I tactfully explained. 'Although a lot of patients survive heart attacks, as many as fifty percent die instantly, or within a few minutes, unless expert help is on hand to give immediate CPR or defibrillation. You did what you could, and did it very well, at least giving the ambulancemen a chance to use their defibrillator. But even a defibrillator in the best hands is only able to save about twenty per cent of people with a cardiac arrest... and I'm afraid it was not to be for your husband.' It was all I could do—give her a wee bit of support and reassurance to ease the suddenness of her loss.

Back at *Gannet*, Alex Hall the Senior Observer collared me in the Squadron Building. 'Could I have a word with you, Jimmy?' I changed and joined him in his office. Gill was already there, and Don Clark.

'What's the problem?' I asked, although I already had a fair idea.

'It's just to discuss ways of improving your callout time. RCC were getting a bit hot under the collar with the delay while we waited for your arrival.'

'Well, I think you should check the agreed procedures for calling me out.' I countered quickly. 'Gill here didn't know she was going to a heart attack case till she came down and met Phil Hill running out to the aircraft, and she was called by phone rather than by siren. She was quite right in calling for a doctor. My medics have for years now been instructed to call for a doctor if they feel they are going to something they can't handle, and a protocol was drawn up by myself and Dave Duthie when he was SARO, defining maximum delay times day or night. This problem crops up year after year whenever we have a change-over of personnel. Do they ever read these protocols?' I would have been very surprised if they did, given the amount of paper the Navy floats on!

'I've already had a chat with POMA Clark and MAQ Dorman about your first point, and we'll just have to make sure that the MA is immediately informed of a casualty's condition by the duty aircrewman so that a quick decision can be made whether to call you out. But this still leaves a major time delay to be pared down. How long does it take you to get here?'

'From the house or surgery, ten to twelve minutes with the green light, then five minutes to change. I can be onboard in sixteen minutes from being bleeped.'

'Could we get you to change on the aircraft? The P2 often gets into his goon suit after takeoff. If the MA was to meet you at the apron side gate for a quick briefing, with your helmet, goon suit, lifejacket and boots—this could save a lot of time.'

'Probably about four or five minutes. It's a good idea and worth a try. If you can find my stolen boots!'

'Doc—about your flying boots...' Don looked rather sheepish. 'I was tidying up your locker last week, and hung them up on a hook.'

Who the hell would expect to find their flying boots hung up at head height, hidden inside a flying helmet bag, when they were in a hurry! Apologies for that slur on their integrity... Officers were still gentlemen after all!

That night, back home, the bedroom was like an oven, as it had been for the past four glorious weeks of an exceptional heatwave. All the windows were open, letting in the night sounds, but no cool air. Helen and I tossed and turned, our sleeplessness compounded by the fact that Fiona was out at a party till two o'clock. We were just dropping finally into a settled sleep when a nearby burglar alarm went off around 0530. Cursing, I got up for a look out the window—no sign of activity. 'Should I go out and have a look?' I suggested half-heartedly.

'Don't be stupid! Come back to bed and get some sleep!' was the peremptory reply in a tone I dare not defy—not that I felt like it anyway. Ach, to hell with the Neighbourhood Watch scheme! An hour later, the phone went: 'Doctor Begg?'

'Yes...' I intoned sleepily and with a degree of grump.

'Neil Goodenough here, from *Gannet*. I'm afraid we've got a report of another heart attack—an elderly man on a yacht again. Can you come in?'

Helen, to her eternal credit, rose to the occasion, literally, and met me at the front door with a cup of tea as I pulled on my ovies. 'You can't go on an empty stomach!'

'Thanks, love. At least I'll have something to throw up!' The prospect of boarding a small yacht always filled me with foreboding. Outside, it was a beautiful morning of still, sweet air and blue skies, which heartened me considerably, although I wondered what the lads would be feeling like, getting another job right at the end of their twenty-four-hour shift.

The new arrangements worked a treat. Gill met me at the gate with my gear, and in the five minutes saved as I dressed on board, we were ten miles up the Clyde and well on our way, our destination somewhere west of Mull, a two and a half hour trip. Shit! My Friday morning surgery! A message was quickly relayed back through ops room for Helen to do my dirty work for me and inform the practice I wouldn't be in for a few hours. Sadly, the low morning sun had to be banned from the observer's radar screen, and I saw nothing of the running commentary from up front of places of stunning beauty as we overflew Arran, Kintyre, Jura and Mull in a blacked-out rear cabin.

Gradually, through Clyde Coastguard, then Oban Coastguard, we picked up more details of our casualty—an eighty-four year old man on a yacht five miles beyond Staffa at an anchorage in the Treshnish Isles. He had a history of angina and had numbness of his left arm. However as we flew, it was reported that he also had numbness of his left leg, making it more likely that this was some form of stroke rather than a heart attack, as had been first reported.

Eventually, Lt Jules Price, our observer, made radio contact with the yacht on channel sixteen. '*Mistress Malin*... Rescue 177. Can we have your position, please.'

A foreign-sounding female voice crackled over the air, giving co-ordinates which were quickly checked on the map.

'*Mistress Malin*, Rescue Helicopter. Can you confirm you are at the island of Lunga—and can you see the helicopter?'

'Rescue Helicopter, *Mistress Malin*. I vill confirm ve are at Lunga, at the anchorage. Ve cannot see you yet.'

'*Mistress Malin*, Rescue Helicopter. Can you please leave the anchorage and head south at your maximum speed. This will help to keep you on a steady course when we are overhead.'

'Can you ask how the casualty is keeping?' I ventured in a lull in the conversation. The observer relayed on my enquiry.

'The patient is not vell. He has a severe headache and is very confused and drowsy. He has been sick and is veak in his left arm and leg.'

'I have them visual at twelve o'clock three miles,' Neil Goodenough reported from upfront. 'We'll have to do a high line transfer. It looks too small a yacht to take the stretcher down. How are you going to work it, Phil?'

Phil Hill looked at me. 'Have you ever worn one of these?' he asked, brandishing a multistrapped harness, not unlike the kind of thing you would get in Mothercare for a baby bouncer.

'No. I've usually been stropped.' The body harness was routinely used by the aircrewmen for double lifts, as it allowed them to have both hands free.

'Well, you go down after me, wearing this harness, and take it off when we get on board... We'll use it to bring the old boy up instead of the stretcher.'

I was a bit dubious. 'If he's semi-conscious, won't he fall out? And if he's vertical, he might go unconscious due to lack of blood flow to his brain.'

'No problem. You can carry someone almost horizontal in this harness. Remember I've got both hands free to position him. And he won't fall out!'

Reassured that I wouldn't fall out either, he strapped me into this oversized nappy with braces, and I sat back in the bulkhead seat ready to go. Phil pulled open the backdoor, and blinking in the sunlight, I got my first glimpse of a Hebridean summer morning at its most magical. We were flying down the eastern fringe of the chain of small islands which make up the Treshnish Isles. Low, flat-topped, with fluted clifflets of Staffa basalt columns, their green wind-cropped grass was bespeckled with white sea-birds, while beneath us, a still sea swirled as a dolphin or large seal sounded the glassy depths to escape the unwelcome roar of the great grey monster overhead. A small yacht motored ahead. Three people on deck gazed motionless as we overflew.

'D'you think that is the yacht? We're gettin no bloody response from them. I don't want to be reported in the *Daily Record* as going down to the wrong boat and being told to sod off!'

'*Mistress Malin*, Rescue Helicopter. Can you confirm that you are the yacht directly beneath us, please?' Affirmative.

'Well, we are about to do a highline transfer. We will lower a sandbag on a long line first. Can you grab it and haul it on board... Do not, repeat, do not tie it to your vessel.'

'Rescue Helicopter, *Mistress Malin*. I am sorry I do not understand. Your message I cannot hear clearly.' Despite trying again a couple of times, reception remained crackly poor. Then suddenly Oban Coastguard butted in as clear as a bell and repeated and reinforced our instructions to *Mistress Malin*.

Phil lowered the weighted line overboard and edged instructions to the pilot till we were directly overhead and the line was grabbed by a man on the stern of the yacht, which was being skewed all over the place by the force of our rotors. The observer took over winch control as Phil was inched slowly down and guided on to the small craft by the high line. Then it was my turn. The winch hook was thrust towards me and I snapped on the body harness. It was a different experience going down, like the wee boy on the bike—'Look Mammy, nae hands!'—seventy feet above the sea, but I still had my teeth at the end of it, and landed safely with an undignified sprawl into the small cockpit.

A middle-aged woman at the wheel, concentrating hard to control the yacht's course, was the owner of the foreign voice we'd heard over the radio. Her husband was Scottish, as was the spry elderly lady who eagerly and thankfully greeted our arrival. 'I'm Mrs Scott. My husband Douglas is down below, in the forard bunk. He has been unwell since four o'clock yesterday. He is normally very fit for eighty-four. He's a climber, and yesterday he was chopping wood all morning before we left.'

'What has happened to him then?' I asked, mentally noting that the aerial 'glassy calm' as seen from above, in fact belied a three foot swell... and I was going down below—and forard!

'He started complaining of a headache, then a numbness in his left arm which did not respond to his angina treatment. Then his left leg became weak, and he started to be sick and became drowsy and confused... and that's the way he has been ever since.'

In the dim depths of the tiny fo'csle, a smallish, lean, old man lay curled on his side, moaning with pain, and retching into a dish as the yacht's bow rose and fell in the swell and she rolled and slewed in the Sea King's downdraught. Engine noise roared through the open hatch overhead. The retching and heaving was powerfully autosuggestive. I began to sweat a bit under the collar, and tried to persuade myself strongly that it was just the heat!

Closing the hatch to deaden the noise, I checked his blood pressure which was reassuringly normal. But he was confused, and awkwardly resisted attempts to assess his limb weakness as he retched repeatedly. There was no doubt he had had a stroke, and we were obviously going to have problems getting him off the yacht. I beckoned Phil to come forard and help. There wasn't enough room for both of us to work in the cramped space, so I very unselfishly let him share the uplifting experience of a heaving patient and a heaving boat as I retreated rapidly to the fresh air and relative safety of the stern, while he struggled to attach and adjust the body harness.

We still had the tricky problem, between us, of manhandling our patient up on to the deck. Phil was having some bother getting a secure grip to carry him clear of the fo'csle till I showed him the ambulanceman's underarm wrist-lift technique, which gave him a secure purchase. As he dragged the old lad out of the bunk, I squeezed past and grabbed his knees and together we carried him aft to the cabin door, where we were faced with a five foot heave up to the deck. With assistance from above, we pushed and pulled till we had Douglas outside and lying straddled across the cockpit.

It was only then that Phil and I realised that we were on our own in a silent world... there was no sight or sound of the helicopter! Where the hell could they have vanished to? The yacht rocked gently in the swell, and the swell gently slipped along the seaweed fronded skirts of Lunga as the seabirds resumed their endless quest for food and space. It was really most pleasant sitting there in the stern being slowly seduced by the charms of the Hebrides. And it was not at all difficult to see why so many yachtsmen succumb to the enchantment of the Western Isles on a day like this, though doubtless they would have preferred an exhilarating Force Five!

Phil picked up the hand radio. 'Rescue 177, *Mistress Malin*. Where the hell are you? We have our casualty on deck ready and waiting!' A couple of minutes passed and the Sea King thubb-thubbed into view from the other side of the island, where it had gone to perch, and minimise noise and wave disturbance, while we were working with our patient.

Within seconds our perfect calm became a maelstrom, as spumes of driven spray whipped across our faces and Mrs Scott huddled over her husband to protect him, while her friend wrestled with the yacht's steering as it spun and slewed out of control in the downdraught. Phil hauled in the high line and I grabbed and slipped on the attached strop before being unceremoniously yanked off the stern and jerked skywards into the Sea King's doorway. Minutes later, Phil's bone dome appeared above the door sill, and he and his horizontal but angular charge were grabbed by Jules Price and manhandled to safety, and the door slid shut.

Mr Scott seemed none the worse of his spin in space as we loaded him on to the stretcher and insulated him with the flectron blanket—as a climber he had probably dangled on the end of more ropes in the past sixty years than we'd had hot dinners. Gill, who had been supernumerary so far, fixed him up with some oxygen, and we headed for the new Lorne and Islands Hospital at Oban, where the long-awaited helipad was now in operation. Leaving the pair of us behind to provide casualty details, as our man was still too confused to be accurate, the helicopter set off to refuel at North Connel airstrip.

We rejoined them half an hour later, to find Neil gabbing into the mobile radio while the rest lounged lazily on the grass verge. 'We've gone Downbird! Neil's on to the Chief Maintainer who is running through a check list. With a bit of luck we'll get home sometime.'

Looking beyond Ardmucknish Bay, past white-sailed yachts ghosting along in the Firth of Lorne; eyes gazing over the long low outline of Lismore to the distant hills of Mull; a hot mid-morning sun drying out damp backs now stripped of their sweatbag goonsuits; there were worse places on earth to go Downbird. All we needed now was a thirst quencher—a wee picnic. 'I'll call Oban Coastguard and see if someone could bring us out some eats and drinks.' volunteered Phil Hill.

'While you're at it, it might be nice to ask them to call up *Mistress Malin* and tell Mrs Scott her husband has arrived safe and well at Oban. She has still a four-hour drive round from Ardnamurchan once they make their landfall, and I'm sure she'd be glad to have news. Oh, and ask her to post on your sphygmo… I think I left it on a wee shelf on the port side of the cabin!' Phil had not been too chuffed when I confessed in flight that I had left my blood pressure machine on board—and then discovered that it had been his!

Sadly all good things had to come to an end. The malfunction was finally identified and clearance given to fly out. Overflying Oban, as we headed south over Loch Avich and Loch Awe, Phil waxed wistful and lyrical about leaving these beautiful surroundings, and intimated to a chorus of 'Awwws' that this was his last SAR before returning to the ranks of God's Chosen Few, posted to RAF Valley in North Wales.

'Never mind, you'll have a few square miles of wee hills to play in down there, but nothing of this quality.'

'Well, this is a momentous occasion for me too, Phil,' I chipped in, 'This is my fiftieth SAR today!'

'Fifty, Doc? Well done.' And then the inevitable probing question from Neil Goodenough, putting it all into perspective. 'And how long did that take you?'

'Oh, about eight years.' I replied half-apologetically, then rallied, lying in my teeth, 'But they were all high quality jobs, mind you, none of your empty airbeds drifting west off Saltcoats beach sort of rubbish. It's just that you don't call me out often enough, that's all!'

'Can't do much better than twice in twenty-four hours, Doc… Can we?'

18

28th August 1995

CAPTAIN COURAGEOUS

I should have kept my mouth shut. Ten short days later, I was entering Ayr ambulance depot to replace an empty oxygen cylinder on my way back to the surgery from *Gannet*, when my bleep began to sing like the lark ascending. Perfect timing, with Rotary lunch only half an hour away. I grabbed the nearest phone and got Pete West in the ops room.

'We've had a report of a man on a fishing boat in the Solway with a winch wire wrapped round his leg—they think he might have lost his leg! Can you come in quickly? The aircraft is burning and turning just right now.'

'I'm just on the outskirts of Prestwick, and can be with you in five to seven minutes.' An amputated limb! This was my worst nightmare scenario. Tearing past Prestwick Airport, wondering how the hell I was going to cope: was it completely off? Would I have to cut it off myself? Would the guy have bled to death by the time I got there? The bleep suddenly went off again. Shit! They've probably been stood down. Or they've been pressurised by RCC into going without me. How will Wendy cope with this job on her own?

With these thoughts birling through my head, I swung to a stop beside the perimeter fence. There was a Sea King, engines running, still on the tarmac, but it was well away from the SAR cab stance which was empty, and there was no MA by the apron gate to meet me with my kit. Convinced they had gone without me, I ran up the squadron building steps, to be met by Dusty Rhodes, the LACMN, coming out carrying my goon suit and helmet.

'Here's your kit, Doc. We're not taking Wendy because of the weight.' Poor Wendy, she wasn't that heavy! 'Can you change in the cab?' Thrown off balance by this change of routine, I had only time to grab the holdall containing my ovies from the car boot, and ran white-shirted but bone-domed out to the aircraft, stupidly leaving behind, in the glove compartment, my instrument holder, with scissors, artery forceps, and stethoscope—probably the very things I would be needing!

Stripped to my Y-fronts and slipping on overalls and goonsuit, I was deafened by the roar of the engines as I took off my helmet to pull the rubber neckseal over my head. It was most uncomfortable, almost painful, on the eardrums, and a salutary reminder of the need to put ear protectors on every casualty. I could now understand the reason why one drunken head injury we flew to the Southern General had become so agitated and restless without his earmuffs that he wanted to jump out of the aircraft—all this noise on top of a hangover and a fractured skull!

Trev Steele, the observer, busily observing my wrestling match with the flying suit, turned round in his seat and gesticulated he wanted to say something. I pulled on my helmet and plugged in.

'You won't need your goon suit, Doc. We are all in overalls, for the water temperature is still high enough. We're flying over land anyway, and the casualty is on a boat close to the Solway shore near Annan. The Silloth inshore lifeboat is heading for her just now.'

'Thanks, Trev, but I'm quite happy in my goon suit, especially if you're going to winch me down on to a lifeboat. I don't want to get soaked if I can help it. Anyway, all my bits and pieces are in my pockets.' I should have remembered that later—up to my knees in the Solway!

By the time I was respectably dressed, we were well inland, and familiar landscapes took on a new perspective as we overflew the village of New Cumnock, and the farms and rolling hills of my boyhood stomping grounds. Thereafter, I was too busy assembling a collection of essential equipment, spare stethoscope, sphygmo, and i/v giving sets, to be able to sit back and enjoy the winding beauty of the Nith valley. Fresh snippets of info came percolating through from time to time, as Liverpool and Kirkcudbright Coastguards vied for territorial control of the incident as if it was some border dispute.

'Listen to them! Everyone wants a piece of this action—and probably none of them knows what's really going on, for I certainly know we don't!'

'Something coming through from Liverpool Coastguard, just now.' reported Trev. 'The lifeboat is in attendance, and they have put a paramedic on board.'

'Could you ask them for a sitrep on the casualty—ask if the paramedic has put a drip up?' There was a long pause.

'No drip up, Doc. They've only got basic equipment on board the lifeboat. But the casualty is conscious. The lifeboat is heading for the Scottish side of the Solway, near Annan.'

'Should we put Dusty and Doc down on to the lifeboat, and winch the guy up from there?' came a query from 'Alf' Ridd, the Aircraft Captain.

'No, if they've only a mile to run it would be quicker and safer to lift him from the shore. They should have reached it by the time we are on scene. Destination is a place called Waterford, at the mouth of the River Annan. Have you got it on the map? We've five miles to run.'

'Yeah. Got it… and got it visual.' The aircraft swung round in a big arc over the Merse, that vast area of flat green salt marshes of the inner Solway, creek-veined and pockmarked with countless stagnant brackish pools. Alf Ridd sat us down gently on a raised ridge of short firm sea turf. A hundred yards away, the inshore lifeboat lay bow-beached on a mudflat at the entrance to an inlet. Behind us, we were surprised to find a crowd of spectators already gathered with their vehicles at the end of a dirt track.

Travelling light, with a small satchel of equipment clipped to my lifejacket, I stumbled and leapt across several small muddy runnels to reach the lifeboat, whose bow was raised high in thick sticky mud, with its stern still afloat in a racing, ebbing current. Thank goodness for my goon suit, I breathed as I opted for the cleaner option—a knee-deep wade through the swirling water to reach the stern, across which was straddled a stretcher. Clambering aboard with a helping hand from the crew, I was met by the local GP, Dr Lapka, looking all the world like a Glasgow Fair holidaymaker in his shirt sleeves and bare feet, with his trousers rolled up to his knees.

'He's in amazingly good shape. Normal pulse and BP, and not in much pain at all. I've given him some diamorphine while we waited for you and the ambulance.'

'He' was a ruddy faced middle-aged man, fully alert as he lay seemingly unconcerned in the stretcher, taking an interest in what was going on around him. His left leg protruded from the end of the stretcher, and a clean, blood-free, neatly bandaged right stump peeped from a gap in the covering blanket. The lifeboatmen had done a wonderful job on board the fishing boat under very difficult circumstances. Luckily for them, and for their casualty, the major arteries in the stump had clamped tightly shut in spasm, as often happens when a limb has been torn off rather than cleanly severed, and there had been very little blood loss. He was not the shocked, ashen, exsanguinated, terminal casualty that I had been expecting, and dreading. I spoke to him.

'Hello. I'm the doctor from the helicopter. How are you? Are you in much pain? What's your name?'

'Tom... Tom Willacy. I'm fine, doctor. Don't feel a thing!'

'He's an amazing man.' said Dr Lapka. 'I've never seen anything like him... so relaxed about everything—even before the diamorph.'

'I think we had better put up a drip on you, Tom, before we lift you off the boat and on to the helicopter.' I explained, crouched in the cramped stern, rolling up his right sleeve.

Grabbing a cannula from the i/v box, I sought out a good vein, stuck it in, and started to withdraw the needle. Nothing happened. To my horror, there was no plastic cannula over the needle! It threw me. I was bewildered. I had automatically pulled the thing from its sealed wrapper. I checked the wrapper quickly, to see if by accident I had left part of the cannula in the package when I withdrew it. There was nothing there. Could it have dropped off the end of the needle? No sign of it on the floor of the boat. I could only conclude it had been faultily assembled. And of all the bloody times to discover a duff cannula! And with the local doctor standing overhead. And a newly arrived ambulance paramedic busy working on the other side of the stretcher to put up another line. I cursed inwardly and, selecting a second cannula, popped it home just as the paramedic shouted he had venous access, and his mate borrowed my giving set and bottle of Hartmann's fluid, leaving me in the lurch till they assembled another for me. Then I discovered there was no sticky tape in the i/v fluids box to secure the drip tubing, and had to borrow some from my ambulance friends across poor Tom, who all this time had lain unflinching and uncomplaining. I would have somebody's collective guts for garters when I got back to sick bay and found out who had not been properly checking my equipment!

With both drips running, and happy now that Tom was properly stabilised for the short flight to Dumfries and Galloway Royal Infirmary, I jumped back into the water to assist the three lifeboatmen and other helpers to carry the stretcher across the mud to the safety of non-slip sea turf. As we left the lifeboat I vaguely heard someone mutter 'What about the leg?' But our priority was to get this man quickly on board the aircraft, so we steadfastly kept on going.

On board the aircraft, as I tied the drip bottles to a roof support, I remembered that I had left my emergency satchel on the lifeboat, and asked one of the lifeboatmen to fetch it up for me, which he duly did. Seconds later, Dusty appeared at the aircraft door carrying a large welly boot which he stacked against the bulkhead. Busily engrossed with making sure Tom was comfortable for the flight, I glanced up and momentarily and vacantly thought to myself, 'That's strange, bringing the guy's boot with him.' Then it dawned. 'Shite! There's a bloody leg in that boot!'

It looked so incongruous and surreal, this big black boot with the leg still in it, standing there on its own, beside its ex-owner, who lay quietly and gazed upon it as if he couldn't have cared less!

As we took off, Dusty diplomatically moved the boot forard out of sight for the trip to Dumfries. After five minutes, Tom's face began to grimace, and he signalled that his pain was returning. Entonox proved inadequate, but ten milligrams of i/v morphine soon restored his equanimity. At the landing site on the local golf course, he was transferred to a waiting ambulance, and I accompanied him to the hospital. He was as relaxed as ever, and dumbfounded me when he spoke.

'Where dae ye come frae, doctor… Dunure?'

'No, Ayr.'

'I wisnae faur oot… juist twa or three miles! I kent by yer voice that ye were frae up there somewhere?'

'Hou did ye ken that?' I replied, amazed that someone who had just gone through the terrible trauma of having his leg torn off, could still be alert enough to recognise my native Ayrshire tongue, and follow it up with a matter-of-fact conversation as if we had been a couple o locals bletherin awa at the pier-heid!

'I uised tae ken lads frae Dunure. I fished wi them. There were the Gibsons, I mind James… an Will Munro. But I think he's retired nou.'

'I've fished for prawns an queenies mysel wi Stuart Gibson on the *Mari-Dor*—did ye ken him?'

The beep-beep-beep of the reversing ambulance drew this amazing conversation to an untimely close. It was almost as if Tom was chatting away to keep my spirits up, rather than the reverse! The back doors opened, and the ambulanceman quietly slipped the boot to a waiting staff nurse who, completely unfazed by the nature of her burden, marched like a standard bearer at the head of our wee procession into the A&E Department, where I handed Tom and his boot over to the care of the casualty surgeon.

On the flight home, I just could not get over Tom's superb, unflinching composure. I had previously read, with some disbelief, fantastic tales of self-induced anaesthesia occurring in the heat of battle, when a soldier, all fired up and laying about him at close quarters with sword or bayonet, finally stops for a welcome victory drink, only to discover he's lost his other arm! Tom's stoicism in the face of such a horrendous injury must have been of this nature—helped by an outpouring of cerebral endorphins which numbed his pain centres and gave him protection.

Sadly, despite the salvage attempts of the lifeboatmen, and a rapid transfer to Canniesburn Hospital in Glasgow, the surgeons were unable to reunite Tom with his leg and thus provide a fairytale ending to a superb display of courage.

Postscript:
Tom Willacy's great courage and resourcefulness was later acknowledged by the BBC in their '999' series, when his amazing exploit was featured and the full incredible story revealed. How his leg had been caught and severed in a bight of winch cable, as he was hauled upside down and left dangling from a pulley. How he had cut himself free from his thigh boot with his fisherman's knife and dropped headfirst on to the deck, leaving his severed leg hanging from the wire. How he had dragged himself to the wheelhouse and called his wife on his mobile phone to tell her he had lost his leg and could she alert the emergency services. How when the lifeboat came alongside, they had thought they had rendezvoused with the wrong boat, for here was a man in the wheelhouse steering it towards Annan, and there was only meant to be one person on board. This was Tom, standing on one leg and heading for home himself! Ours had been a minor bit-part role at the tail-end of a momentous drama.

And finally, how only six months later, fitted out with his artificial limb, he was back at sea on the *Patricia Willacy*, fishing the Solway for shrimps—on his own!

PPS:
On the 20th May 1997, just a few weeks after the '999' programme was broadcast, having been drafted south from 819 Squadron, LACMN Dusty Rhodes lost his life in a diving accident during routine training at the Royal Naval Diving School on Horsey Island near Portsmouth. Back at *Gannet*, we were all profoundly shocked by the tragic loss of yet another fine aircrewman, colleague and friend, who died while practising those professional skills so vital for ensuring the safety of others.

19

14th September 1995

STRESS

When the phone went at four o'clock on Thursday morning, and the anxious voice of Gill Dorman told me that RCC had requested a doctor for a medevac from Machrihanish, I could have crawled under the bed and died. I knew exactly what the forthcoming response would be, as a slowly stirring shape under the quilt heaved herself round on her pillow to confront me with a look of total exhaustion and deep despair, welling up into a real cold anger.

'Not again! I thought you were not doing any more of these bloody calls after midnight. You'll kill yourself. Look at Martin McLean and Robbie Duncan, with their coronaries and heart bypasses. I can't handle this with all the other problems we've got… It's got to stop!'

Helen was nearing the end of her tether. For herself and her family, nineteen-ninety-five had been—in those immortal Christmas Message words of our Head of State and dear Monarch—an 'Annus Horribilis', which could I suppose be coarsely and phonetically translated from the Latin, with some accuracy, as a right horrible arsehole of a year!

Both her parents were rapidly becoming increasingly frail and dependent, and, as is often the case, were going through that phase of proud denial of the fact they could no longer cope. Struggling with this dilemma, plus Fiona's stresses and self-doubts during the run-up to her Highers, plus my own increasing practice workload—

and the fact that two of my contemporaries had just had coronaries in their early fifties—had, not surprisingly, left Helen feeling very low during the winter months.

By the end of June, happily, this had settled, and we both had been greatly uplifted by the fantastic hospitality we had enjoyed during our three-week tour of the eastern states of America with the brilliant youngsters of the Ayrshire Fiddle Orchestra. The intense feeling of pride in watching these young musicians play the White House Lawn, the Shea Stadium in New York, and the Payne Hall at Harvard, had more than offset the minor problems of the acute appendicitis I had to deal with midway across the Atlantic, the articulated lorry/school bus shunt resulting in six whiplash injuries and two hysterias, and the five hours spent in a Washington ER dept while one of my partner's daughters was brain-scanned after a swimming pool accident. And Fiona lost her contact lens down the loo… and broke her violin! What more could possibly happen? You name it.

As we contentedly unpacked the car on our return home from the Relais Chateaux comfort of the Airds Hotel at Port Appin, where we had gone for a couple of nights' luxurious relaxation to recover from what had been really a very strenuous tour, the phone rang to say that Helen's father was en route to hospital with a broken hip. Eight weeks on, exceedingly frail and helpless, he had just been discharged, to join her Mum in requiring twenty-four hour home nursing care. And in just the same week her younger brother Will had been admitted to the Southern General Hospital for investigation and treatment of a brain tumour.

And now here was I, selfishly farting off on a bloody helicopter into the middle of the night!

'What is it this time? I'm just not sleeping well… and now to be woken by this! Probably be a bloody waste of time as usual!'

I cringed. 'It's a sixty-two year old man who has had a cardiac arrest, is unconscious, and RCC say there is no doctor available in Campbeltown to go with him to hospital.' Feeling absolutely dreadful and guilty as sin, I sneaked down the stairs and out to the car in my vest and Y-fronts to retrieve my kit bag and overalls from the boot.

Gill was waiting for me at the side gate with my helmet. 'Your goon suit is on board, Boss. We're going to Machrihanish to pick up this patient. Apparently he is unconscious, and intubated.'

'Intubated!' I didn't relish this prospect one bit. This was really a job for an anaesthetist.

Onboard, in my goon suit, I discovered I had no flying boots—again! Gill didn't know where they were. She had looked. I had left them to dry on top of my locker after their Solway soaking. Don't tell me somebody really had nicked them this time. Wearing my good tan shoes again!

Busy rummaging about in the half-dark of a noisy, smelly helicopter pulling on kit and checking medical gear, the usual directional chit-chat by and large went over my head. I vaguely recalled Neil Goodenough asking for a heading round the tail of Arran to avoid low cloud over the hills, then a comment that we had overflown Davaar Island at the mouth of Campbeltown Loch. In no time we were within the perimeter of Machrihanish airfield and Neil was floating us gently along the runway towards the control tower. A slightly-built, dark-haired, mild mannered, gently-spoken lad, Neil's flying mirrored his personality. His very delicate touch as a pilot always inspired my confidence. His landings were so smooth and imperceptible that it was often difficult to know if and when we had landed, and when to unbuckle our seat-belts!

As we drifted along, lulled by this knowledge into a false sense of security, he suddenly and quietly announced, without raising his voice one semitone: 'Bird strike! Something has just flown into the rotors. I'm just going to put her down and shut down till we've done an inspection.' And down we went, as delicately as ever, on to the helipad a hundred yards from the control tower.

Typical bloody SAR! Gone downbird, with a gravely-ill patient waiting, and perhaps depending on our presence to save his life. Fortunately he was still in the hospital at Campbeltown, and not lying stretchered on the runway.

Gill, myself, and the aircrewman set off to establish contact at the control tower, while the two pilots checked the rotors and jet intakes for evidence of damage. The aircrewman was Warrant Officer John

Sheldon, a huge mountain of a man at six-foot-four, who towered over wee Gill at five-foot-three, and me, at somewhere in between. With a rapid John Wayne walk, he led the way at fast rifle pace through the rough grass, while we trotted behind trying to keep up with him. Looking for the entrance, we circumnavigated the control tower once, then twice—after consulting the airfield fire tender driver—then a third time, before Gill finally spotted a small unlit door tucked away in a dark corner, which opened on to a steep staircase leading up to the control room.

Introducing ourselves to the three controllers, WO Sheldon commandeered one of their phones for an up-to-date weather forecast for Glasgow Airport, after learning that the fixed-wing air ambulance had not been able to make the flight down because of fog. The visibility was still only three hundred metres at Glasgow, probably ruling the airport out for our Sea King as well. Meanwhile, on the other phone, I was put in touch with Dr Lazarus in the Campbeltown Hospital.

'Oh, I won't need to come with her then,' was his opening remark. Funny, I thought. RCC had said there was no doctor available—and had dragged me out of my bed. I quizzed him.

'Well, originally there was no one available, then I said I would go if no one else could.' RCC might have saved me a night's sleep—and a pending divorce—I grumbled to myself. 'The patient is a sixty-two year old man who has been in chronic hepatic failure. During the evening, he developed respiratory problems, and then arrested just as the ambulance arrived. The ambulancemen managed to get a tube down, start defibrillation, and get him into hospital. He is still deeply unconscious, but his BP is normal and his pulse rapid but regular. We've arranged for him to go to Glasgow Royal Infirmary.' With a history like that I could only pray that there would still be enough fog in and around Glasgow to give us the short and sensible option of taking him to Crosshouse and saving twenty minutes flying time.

Just then, Neil Goodenough clambered up into the control room, and we gave him a quick heads up on what was happening. He spoke briefly over the phone to the Duty Chief Maintainer at

Gannet, informed him that checks of the rotor blades and jet intakes had been negative, and was given the all clear to proceed. Glasgow was now closed due to fog, so it would have to be Crosshouse. The local hospital was informed and we descended to the runway to await the ambulance.

It was a lovely mild still night with the stars showing through large gaps in the cloud cover. John Sheldon remarked that there were worse places on earth he could think of to be sitting outside in the dark. And I could well believe him. Gill stood gazing around, wondering from which direction the ambulance would come. I teased her gently. 'Are you lost, Gill? Well, I'll show you how to find north next time you're stuck out in the middle of nowhere. See, up there… that's The Plough. And if you follow the line of the pointers, it will lead you the the Pole Star. Do you see it?'

John Sheldon laughed. 'Reminds me of the Falklands. When we looked up and saw all these stars and didn't know any of them except Orion. It was very strange.'

'And over there,' I pointed to the east, 'you can just see the lights of Campbeltown faintly reflected on the clouds, so I suppose the ambulance will come in from somewhere over in that direction…' pointing authoritively to the south-east.

A few minutes later and the flashing blue ambulance lights appeared—from the north! Field craft skills are fine, but a good knowledge of the local road layout would have been much more impressive.

In the back of the ambulance was Dr Lazarus, a youngish chap in his thirties, tending a deeply unconscious, middle-aged man breathing oxygen normally through a Hudson face mask. His colour was good. He handed me a letter addressed to The Royal.

'Do you know he's going to Crosshouse?' I checked.

'Yes. We got your phonecall, and I have already phoned Crosshouse with details.' He indicated backwards with his head as he climbed down from the ambulance, 'I'm a bit concerned about him. His conscious level is rising a bit and he's getting restless with that tube in.' Thanks a bundle, pal, I mouthed inwardly, this is all I need!

'Can his son come with him?' asked the ambulance driver. WO Sheldon checked and confirmed, and the young fellow was kitted with a lifejacket and ushered forard well out of harm's way.

Attached to HeartStart and pulse oximeter, and breathing ten litres per minute oxygen through his mask, a few minutes into the flight, Mr Mathieson began to cough and retch, then settled, only to repeat the cycle shortly afterwards. This time his oxygen saturation began to drop steadily from 90 per cent down to the low seventies.

'Turn the flow rate up to fifteen litres a minute,' I instructed Gill. It didn't work. 'I'll have to bag and mask him. Get me out the Ambubag, and the connector for the endotracheal tube.' Shit! There were bits missing—or not where they should have been—but which were found speedily and connected up. I would have someone's guts for garters—whoever had done the kit check this morning—when I got back.

Meantime there were more vital tasks to attend to. The endotracheal tube had been cut too short when inserted, and the tie cord had slipped off, leaving it poised to slip down and be lost in his lungs. And the end had split, loosening the ferrule connecting the tube to his oxygen supply. We tried micropore tape, but the tube was slippy with saliva and it would not stick. Gill had to press the connector firmly into the tube and hold it there throughout the flight while I worked the Ambubag, spelled from time to time by John Sheldon, who took over when I was checking the patient's vital signs. His pulse was rapid during some of the restless episodes, and occasionally there would be some resistance as he exhaled against the pressure being applied through the Ambubag. Initially his oxygen saturation levels did not budge, then slowly they began to rise till we achieved a very satisfactory 93 per cent, and thankfully held this level till touchdown at Crosshouse, where a full team of Intensive Treatment Unit staff were waiting to take over.

But sadly, both our efforts and those of the ITU were hopeless, as doctors found that he had suffered irreversible brain damage during his initial cardiac arrest, from which he died several days later.

Dawn was breaking as I headed for home to face the unknown, slipping into bed for a short ninety minutes' rest before my morning's session at *Gannet*. Helen was only half-awake when I slunk out at 0815, and simply mumbled a few inconsequential remarks/queries/ observations as I whispered goodbye. I felt I had got off lightly… and I would make it up to her at lunchtime by going home specially to run Fiona up to Ayr Hospital for her job experience interviews at Physio and A&E.

◉

I found the culprit! Or at least he owned up before I got to him. Neil Hodgson had checked the resuscitation case that morning, had found it difficult to shut with the Ambubag fully assembled, so had disconnected and stowed the parts separately, but in the same compartment.

That's all right in broad daylight, I told them all, but in poor cabin visibility during a night SAR, when there's a bit of a panic on, it is very difficult to locate items of kit in a hurry. And, I added for good measure, the back of the cab had been cluttered up with crew rucsacs and non-essential items which were a distraction, and a misuse of valuable stowage space badly needed to lay out any equipment being utilised to treat a casualty.

It was about eleven-thirty, and Fez Parker appeared in the office doorway, having just returned from the morning training flight. 'Fez. You're duty MA. I was just telling the others about the problems we had last… ' My voice was lost in an almighty clamour as a green-flashing siren erupted on the wall just above his head. Gill and Rob, on the phones, covered their ears as they tried to continue with their conversations. Fez abruptly terminated ours and ran for his Rapid Response Vehicle—the mountain bike. So this was the new SAR callout system—and it was programmed to wail for ninety seconds!

An eternity later, the din ceased, and the phone rang. 'It's your surgery, Boss.'

'Doctor Begg. There is one visit down for you, and another spare one which no one else has taken. Do you want to take them both? One is in…' 'Could you please clear your line, there is an emergency call coming through.' I put down the phone, guessing spot-on what was about to happen. The phone rang immediately. 'It's Fez, Boss. Another heart attack. Can you come down straight away?'

'Could you tell the surgery I'm off on a SAR.' I shouted back as I rushed out of the room, not knowing how long I would be gone. Fez met me with my goon suit—and no boots!

'I'm sorry, I couldn't find them, sir. It's Captain's Rounds this morning and they've probably been tidied away out of sight till he's gone.' I wondered if the Navy would come good for new shoes if this pair got any more oil on them! Shirt-sleeved and carrying my holdall as we dashed for the aircraft, Fez shouted in my ear that we were going to Inveraray where a man had been reported as having had a heart attack on top of a steeple. Well, that's novel—haven't had one of these before, I mused as I noticed that all the crew were ovie-clad because of the warm sea state. So I did likewise. Most comfortable!

In fact, we flew very little over the sea as Lt Mick Whitelock, the Captain, preferred flying a more direct route, up the Clyde coast then over the Cowal hills to Strachur and across Loch Fyne to Inveraray. During the flight, Lt 'J-P' Mercer, our observer, confirmed that the casualty was still up on the steeple, and that two ambulance paramedics were in attendance but could not get him down. He was not a steeplejack as had earlier been thought, but a middle-aged tourist with a history of angina.

The steeple, we discovered, was not a steeple, but the Inverary Bell Tower, a well-known prominent landmark and viewpoint, situated on the landward side of the village. Built of red sandstone, it had a flat lead roof on which we could see a huddled group of figures. 'I'll do a circuit to find the best approach, and then we'll winch down the aircrewman with the stretcher… I don't think there is any need for Doc to go down just now, for I gather the casualty has no chest pain and is quite stable.'

Lt Mercer was quickly lowered on to the tower roof and confirmed there was no need for either Fez or myself to join him. The paramedics had the patient, a fifty-nine year old man, wired up to their HeartStart, and his BP was normal. While he was being prepared on the stretcher for winching, we circled the village and Inveraray Castle.

Below us, in the field next to the Bell Tower, one of the locals, obviously a keen photographer, had got himself a good vantage point leaning against a telegraph pole, and was busily filming the rescue. But would it make the *Daily Record*? Adjacent to the tower was the local primary school. The kids should all have being inside doing arithmetic, but this was too good an educational opportunity to miss! The whole school, teachers and all, were gathered outside in the playground, watching the performance. Real drama! Right on their doorstep. 'And what did you get at school today, Calum?' 'We watched a helicopter rescue a man from the Bell Tower,' followed by a gushing half-hour of enthusiastic detail. A pleasant change from the usual 'Nothing much—sums and writing.'

Guided in to the hover, just twenty feet above the grey leaded roof, I gulped in alarm as a small corner spire, topped by a lightning conductor, passed by the open door a few feet to our right. LACMN Lee Norton was lying flat on the floor with his head out the door, intently looking forward and down, edging the helicopter three yards forward, steady, up four feet, a yard to the right…

To the right! Did he not see that bloody spire… the tail rotor must just be level with it now! I hope the pilot knows where the arse of his helicopter is.

'Steady there. You are directly above the casualty. The winchman is connected to the stretcher. They are both clear of the tower… and coming on board… now.'

It was with great relief, as I helped drag the stretcher into position on board, to watch the Sea King finally veer well clear of the Bell Tower. A ruddy-faced, stoutish man smiled up at me once the worried look had left his face. J-P handed me a letter. 'His name is Bill Anderson… on holiday from Redcar. Thought he'd climb the hundred and fifty steps and try the view from the top of the tower. Got to a hundred and forty and felt unwell with chest pain. He couldn't face going down again, so his wife helped him up the last few steps to the top where he collapsed and passed out.

'The paramedics checked him over and his blood pressure is normal and so was the tracing on the monitor. But you should have seen his pulse rate shoot up through the roof when the helicopter arrived overhead!'

'Do you have any chest pain?' I signalled, rubbing my hand across my chest. He shook his head no.

'Can you take aspirin?' I mouthed the words silently, holding a small bottle of pills in my hand. Again he shook his head sideways, and rubbed his stomach, mouthing the word 'ulcer'.

Lee Norton fetched me the oxygen cylinder out of the new air-crew ready response bag which we had just brought into operation, and I slipped a mask over Bill's face. Meantime, Fez sat steadfastly up front—having a day off!

'Where are we taking him?' I asked. 'He seems to be quite stable.'

'Alexandria Hospital, Doc.'

'Do you mean the Royal Alexandria Infirmary at Paisley on the south of the Clyde… or the Vale of Leven Hospital at Alexandria on the north of the river?' You could never be too sure about these all-English crews and their sketchy knowledge of local geography!

'OK. Vale of Leven, Doc… If that's all right with you.'

We were there in jig-time, landing in grassy parkland where an ambulance was waiting. On board the vehicle, I had a chance to have a word with Bill, who was getting more relaxed by the minute. 'Where is your wife? Sorry we couldn't bring her with us. I don't think she would have fancied being winched off the top of a hundred foot tower!'

He laughed. 'The police are bringing her by road from Inveraray. 'We are staying at a caravan site at Balloch.'

'That's handy! Balloch is only a couple of miles up the road. Did you plan this caper just to get home quicker?'

He looked pleasantly surprised. 'Oh, that's good. I didn't know the hospital was near Balloch.'

'Just part of the rescue service! We always like to keep our customers happy! But just thank your lucky stars we didn't decide to take you to Oban… the same distance from Inveraray in the opposite direction.' I reckoned he would be discharged in a couple of days.

I had never flown in or out of Vale of Leven before, so it was quite an experience to overfly Dumbarton and the ancient rock fortress from which the town took its name—Dun Barton—the fort of the Britons—a settlement since Roman times, and no doubt for long before that. Nestling under Dumbarton Rock, situated on the winding bends of the lower River Leven flowing out of Loch Lomond, lay several flattened, derelict industrial sites. Shipyards. Dumbarton had once been a world famous ship building town. Ships that were the pride of the Clyde had been built there. At one time, a third of all the world's ships were Clyde-built. I wondered how many of these English guys knew that. Helen's father, born and bred in Dumbarton, had trained as a doctor, and had spent his war service as a young Surgeon Lieutenant on the escort Destroyer HMS *Watchman* on Atlantic convoys. Ships and the sea had been in his blood. His father and grandfather before him had worked as engineers in Denny's shipyard. And there was the site of Denny's directly below. Derelict. Stood directly behind the two pilots, my thoughts burst out aloud.

'Down there, at nine o'clock. That's Denny's shipyard where the *Cutty Sark* was built.'

'Was it, Doc? Didn't know that.'

'Just because it's now moored at Greenwich doesn't mean it was built by you lot down in England! It was Clyde-built.'

'Oh, you mean British-built, then, Doc?' Someone was gently winding me up.

'No chance. Scottish-built. You lot only call something British when it is an English football hooligan.'

Suddenly the aircaft did a violent right and left swerve which almost threw me off balance.

'Bloody shitehawks!'

'Why did you do a right, then a left, when they were coming from that direction?' complained Tim Eldridge the co-pilot.

'Thought they might as well hit your windscreen rather than mine!' joked Mick Whitelock. 'Could have used the other option though...'

'What's that?'

'Fly straight at them. Play chicken. Get out of my way you bastards... I'm bigger than you!'

'Did you hear about the goose and the jumbo?'

'No.'

'It's true. This seven-four-seven was flying at thirty-five thousand feet when a goose went right into one of his engines. Imagine the surprise for the pilot… flying his aircraft at that height and hitting an arse-up duck! The investigators thought it must have been driven up to that altitude by a thunderstorm.'

'Imagine the surprise for the friggin goose, flying along quite happy, thinking "Thank god I'm away from that bloody hail and lightning", when WALLOP, you're minced through a jet engine.'

Thank goodness it was only a bird the size of a sparrow last night, I thought to myself. Last night! Helen! Shit! Fiona! I'm supposed to be taking her up to the hospital at two o'clock and it's now a quarter to one!

We landed on at Prestwick about one-fifteen, and I dumped my kit in the locker and grabbed the phone in the SAR duty room. It rang and rang. No reply. Maybe she's down at her mother's.

Twenty to two. No time to phone again. Into the car and down the bypass, burnin' rubber! Into the house at five to two. No Helen. In the shit!

Phoned mother-in-law's house. Mrs Mossie, their daily help, answered. 'She's just left to pick up Fiona from school this minute. Hold on and I'll see if I can catch her before she drives off.' That horrible sinking feeling—deeper, ever deeper, in the excrement! 'No. Sorry, she's gone.' Neck deep!

God! And I'd better phone the surgery too, to let them know I'm back and not to cancel my three o'clock appointments. 'Oh, Doctor Begg. Your wife is just off the phone looking for you five minutes ago. I told her you were away on a SAR and we did not know when you would be back.' Adding, in a very apologetic and feeling-for-you-much tone of voice, 'She didn't sound very pleased.' Above the nostrils and drowning in it!

Maybe if I rushed up to the hospital, I could meet them there and take over from Helen. Throwing myself a lifebelt. But do lifebelts float in shit? Screamed along Belmont Road. A white Metro, travelling almost as fast, passes in the opposite direction. Two strained faces behind the windscreen. Signals to stop. A menacing figure steps out of the car and looms over me. Feels like I'm about to be done by the polis! And she's only five-foot-two! The inevitable and venomous, 'Where have you been!' Any permutation of emphasis in the spitting out of these four fateful words would work equally well in reducing me to a quivering wreck. The lifebelt is blown beyond reach.

I grovelled abjectly and followed the white Metro home to thole my assize—accusation, interrogation, explanation, plea of mitigation, adjudication, castigation, subjugation and probation—castration deferred! Extricating myself slowly from the *merde* I drove Fiona up to Ayr Hospital. I deserved all I got—and prayed I would never have to do two SARs in eight hours again!

◉

Bill made a good recovery, and was soon back home—to star on television when his escapade was featured in the BBC's '999' series.

20

6th February 1996

PREGGEVACS

Tuesday again. Terrible Tuesday. And the portents were bad from the moment I rose and peered through the curtains at a dreich grey dawn, lightened vaguely by a two-inch covering of fresh snow. It was a quarter to eight, and I was late for work. Last night, old Betty Lindsay had been gey breathless when I had sounded her chest on my way home, and I had promised to drop in and see her just after eight o'clock, en route to the surgery.

Dressing quickly, my ear caught the tail-end of a Radio Scotland road report as I simultaneously filled the kettle, piled my plate with cereal, and fed the dog. Overnight, apparently, the heaviest blizzard for decades had hit South West Scotland, and left Dumfries and Galloway region under two feet of snow. Hundreds of vehicles had been trapped on the M74 between Scotland and England, and all roads were impassable. Someone, somewhere, was going to have big problems today, I mused, but consoled myself that the sheltered five-mile radius around Ayr seemed to have missed the worst of it—as usual.

Seconds later, the phone rang. Two minutes past eight! It was the surgery. Mrs Robinson had collapsed with breathlessness and chest pain. Could I attend ASAP. Five spoonfuls of branflakes and a half slice of toast stuffed sideways into both cheeks as I made for the door, hardly constituted a substantial breakfast for a cold morning, but it would have to keep me going till I got a mid-morning coffee at the surgery... and Betty Lindsay would have to wait a wee while. Fortunately, Mrs Robinson did not have the anticipated heart attack, though a lobar pneumonia and pleurisy certainly justified the early call and her immediate admission to hospital. Old Betty's heart failure had stabilised overnight, and she was up and about with a smile on her face when I arrived.

With two worthwhile calls before nine o'clock, I was suffused with the rare, warm glow of the 'feel-good-factor' as I strode across Cathcart Street to pick up the Vodaphone for the rest of the incoming morning visits. The *Gannet* bleep trilled as I stepped through the surgery door. Switchboard put me quickly through to the SAR Ready Room. Neil Hodgson, the duty LMA, answered. 'I asked them to bleep you, Boss. Just to give you a heads-up on a job we might have on—a preggevac from Stranraer to Glasgow. A woman who's twenty eight weeks pregnant, with complications. RCC are asking about a doctor.'

'Do you want me to make my way in, just in case?' I asked, mindful of the risks of an unnecessary delay in deteriorating weather conditions.

'Yeah. Might not be a bad idea.'

Apologetically leaving our long-suffering girls to sort out the appointments mayhem which inevitably followed these sudden departures, I green-lighted for *Gannet*.

A knot of aircrew, still in their flying overalls, hovered expectantly around the SAR telephone as I arrived. Jon Bird, the observer, saw my puzzled look. 'We are still waiting for the go ahead from RCC, Doc. Probably just as well for you to get kitted up and ready.' As I waddled back along the corridor to a mocking chorus of 'Very fetching, Doc. It's just you to a tee!', confirmation came through that the job was on.

The weather was foul, with driving snow on a strong south-easterly wind, and a cloud level of less than three hundred feet. There was no way that we could shortcut our journey by flying overland. As the visibility worsened, Paul Farrant, the Aircraft Captain, instructed his P2, Adam Carr, to fly low over the sea at 150 feet and to use each faint, emerging headland as the next flight reference, keeping the aircraft as close inshore as possible. In this fashion, Stranraer was reached in half an hour, and a wide circuit over the ferry terminal finally lined the Sea King up with a football field landing site near the Garrick Hospital.

From the waiting ambulance, a man emerged wearing the familiar green and yellow protective overalls of a BASICS doctor. I recognised him immediately—Gordon Baird the Sandhead GP—in whose congenial company I had swallowed my first ever oysters in a bar on the Leith Walk several years back, during a BASICS conference in Edinburgh. I survived. He didn't recognise me.

'Hello, Gordon, how are you?' Surprised, he peered under my bone dome.

'My God. It's Jimmy Begg.' He grasped my outstretched hand. 'How are you doing? And here… congratulations on your MBE! My father has just got one as well, for his work with the Portpatrick Lifeboat.'

'Thank you very much.' I acknowledged awkwardly. It took a bit of getting used to this, now being a member of the 'aristocracy'! 'What's the problem with your patient? All I've heard is that she's twenty eight weeks pregnant with complications.'

'And some!' He grimaced. 'She's had a bad antepartum haemorrhage. She was unconscious when I got there, but came round quickly when I got a line up and pumped in some Haemaccel. She's potentially unstable, but OK at the moment.'

'Are you flying?' I asked, as a midwife emerged from the ambulance.

'Yes. I phoned Jim Ramsay at the Southern General, and he wanted an obstetrically trained doctor to accompany her… but if I'd known you were coming, I wouldn't have bothered.'

An unstable bleeding patient, who could suddenly lapse into shock or premature labour—or both—in a lurching helicopter, in a blizzard, half way between Stranraer and Glasgow! Two doctors are better than one, I thought thankfully. Glad to have you on board! Gordon introduced me to Linda, as we transferred her on to the lightweight stretcher. Outwardly, she was quietly composed, and managed a weak smile. Her colour was reassuringly good. We loaded her on to the Sea King.

This was my first SAR on the new stripped-out mark 5 Sea King, the aircraft we all had been shouting for, for seven long years. Sans sonar, and similar to those flown by the Crabs, and the Navy at Culdrose, it was a SAR pilot's dream. A tonne lighter, infinitely more manoeuvrable in the hover on mountains or over fishing boats, plus an increased fuel-carrying capacity and range, meant a much safer operating margin in extreme conditions, and that was good. Likewise, it was a medic's dream. We had space! The rear cabin for stretcher cases, and forard for walking wounded and relatives.

Gordon and the midwife were ushered forard for take off, while Neil and I secured Linda and her drip fluids at the back. With a following wind, within minutes we were well up Loch Ryan, and hugging the cliffs of Bennane Head. I checked the drip. It had blocked. I called to Neil who had retired up front for some strange reason. It was only when we got back to Prestwick much later, that I learned he had already done twenty-four hours on SAR duty, but had agreed to continue on standby to let Don Clark take his youngster to a hospital appointment—and had been tasked! He was dog-tired.

'Could I have a ten mil syringe and some sterile water to clear this drip.' He seemed to take an inordinate time to fetch these items, and I suddenly realised that no real thought or logic had been applied to the siting of the medical kit in the new aircraft. As of necessity, it had had to be stowed forard in the standard operational mark 5, but here I was in the new cab, surrounded by irrelevant aircrew survival Bergen rucsacs, while vital medical equipment was planked five yards away.

'And while you are at it, bring down the Propaq, and also start her on ten litres of oxygen. We've just acquired a new Propaq monitor, Gordon, which we can use to keep an eye on Linda's blood pressure.'

'Sounds great, Jimmy, but for heaven's sake watch that drip. It took me a long time to find that vein, and if it goes, we are in trouble!' I drew up ten mil of sterile water and was on the point of injecting it into the Venflon, when the aircraft pitched violently as it hit turbulence and I was almost flung on to the patient. I glanced out of the cargo door window. We were within fifty yards of the Bennane cliffs. 'For God's sake, can you move away from these cliffs and give us a steady ride!' I shouted in exasperation.

'Sorry, Doc. We'll soon be out of it. We've got to keep close to land under these flying conditions.' But not that bloody close, I mumped to myself, as I eventually succeeded in clearing the blockage. The Haemaccel ran sweetly free, and the Propaq recorded stable pulse, blood pressure and 100 per cent oxygen saturation. Magic! What a relief it was now to have this superb monitor, instead of a shaky finger on a weak pulse, after years of shouting and pleading to be allowed to trial it.

But marvellous monitor or not, Linda still looked uncomfortable. Neil leaned over, lifted the corner of her ear muff, and shouted something in her ear; then put his head close to hers for the reply. He looked up. 'She's in pain, Boss… level five out of ten.'

'Could you fit her with a talking headset?'

'It will overload the intercom, Doc.' interjected Jon Bird. 'There are seven in use already.'

'Doesn't matter. I need to talk to her. Someone else can unplug for a minute.' Neil fitted the headset and unplugged himself.

'Are you having much pain?' I asked. Linda nodded.

'In a scale of ten?'

'Six.'

'Contractions?

'Yes.' Oh shit!

'How often?'

'Every five minutes.' I unplugged her.

'Do you want me to give her something, Gordon? And could you come down and give me a hand?'

'What have you got?'

'Pethidine.'

'OK.' I slowly injected 100mg pethidine intravenously, as Gordon clambered to the far side of the stretcher and took her hand. Slowly her face relaxed as the pain subsided. Gordon checked. There had been no fresh blood loss. So far so good.

By now we were well up the coast, passing Hunterston Nuclear Power Station, Largs and Inverkip. The weather closed in rapidly as

Paul Tarrant took the aircraft slowly up the Clyde past Greenock and Port Glasgow. In the lee of the Renfrewshire hills, out of the driving east wind, the snow lay thick and still on bushes, trees, and rooftops, creating a picturesque vista which might have been most enjoyable had we been in a position to appreciate it. As it was, the flying visibility was only a few hundred yards. Getting into Glasgow Airport would be tricky, and going under the Erskine Bridge was out of the question.

'We'll have to follow the M8 from junction 31 to junction 30, and then on to the airport which is just before junction 29.' instructed Jon Bird. 'But watch out for two sets of power lines crossing the road just after junction 30.' Traffic was moving slowly but steadily on the twin black ribbons of road beneath us, while we ourselves were flying only marginally faster as Adam Carr twice eased the Sea King, like some big lazy hurdler, over the 360,000 volt cables slung across our track.

Leaving these hazards safely behind, within a few minutes we were skimming low over the perimeter fence and along a runway thick with slushy snow. The airport seemed almost at a standstill, and uncannily quiet once the aircraft engines were shut down. We sat and waited, and waited. No ambulance appeared. We knew the roads were open. Linda was quietly stable, and under the influence of her sedation her contractions had settled. But she could go off again at any time. Surely it could not take half an hour for an ambulance to come from the Southern General,even in this weather. But half an hour we did have to wait before it showed up, and I made a mental note to request RCC to ensure, in future, that any Sea King carrying an unstable patient would be met on arrival by an waiting ambulance.

'How are you both going to get back to Stranraer?' I asked, as Gordon and the midwife clambered into the ambulance beside their patient.

'I don't know yet. Depending on the weather, I'll phone Anne and see if she could drive up to Ayr or Girvan to meet the train. See you again sometime.'

The weather was still worsening as we retraced our route and gingerly renegotiated the high tension pylons as we sought the safety of the open waters of the Clyde. The intercom was buzzing. There seemed to be a lot going on down in the south west, involving a train stuck in snowdrifts, and a helicopter with a strange call sign.

'What the hell's going on, Jon? Who is Rescue 137, and what is he doing in our patch?'

'It's a Crab Wessex—over from Northern Ireland, and he's been tasked to lift passengers off a stranded train south of Girvan.'

'Not much hope of Doctor Baird and his nurse getting home by train, then!'

'Quiet!' We shut up.

'It's RCC. They've got two jobs for us. Another preggevac, and a sick baby to be transferred from Ayr Hospital to Glasgow.'

'Where is the preggevac?'

'Gretna... A woman in labour with twins, to be transferred to Dumfries.'

'Gretna! Twins! Bloody hell, that will mean going all the way back down to Stranraer and right along the Solway coastline to Annan. It'll take three hours in these conditions, and there is not a cat's chance in hell of flying overland.'

A woman in twin labour, and a sick baby! Some medical prioritising would have to be done.

'Probably more urgent to go for the pregnant woman.' I volunteered, though not relishing one teeny bit the thought of another rough trip down the Ayrshire coast, followed by a ninety-mile slog east into a blizzard before we even got to our patient. And the prospect of delivering twins in a helicopter didn't even bear thinking about. At least the sick baby was under specialist care in a warm hospital at present.

'I'll check with RCC, and ask them what they want us to do.' said Jon. There were a couple of minutes of strained silence before he came back with the welcome information that the Crab Wessex had been sensibly tasked to fly on to Gretna after completing the railway rescue, and that we were to transfer the sick baby to Glasgow. It's not often the boys are happy to have a job snaffled from under their noses, but this time they seemed quite chuffed at avoiding such a long transit.

We overflew Prestwick and landed a few minutes later on the helipad at Ayr Hospital. I noted with interest a ten-feet wide trench which was being excavated round the pad perimeter. It had only taken them three years, but at long last the Hospital Trust Board were implementing my recommendation about enlarging their helipad, to allow stretchers or trolleys to pass safely round the nose of a Sea King without having to struggle and slip across a treacherous grassy surface to the waiting ambulance. Still, better late than never!

But there was no waiting ambulance. Up in the hospital, a paediatric staff nurse and young SHO were gathering a baby bag and mask and a pocketful of vital bits and pieces from Leo Murray, the A&E consultant, as they awaited the arrival of the incubator from the paediatric unit upstairs. With the nurse only dressed in her tunic and the doc in shirt sleeves and light jacket, they were both totally ill-clad for a trip in a Sea King in a blizzard. I quickly pointed out that, unlike ambulances, our beast had not the luxury of a heating system... if they wanted to avoid hypothermia... Heavy jackets were speedily borrowed, and the Vickers incubator, its four-week-old occupant and his anxious mother loaded aboard and secured for take-off.

Almost immediately we hit a problem. The staff nurse, who seemed much more au fait with the workings of her incubator than the young doctor, looked worried as she switched on the controls only to get a message to 'Connect to Mains Supply'! I had thought all these incubators had several hours of in-built battery supply, but this one didn't seem to have one—or had they thrown the wrong switch? SAR flying is one long series of constant learning curves, from which hopefully stem equally constant modifications to equipment and procedures. This was another point for checking with Leo Murray when we returned.

But the problem remained. Only the oxygen system worked. The incubator could no longer heat and monitor the baby, who had a serious congenital heart condition, during a long transit in sub-zero temperatures.

'Do you want to try our Propaq monitor? At least you will be able to get pulse rate and oxygen saturation levels if nothing else.'

The staff nurse eagerly took up this offer, and was as delighted as we were to see it work perfectly. Temperature control was another matter, however, as we watched the thermometer slowly drop from 25 to 15 degrees Celsius over the next twenty minutes. Fortunately, the baby was well-cocooned in blankets, and hopefully still as snug and warm as any wee Eskimo papoose. Still, given the time delays of our last trip, I was taking no chances, and asked Paul Tarrant to insist that an ambulance was on the apron to meet us on our arrival at the airport.

Our approach to Glasgow was even more hazardous this time round. Blizzard conditions brought visibility right down to a hundred yards at times, and made spotting our user-friendly high tension cables even more difficult than before. Guided in by the combined skills of observer, pilots and Air Traffic Control, it was with immense relief that we felt the reassuring jolt of landing wheels as the aircraft touched down and rolled to a halt beside the terminal building. This time an ambulance was waiting. The incubator was quickly manhandled into the ambulance where it could be plugged into the vehicle's electrical supply to restore heat and monitoring function for the baby's cross-city trip to Yorkhill Sick Kids' Hospital and cardiac specialist care.

Amazingly, even in these horrible conditions, aircraft were still landing and taking off, on slush-covered runways with six to eight inches of snow on the perimeter. The marvels of blind landing approach technology was something Sea Kings did not possess, and as soon as a minor gap appeared in the snow curtain veiling the airport, Paul made his difficult decision to head back for Prestwick and over these bloody pylons for the fourth—and hopefully last—time. There was no let-up in the weather till we were almost back at *Gannet*—and no let up for the crew either when we arrived to find another potential job—at Dumfries!

I was exhausted, and I hadn't been flying the aircraft. Neil sloped gratefully off to his kip, while Don Clark slipped into his goon suit. At least he would be fresh for the job—a medevac to transfer a severe back injury from Dumfries to Edinburgh—but I was heartfelt sorry for Paul, Adam, Jon and Lee Norton, faced with the prospect of another trip down the coast to Stranraer and all along the Solway to Dumfries, in the dark, in a blizzard! Mind you, I was heading back to an evening surgery. I wonder if they felt sorry for me? Nae chance.

Home for the evening, I was drifting off in the chair by a roaring fire when the phone rang. It was Faither. 'I heard ye've been gallivantin in that helicopter o yours again! Haes yer sister been on the phone tae ye?'

'No. Whit sister?'

'Marjorie. She wis workin in the music shop this efternuin when a young wumman came in an asked for some music. Her accent sounded familiar an Madge asked her whaur she came fae.

"Stranraer," says the lassie. "Oh," says Madge, "ye're faur fae hame. Hou did ye manage tae get up here in this wather?"

"I flew," she said. "I'm a midwife an I've juist taen a pregnant patient up tae Glesca fae Stranraer in a Navy helicopter this mornin. We got the train back tae Ayr, an we're juist waitin on a lift back doun hame."

"My brother would be on that helicopter," says Madge.

The lassie looked dumfounert. "Your brother?" she said.

"Aye," says Madge. "He's a doctor."

"Doctor Begg?"

"That's my brother!" '

Faither chuckled. 'It's a sma world—is it no!'

Two weeks later, Linda gave birth to a 'very special' baby boy. Kieran was only a shade over two pounds at birth, and it was a further three months, and many long , weary and worrying journeys back and forwards to Glasgow for Linda and her husband, before he had gained enough weight, and was well enough, to go home to Stranraer. Now he is at school, and a sturdy 'wee terror'!

By another strange coincidence, Linda's brother Duncan, heading for a routine hospital appointment in Glasgow, was one of the passengers airlifted to safety by the Wessex that same day, from the stranded, snowbound train on the moors south of Girvan.

21

29th February 1996

VICTOR THREE

'Good morning, Boss. You're going to have a quiet morning. Two of the fresh cases have cancelled, and so has the medical.' Craig Menzies was a pleasant young bespectacled lad from Glasgow, who had just joined sick bay from the Royal Marine base at HMS *Condor*, having recently gone through all the usual aircrew training drills before he could be put on the watch bill for SAR flying. Tragically for him, he had quickly discovered he had a major handicap—severe motion sickness. Never having had a sea draft, he had never been put to the test on board ship, and the problem only came to light on his first training flight.

He had been distraught, feeling he was wimping out and letting the other guys down. Due to Fez Parker and Neil Hodgson leaving to take up POMA appointments, we had been under-strength, with Don, Rob Smith and the new MA 'Scouse' Williams working a virtual one-on, one-off twenty-four hour rota. Craig had tried hard to fulfil his SAR duties, but had been beaten by turbulence, especially in the mountains. I had prescribed Hyoscine and Stugeron, tried relating to him my own experiences of disgracing myself, and told him I had seen senior PO aircrewmen throwing up, and even some observers looking much the worse of wear. He had been on the point of giving up, but had been persuaded to hang in there and try to become acclimatised by participating in regular navex training flights where he could relax, knowing he was not going to be a liability to other crew members if he was sick. Hopefully, this would gradually build up his confidence and allow him to return to full SAR duties. With selfishly more than Craig in mind, I had asked Andy Holley, the SARO, to remind his pilots to try and avoid swinging their aircraft about too much, both on the outward flight, when a sick doc or medic arriving on scene would be of little use to a casualty, and on the return leg, when a seriously ill patient always needed delicate handling to avoid the risk of inhaling vomit. Only time would tell if the lad would crack his problem.

I was quite glad to have a slack morning, for I had just completed a challenging two and a half day Advanced Trauma Life Support course to re-accredit my ATLS Certificate, and this had stimulated me to overhaul the contents and layout of my doctor's grab bag. New equipment had to be stowed, and old items discarded, and the whole lot was strewn over my examination couch ready for its final packing in a brand new red bag. This was the standby gear, which would eventually become the first line kit when I had finished.

With only one patient still to come, I went through to the main office to ask Scouse to pour me a wet. Some medics are better than others at brewing tea, and Scouse seemed to have the knack. He was on the phone, cheerily gabbling away in that adenoidal accent peculiar to Liverpudlians. 'Yeah, yeah, ee's 'ere. Ah'll get 'im to come down straight away.' He put down the phone and looked up. 'It's an appendix case, west of Arran. They want you on board now. Will I phone your surgery?'

'Hardly worth while, Scouse. If it's only west of Arran, I'll be back in a couple of hours.' It was only half past nine. Why on earth did they want me for an appendicitis west of Arran? Unless it was a fishing boat. But surely Rob Smith, who was duty MA, could handle that. As I ran up the Squadron Building steps, my bleep went. Was this to stand me down? Tim Eldridge met me at the duty desk.

'Could you get changed quickly, Doc. We've got an appendicitis on a Russian submarine.' That explained it—but west of Arran?

'How far out is it?' I asked.

'About one hundred and sixty miles.' So much for west of Arran. So much for Scouse's communication skills. He had either interpreted 'west of Ireland' as 'west of Arran', or just pronounced it like that. Either way, the surgery would have to know now that I would be gone for a while.

A Russian sub! This would be another first. Intriguing. The intercom crackled constantly with signals as we headed past Pladda and crossed the Mull of Kintyre just north of Campbeltown. At least the weather was good for a winching, with a large anticyclone out to the west, and a ten to fourteen knot wind and gentle sea. I had time to look around. Tim Eldridge was Captain, and Al Falconer the co-pilot. The hunched figure over the radar was Lt Cdr Gordon Wright, on RNR secondment duties. Gordie worked as an environmental biologist with the Scottish Natural Heritage based in Perth, and filled in frequently during the winter months on SAR duties. And the guy in the fancy red wet suit? POACMN Ian Copley… fresh from his Man of the Year Award in London, when he and Lts Andy Aspden, Diccon Murphy and Andy Naylor from *Gannet* had been honoured for rescuing eleven members of a Norwegian fishing boat while on exercise with 819 Sqn off Norway last year.

'Is this you joining the Red Navy, Ian? Or is it an anti-radiation suit?'

'It's just to make them feel I'm one of them if I'm winched onboard, Doc.' He grinned as he pulled on his flying jacket and fastened his PLP.

Gordie Wright swore. 'I wish to hell they would make their minds up. They've given us two sets of coordinates for this sub. The first is fifty-five degrees thirty north by eight degrees thirty west—that's west of Donegal—and the second is fifty-seven thirty north, eight thirty west—level with Benbecula! What's the best place to refuel? We've a long search ahead.'

'Well, you've got Ballykelly in Northern Ireland, it's an Army base, but with the Canary Wharf bombing and the new security alert you'll need to give them advance notice.'

'If we've got to search further north, it might be worth while heading for Benbecula to refuel when the time comes. Call Rescue 11 and ask him.' By this time we were passing south of Islay heading for the search area off Donegal. Somewhere above us, Rescue 11, a Nimrod from Kinloss, was coordinating the sea search.

'Rescue 177, this is Rescue 11. Please continue to search area fifty-five thirty north, eight thirty west. Confirm refuel at Benbecula, not Ballykelly. Rescue 119 will proceed to fifty-seven thirty north, eight thirty west.'

'Rescue 119—that must be the Coastguard cab from Stornoway being tasked to cover west of Uist. It'll just be like the thing if the bloody sub pops up there and we lose the job! Let's slip north a bit before we get to the westing. Then we are in a position to go either north or south should the submarine decide to surface.'

'What do the Russians think they're bloody playing at anyway? You would think that if they'd shouted for help, they would have the decency to let us know their exact position and pop their heads up straightaway.'

'It's a bit more complicated than that.' voiced the observer, knowingly. 'We are only getting half the story. Just as much as Northwood want us to know. I keep getting snippets of information from the different signals. The request for help came from the Russians via the British Embassy in Moscow, who spoke to the MoD, who spoke to GHQ Northwood, who passed it down the line to RCC Kinloss—and COM Clyde are also putting their tuppenceworth in. So we are well down the line of command, just doing what we are told, and farting about out here looking for a tube which could be anywhere along a two-hundred-mile line! With that chain of communication from Murmansk to Kinloss, the bloody reference has probably changed three times en route.' Send three and fourpence all over again!

'The bugger is probably playing hide and seek with us,' grumbled Tim Eldridge. 'He's probably been spying on the NATO exercise for days and wants to get as far away as possible before they ping him.'

'I can't believe they don't know where he is. It's probably bluff and counter bluff. The Russians think we don't know where he is. The Navy knows where he is, but don't want the Russians to know that we know where he is, so they pretend they don't know where he is... and leave us poor sods to bugger about for hours looking for nothing.' It was beginning to sound like something out of Red October, or a Bond movie. We were but small pawns in a great political chess game—but it was quite exciting.

'Or it could be that the Russian commander is scared to act on his own initiative and surface straightaway,' added Gordie Wright sagely, with the weight of years of experience behind him. 'Their chain of command probably starts somewhere in the Urals, runs through Moscow, all the way up to Murmansk, and then to sea. A sub commander would hardly be allowed to as much blow his nose without authorisation from the top. And by the time his references are passed up the line and back down again, plus all the signals from this end, it could be hours before anything happens, if ever.'

'So we could be here all day, Gordie—is that what you are saying?'

'Sounds as if he knows more about this than he is letting on. Do you all know what day this is? February twenty ninth.'

'What's that got to do with it?'

'Leap year, you stupid sod! Gordie has probably organised this whole scam to get away from his girlfriend, so she can't ask him to marry her!'

'To change the subject, chaps,' retorted the sage under seige, '*Monmouth* is close to fifty-five thirty north, and is putting out her Lynx to look for the sub. I suggest we head north up the Minch for Benbecula to refuel, for I've just had another bloody reference putting the submarine at fifty-nine thirty north, nine west.

'For Chrissake! That's well out of our patch... away to the north of the Butt of Lewis. That is Coastguard territory. They're sure to be tasked for this job now.'

'Look, the bloody thing could be in any one of three sectors, and they are all still to be covered. Nobody seems to have a bloody clue.'

'God, by the state of some of those old Russian subs on the telly last week laid up at Murmansk, you would think that tracking one of their tubes would be no problem. You should be able to see the pink glow from its reactor in thirty feet of water... and follow the trail of steam!'

'Yeah. I hope the Doc's got plenty of protection if he's winched down on this one.'

'The least he will need is a lead-lined jockstrap!'

Gordie Wright silenced us again. 'I spoke to Rescue 11 about refuelling at Benbecula. They have asked us to proceed straight to Stornoway to refuel. It looks more and more like it will be surfacing in one of the northern sectors. I'll give you a heading which will take us over the north west tip of Skye.'

'Rescue 11. This is Alpha Juliet India Quebec. What assets have you for your search to the north of fifty-seven thirty? I am at present fifty-eight north, nine west and am in a position to assist.'

'Who the hell is that?'

'Dunno. But it's not a fishing boat… "What are your assets"—he seems to know what he is talking about.'

'Alpha Juliet India Quebec. This is Rescue 11. We have two helicopters searching areas fifty-five thirty north and fifty-seven thirty north, eight thirty west. Proceed on your present course.'

'Ask him to identify himself, Gordie. The Crabs seem to know him.'

Gordon duly obliged, and quickly came back with the information that it was HMS *Glasgow*, a type-42 destroyer and Falklands veteran, taking part in the NATO exercise. Well, at least there was one helicopter searching, but it wasn't us—yet. At this point we were passing five miles west of Skerryvore Lighthouse which, in a gentle swell, looked much more appealing than when I had last passed it—lashed by mountainous seas in a Force Eleven January storm. Flat Eigg, mountainous Rum, and tiny Canna slipped past on the eastern horizon as we skirted Dunvegan Head and passed Loch Snizort, from where the ferries sail on the road to the isles—from Uig to Lochmaddy—and the bonny trout lochs of the Uists.

Gordie was a fisher. 'How is the fishing on Loch Leven, Gordie? Has it improved much?'

'Tremendous. The best season for years, last year. The brown trout are almost back to their best, and the algae problem is almost gone.' I made a mental note to speak to Peter Galloway, now based at Faslane, and arrange for the three of us to have a day to remember on

Loch Leven. Before I could say more, Gordie sat erect in his seat, a concentrated look on his face, his right hand held out in a command for silence. Then he scribbled furiously on his kneepad. We all sat expectantly. He looked up, grinned from ear to ear, and stuck up a triumphant thumb.

'We've got it!' he cried. 'Word has just come through that the sub has arranged to surface at fourteen-thirty hours at fifty-nine thirty north, eight thirty west. Rescue 119 has been asked to return to Stornoway and is being stood down. We've to proceed to Stornoway, shut down and await further orders.'

'What a steal! The Coastguard boys won't like that—for us to come up and nick a job like this from under their noses—right at the top of their patch!'

'Yeah. And we leapfrogged them too. With them being sent down to fifty-seven north while we sneaked up past them to Stornoway.'

'Sounds as if it has all been part of a cunning plan. I think we must have been pencilled in for this job from the start, because of its political implications. The military were never going to let a civvy helicopter steal their thunder—or cock it up—when the profile was so high.' By this time we were past the Shiants and running along the Lewis coast with only a few miles to go. We had already been flying for almost three hours.

The midday British Airways ATP flight to Glasgow left shortly after we touched down, leaving Stornoway airport deserted. The Coastguard Sikorsky 61 had not yet returned. We were ushered into a huge hangar which could have housed the whole of 819 Squadron with room left to spare—a relic of the Cold War when Stornoway airport runway was enlarged to take large NATO military aircraft and fast jets. It was now home to Bristow Helicopters, who ran the Coastguard SAR service—with one helicopter. Along a painted brick corridor, left turn and upstairs to the spartan comforts of the Coastguard aircrew's ready room for a welcome mug of coffee and a comfy seat.

Al Falconer switched on the TV for the one o'clock news. The first item was of a major sea search involving warships, a Nimrod and two helicopters, now under way for a Russian submarine off

Ireland and the Western Isles. This was the first time since the end of the Second World War that the Russians had asked the West for assistance in rescuing one of their servicemen at sea, the request coming—as we already knew—via the British Embassy in Moscow. It was a weird feeling, being part of the news and, in a small way, part of history.

The only problem was that we were well ahead of the news—there were no helicopters out there searching for the beast. The Sikorski arrived back, with a very disgruntled aircrewman tugging angrily at his goon suit zip and sounding off about what a bloody waste of two-and-a-half hours that had been, looking at grey sea! 'Don't take any notice of him,' said his relief with a grin, 'he's a Crab!' The Coastguard crews seemed to have been recruited fifty-fifty from the ranks of ex-Navy and RAF fliers, and this lad turned out to have been a mate of Ian Copley—small world again! It was, however, a wee shade embarrassing to be lounging around in their easy chairs, enjoying their coffee and home comforts, while poaching a major job from under their noses.

Gordie tried the landline to Kinloss, but got little more out of them than we had heard on the news. 'Looks as if we will have a long wait, lads, so enjoy your bacon butties. I'm not going to ring them again for a while. They get pissed off if you pester them too much. They will ring us if anything develops.' Tim and Al found an Uckers board and launched with great intensity into trying to beat the hell out of each other, at what looked like a glorified game of Ludo. There was something strangely familiar about the counters, till I looked closely and discovered they were made from the brass detonator caps of twelve-bore cartridges, painted in different colours! Ian Copley uncovered three huge scrapbooks meticulously detailing all the SAR missions undertaken by Rescue119 since they arrived in Stornoway in May 1987, with press cuttings, photographs, met charts and RCC signals, very impressive—and probably the creative consequence of a mega-boredom factor in the long interval between jobs.

'Have you ever seen inside a Sikorsky 61?' I asked Rob. He hadn't, so a quick OK from the Coastguard Officer in Charge, and we were soon ferreting around inside the Sikorsky—a big cousin of the Sea King but a helluva lot more luxurious, with paired rows of plush padded seats in a lined, insulated, commodious cabin. It was obviously one of the oil-rig passenger transport helos modified for SAR by the removal of a few seats to take a basket stretcher. They also had an interesting stretcher variation—a cross between a long spinal board and a Neil Robertson stretcher—which looked ideal for lifts from submarines, for example! A couple of grab bags with similar contents to our own, some oyygen and ventilation equipment, and that was it. No Propaq or HeartStart monitors. At least we were one up in that department. But the infra-red night detection equipment, and the large inboard reserve fuel tank—which gave it an extended range—were huge plus points, especially as many of their jobs were very exposed, at the extremes of their range out in the wild Atlantic. And it must be pleasantly quiet, clean and warm to fly in.

Shortly after rejoining the lads, the phone rang in the Bristow office. Gordie went through to answer it, while we waited, all intent. 'It has surfaced as scheduled, about ninety miles north west of the Butt of Lewis, and HMS *Glasgow* is in the vicinity. Should take us about three quarters of an hour to get there.' We rose and walked out to the aircraft. It was now about three-thirty. The wind was from the north west and the sky was grey and overcast, with low stratus cloud at a thousand feet. Not the best visibility for locating a sub at sea. Flying up the east coast of Lewis, we turned left at Tolsta and flew north west over some of the most desolate terrain imaginable—a giant bogland sieve, with hundreds of puddles, dubs, lochans and lochs, linked together by thin threads of barren moor. But what trout fishing! My young cousin Jim's wife Doleen was born at Ness, right on the tip of the Butt of Lewis, and they often come up on family holidays, but don't fish. He is a golfer. What a waste!

Overflying Ness, a scatter of crofts strung like beads of a necklace on a ring of narrow roads, we headed out over the Atlantic towards Sula Sgeir and North Rona. Funnily enough, I had just been reading about Sula Sgeir in the February issue of *The Scots Magazine*, little dreaming that a couple of weeks later I would be flying past it. Sula Sgeir in Gaelic means the 'Gannet Rock', appropriately named after our home base and epic flight perhaps, but more so for the fourteen thousand pairs of gannets who make a much more impressive epic, annual, return flight each spring from the warm seas off North Africa and Spain to breed there. Lying far to the north of Lewis, it has been a valuable source of scarce food for the folk of Ness for centuries. Braving thirty miles of Atlantic Ocean in open boats each summer, the men of Ness would cross to Sula Sgeir and scale its two-hundred-foot cliffs for their annual cull of young gannets or 'gugas'. This unique and jealously guarded tradition apparently persists to the present day, with a quota of two thousand gugas permitted to the Lewismen by law. I was looking forward to seeing the island.

'Rescue 11... Alpha Juliet India Quebec. I am now alongside the submarine. Our Lynx is airborne and I propose to put our medic on board to assess the casualty. We will then winch off the patient and transfer him on board prior to casevac to Stornoway.'

'What the hell to they think they are playing at! Tell them to bugger off! Their Lynx is not equipped for this type of transfer, and anyway it would mean double handling and a deck landing for us on *Glasgow*. Some tosser hasn't thought this one through.'

I wasn't too chuffed either, for I was already strapped into a double-lift harness, ready to follow Ian Copley down on to the submarine if he felt he needed assistance in preparing the patient for evacuation. And here was some bloody MA from *Glasgow* just about to steal our thunder after we'd flown three hundred miles!

Gordie Wright was quick off his mark. 'Alpha Juliet India Quebec, this is Rescue 177. Our ETA is thirty minutes. It would be better if we transfer the casualty direct to our Sea King from the submarine. By the time your medic has him prepared we will be on scene and will lower our winchman to take charge of transfer.' *Glasgow* agreed, and we flew on.

Sadly, Sula Sgeir never became more than a tantalising smudge on the horizon far to starboard, but beneath us the long white, black-tipped wings of a few early arrivals gliding low over the wave troughs, banked in avoiding action as we flew past. Without the electronics of radar or GPS, these gannets had managed to navigate thousands of miles at low level to find a tiny speck on the ocean. With radar, at low level, Gordie was having some difficulty in finding *our* speck on the ocean.

'Can you take her up to five hundred feet and I'll see if we can make a contact,' he asked Tim. The extra height did the trick. He got a fix and Tim altered course accordingly.

In the back, Ian Copley was completing his checks for winching, and readying the stretcher with the help of Rob Smith. With his back to us, he rummaged around and produced a metal box. 'Right, David Bailey, let's see how good you are!' Out of the box came a couple of expensive cameras. He proffered one to Rob. 'Can you use one of these?' Rob nodded, took the camera, squinted through the viewfinder and simultaneously twirled the focus with an air of apparent expertise.

'OK. When we get over the sub, fire off as many spools as you can. We don't often get the chance to snap one of these buggers!'

I moved up front behind the pilots as a third pair of eyes, and a few minutes later was lucky to be first to spot, in the grey sea under a grey sky, a distant grey shape low in the water at one o'clock. It was *Glasgow*. At first we could not locate the submarine, then as we approached closer, its raked, low-profile conning tower appeared on the lee side of the destroyer, above a long sinister hull which rose and fell slowly in a six-foot swell.

'It looks like a Victor 3?' called Al Falconer. 'I've hunted for them often enough, but this is the first time I've seen it on the surface.' The Victor 3 was one of the newer Russian nuclear hunter-killer submarines, and one about which little was apparently known. *Glasgow's* Lynx was fussily flying round it like a wasp at a jampot, while from the right our Rescue 11 Nimrod made the first of several low level passes. Quite a scene!

'Rescue 177... Alpha Juliet India Quebec.'

'What does he want this time?' We were still some way off.

'We have an urgent package to be taken to the mainland. Could you uplift it first, before you transfer your casualty?'

'What the bloody hell does he think we are, a bloody postal service? We are here on a SAR. If he wants something taken off, that's what his Lynx is for. Tell him we will do our task first, and if we have time and fuel, we will come across and collect his mail!'

Gordie came back to us. 'It's top priority... relevant to today's goings-on. Let's get the PO aircrewman on board the sub first, then we'll work it out.' He left his seat and strapped on his safety harness. Rob did likewise, and positioned himself prone on the floor as Gordie slid open the cargo door and talked Tim carefully and quietly over the tower of the Victor 3, perilously close to a large metal tube with what looked like a closed parasol at its tip, their UHF aerial, which stuck up awkwardly about twenty feet above the heads of half a dozen Russian sailors cramming the hatch entrance. Ian Copley was quickly lowered among them, and gesticulated emphatically for them to lower the aerial to allow the stretcher to be winched down.

This done, we stood off to one side allowing Rob to snap away furiously at the upturned faces of heavy-smoking fur-capped Russian sailors, who returned our curiosity about them in equal measure, with waves, smiles and some equally furious snapping. The submarine, number 661 painted on its fin, had obviously been at sea for a long time, with large strips of anti-sonar cladding fabric peeling loose from the front of the conning tower like the skin of a moulting elephant seal. A long aerial wire trailed away astern from a point on the aft starboard quarter, and its huge protruding rudder was surmounted by a large pod shaped like a jet engine, which I was reliably informed held the towed array used in tracking and hunting enemy submarines—i.e. ours!

After Ian was taken below, and Rob had secured some superb shots of the Victor 3 with HMS *Glasgow* in the immediate background, we backed off and began circling the submarine in a long wait for our casualty to emerge topsides. It was an ideal opportunity to call up *Glasgow* and play postman. The type 42 was manoeuvred into position for our approach, a sandbagged wire lowered on to the flight deck, and a blue mailbag quickly attached and hoisted on board to be stowed away out of view up front. It only took a couple of minutes, an interesting small diversion in an otherwise boring thirty minutes hanging around waiting for a call from Ian Copley.

When it did come, just after four o'clock, the transfer was swift, professional and almost anti-climactic after eight hours of anticipation. My first impression was one of surprise. The patient was only a boy—but I suppose so are many of the young lads I see every week at *Gannet*! You just never think of the other side being the same. Strapped securely with webbing into a canvas stretcher for the vertical lift up through the tower, a look of helplessness and apprehension flickered briefly across his pale drawn face as he waved weakly down to his clustered shipmates, before Gordon drew shut the cargo door and we headed for Stornoway.

Rob clipped on the ECG leads as I fitted the BP cuff and pulse oximeter. All readings were normal, till suddenly he became restless and his oxygen saturation began to drop, and it equally quickly dawned on me that, under the insulating blanket, his chest must have become tightly wedged into the webbing straps during the ascent, and his breathing was now being severely restricted. Grabbing a pair of scissors, I quickly cut through the strapping and within seconds his blood oxygen levels had returned to normal. Ian Copley handed me a letter from the submarine's medic. Written in sloping long-hand, it looked just like any other doctor's handwriting—almost illegible! Apart from recognising a normal BP reading, and a high fever with a temperature of 39 degrees Celsius, I could make neither head nor tail of its contents, till I realised it was all in Russian!

'Did you get much information from the medics on board as to what has been done to this guy, Ian?' I quizzed in desperation.

'Not really, Doc. I spent most of my time being interrogated by the Captain as to who I was and what was my rank, probably in case I was a spy. Just gave him the usual name, rank and number stuff. There didn't seem to be anyone on board who spoke good English or could tell me much about the bloke. the Captain's main concern was to get me to sign for him—like a bit of kit issue—before we took him off the sub!'

Then he grinned and stuck his right hand deep into his lifejacket. 'But here's a bit of kit I didn't sign for!'—and proudly pulled out a black furry Russian navy hat. 'One of the sailors on deck presented it to me as we were leaving. Just what I've always wanted!'

It was almost dark when we made our final approach to Stornoway, and landed in a field next to the Western Isles Hospital where the press were waiting, cameras rolling, as we transferred the young Russian into the hospital Receiving Room and retrieved our equipment. I explained to Sister and the House Officer as well as I could his medical history and background, while taking the opportunity myself to peel back a sodden dressing pad and reveal a foul-smelling, pus-filled, open lower abdominal wound. My guess was a ruptured appendix abscess. The certainty was that, had we not airlifted him to hospital, he would have been dead in forty-eight hours.

Scrutinising the letter again, despite being under good lighting, I could only decipher one other word, which looked like 'Alexander'—probably his name. An interpreter was being called, who would decipher the rest—if he could read a Russian doctor's handwriting. I looked at the boy's drained anxious face. He had had enough excitement for one day, and was more in need of intravenous antibiotics. Quietly signalling goodbye, we left him to the capable care of Mr Duncan McLean, the island surgeon.

For the next few days, the media had a field day, with the story of Alexander Erokhin, the Russian twenty-year-old who had been operated on by medics holding a textbook while his submarine lay on the seabed avoiding detection by NATO warships. He had refused to tell interpreters about his medical problem, or what had been done to him, in case he would be in trouble for leaking secrets! The press had also tried to make capital over the cost and length of the search—'Million Pound Rescue' said the *Daily Record*, with typical hyperbole—and the unco-operative evasion tactics employed by the submarine Captain attempting to hide the fact that they had been spying on a NATO exercise.

Meanwhile, both the Russians and the Ministry of Defence played down any attempt at controversy, simply delighted that this first ever request for assistance by the Russians was a historic breakthrough which showed that the two sides could now, after fifty years of emnity, trust each other to deal positively with such situations.

Ten days later, Ian Copley, who, not surprisingly, had just returned from an intensive security debrief in London, popped in to sick bay to see Don Clark and the boys. 'Have you heard how the Russian sailor is doing, Doc?' he asked.

'I phoned up at the end of last week,' I replied. 'After tests and a course of intravenous antibiotics, they operated on him last Saturday and cleaned up his appendix abscess. He seems to be doing fine and they are hoping to discharge him tomorrow. How's your furry hat? Does it fit?'

'Don't talk to me about that!' he grimaced. 'The Boss wants it.'

'What! You mean like a big boy stealing a wee boy's sweeties?'

'Well, not quite as bad as that,' he grinned wryly. 'He wants it for a squadron trophy—to put it in a glass case with the other flotsam they've picked up over the years. So it's one of these offers you can't refuse.'

'Tough luck, Ian. Well, just make sure it's got a big brass label on it saying "Captured from a Russian sub—Victor 3—North Atlantic 1996—single-handed—by Petty Officer Ian Copley"!'

22

10th April 1996

UP HOROSCOPE!

'You are looking dead beat.' Helen stared accusingly across the hearth as I slumped into the chair by the fire.

'Just a wee bit tired,' I countered defensively. It had been a typical fraught Tuesday, with a grabbed lunch snack at a quarter to two, and a homecoming at six-thirty. An Faither aye came doun on a Tuesday for his tea—an a guid argie-bargie! With his eighty-fourth birthday only two months away, he was still as sherp as a tack, in guid fettle, an aye rarin tae go on some topic or other, be it politics, the evils o' drink, thae young folk, or fitba. Wi a twinkle in his e'e, an his twistit sense o humour, he loved an argument—if only to wind Fiona up about her team, the Rangers; or Helen about his stomach and her cooking; or me about everything else!

And I loved to argue back—we were two of a kind, Faither an me. As Helen often said, 'You can't argue with a Begg!' But it could be gey wearin efter a ten hour day, to muster up the energy for this weekly two-hour verbal sparring match. He had just driven smartly off home, after failing miserably in an attempt to tell me how I should be trimming my cypress hedge—but left me exhausted in the process. Honours even!

'I've just been reading this in my magazine,' Helen began ominously, 'and you should listen to it!'

'Whit nou!' I groaned. She was aye reading things in her magazines.

'Your horoscope! Sagittarius. Listen to this. "You appear to have a lot on your plate at the moment, but how much of what you are doing is necessary and how much is simply to keep others happy? If you burn the candle at both ends, then something will have to give—whether it is your health or your temper that feels the strain remains to be seen, but you have only so much energy to go around, so use it wisely."

'That's just you!' she went on, turning the screw. 'You were on call for the Doctors Co-operative last night till after midnight. you had four committee meetings last week—and now you have one of your bloody talks to do on your half-day tomorrow! You are doing too much again.'

I squirmed under the onslaught. 'Not as much as I used to,' I retorted lamely. 'That was the only Co-op shift I've got to do for the whole of April, when in the old days I would have had four or five overnights on call. At least now I can get an undisturbed night's sleep after midnight—every night—for the first time in thirty years. So you've read my horoscope, then what's yours?' Attack is the best form of defence.

Helen picked up her magazine again. '"With six of the eight major planets appearing to move backwards through the sky this month, you cannot expect everything to be decided in your favour."'

Round one to me!

'"Even compromise solutions have a tendency to unravel for no apparent reason..."'

What's new!

'"What you can expect, however, is for an emotional relationship to keep on improving and support from family and friends to be increasing."'

'Well, that's reassuring. So even if I do a wee bit too much now and again, as long as I take my turn about the house you'll still love me!'

She laughed. 'Let's all try to get to bed before midnight for once, and get a good night's sleep—especially you, Fiona, with your studying!' From Fiona, sat with her back to us at a table cluttered with lab reports and graphs of an as yet unfinished and overdue SYS biology project, came a non-committal grunt.

Typically, my exhaustion disappeared as the evening wore on, and at quarter to twelve I found myself still at the word processor, revising the talk on 'Burns an the Guid Scots Tongue' which I was due to deliver on Wednesday afternoon to the Ayrshire branch of the Scottish Retired Teachers' Association. Mindful of the curfew, I called a halt, switched off the machine, and was in bed by a minute to twelve.

At ten past twelve the phone rang! In terror for my life, I lifted the receiver. As I had feared, it was the OOD at *Gannet*. 'We've a medevac, and a doctor has been requested. Can you come in?' There was no other info available on location, distance, or nature of illness. Helen was one very unhappy lady, and I promised to phone her from *Gannet* with further details.

Expecting a simple heart failure in Campbeltown or Arran, my heart sank when Alex Hall, the SOBS, informed me that it was a one hundred and thirty-mile trip to Barra, to medevac an unconscious man. And it sank even further when he qualified that bombshell by saying it was not really from Barra, but from a fishing boat twenty miles off Barra Head!

'Could you phone home, Alex, and tell my wife I'm off to Barra. But don't mention the fishing boat. She'll have enough to worry about.'

Although calm, it was a miserable night for flying, as black as the Earl o' Hell's waistcoat—and made worse by low cloud and extensive fog over the Clyde. Al Falconer was first pilot, and Adam Carr the co-pilot. To minimise the risks, Capt Steve Roberts, the observer, elected to climb to four and a half thousand feet, thus putting a safe fifteen hundred feet altitude between the aircraft and the tops of Goatfell, the Paps of Jura, or Ben More on Mull, all of which lay more or less on our route to Barra.

Steve was a Canadian on secondment to the Royal Navy, who somehow or other had managed to stretch his two years' stint to three. However, time was catching up fast, and he was due back to his home city of Edmonton in a couple of months. This was the fifth SAR I had flown with him, so it might be my last—figuratively speaking.

But you had to watch it with Steve. His nickname was 'Crash' Roberts, and not without good reason. My first encounter with him had been only two days after he arrived at *Gannet*, when his Sea King had stoofed from twenty feet above the runway after its tail rotor drive failed, and had crash-landed on its side. Steve and the other three lads had miraculously walked away unscathed! Two years previously however, he had not been so lucky when, taking part in an American airshow, his Canadian Sea King had spiralled down from four hundred feet and crashed. He had sustained serious back and leg injuries from which he made a great recovery apart from permanent instability in one knee, for which he had to wear a knee brace when flying. Despite this, he had become a very experienced SAR observer, involved in many cliff and ship rescues during his time at *Gannet*, and had recently been awarded a Queen's Commendation for Brave Conduct in the Air, following one particulary hairy experience guiding his Sea King and crew to safety out of a steep-sided mountain corrie in atrocious white-out blizzard conditions.

Last summer leave, he had had an even luckier escape. He had hitched a transatlantic lift on an RAF Nimrod to Toronto, and had been offered a flight on the same aircraft the following day, when it was due to give a display at the Toronto air show. He had made other arrangements, however, and declined. At the end of its display, on its final pass, the Nimrod plunged into Lake Ontario, killing all on board.

Safely over Arran and Jura, and heading towards Colonsay, a strange burning smell began to pervade the cabin. Up front, Al Falconer voiced his concern, and asked Rocky Sharp the LACMN to investigate. Rocky explored the cabin with a torch, tracing all the accessible hydraulic piping and finding nothing.

'It doesn't smell acrid enough to be electrical,' Al observed. 'Could it be coming from outside?' Rocky opened the cargo door and sniffed.

'Can't say I smell anything particular out here.' he reported.

'It smells kinda sweet,' drawled Crash. 'Could be some of that heather burnin' that's been goin' on in the hills. We've come across it several times during navexes in the past week.' Then he paused and swore. 'But we've got bigger trouble than that. The UHF radio has packed in, so we are going to have trouble making contact with this fishing boat when we get to her.'

Cabin fumes! Duff radio! By rights this should not have been happening. The aircraft we were flying had just come up from RNAS Culdrose, from whose stock of three, 819 Squadron had finally been allocated a long-coveted red-nosed, red-tailed, custom-built, high-profile, mark 5 Sea King. Spacious and functional, high performance and highly photogenic—it was capable of taking on the Crabs on equal terms should the challenge and photo-opportunity arise! And now we had got it, frustratingly, it didn't work.

Fortunately the cabin smell gradually disappeared. Crash may have been right—smoke from the burning moors rising to four thousand feet and mixing with aircraft fuel fumes might well have produced that strange sweet smell. Smell gone, the crew could now concentrate on their other problems. The pilots were flying on instruments, flying blind through thick cloud which swirled past in an uncanny glow of eerie green and hell-fire red flashes from the navigation lights. It was not pleasant, and the wind was rising. The sea state off Barra had been reported as four or five, but the calm conditions we had left behind us in the Firth of Clyde were quickly being replaced by a strong south-easterly wind, the result of packed isobars running tightly up the spine of the Hebrides, as a depression lurching in from the west banged against a static area of high pressure over the North Sea. The wind was already touching twenty-five knots. Crash contacted RCC for an update on the situation.

'The fishing boat is called the *Coromandel*, and her last reported position was fifty-six degrees forty-one north, seven degrees twenty west, about sixteen miles south east of Barra Head. She's apparently heading south-east towards us, although she would have been better heading for shelter on the lee side of Vatersay.'

'We're well clear of high ground now. Just passing Tiree at three o'clock, so you can take her down to four hundred feet on a heading of three one zero, and we'll check the viz when we get below this stratus. Sixteen miles to run.'

The 'viz' was no better below the cloud—if we were below the cloud. It was still pitch black outside. A mist of fine rain slid over the windscreeen, and when Al switched on the landing lights, the blinding white beam bounced back into our faces. He quickly switched them off again, and we throbbed expectantly onwards.

'I've a weak contact, eight miles… on the nose,' came welcome news from the back.

Adam Carr had taken the controls to give Al a break, and I stood behind them, straining my eyes, searching into the black void beyond the sweeping windscreen wipers for something—something which was not a lit-up raindrop or a reflected panel light. Suddenly a tiny, faint pinpoint appeared at one o'clock, which did not roll off the windscreen. Al picked it up simultaneously, and within a few minutes we were circling over not one, but two fishing boats, showing masthead and nav lights only, and paying not the slightest attention to us!

'Bugger this for a lark. These are obviously not what we are looking for… and we've no bloody comms to ask them where it is.'

'Head on at three one zero.' instructed Crash. 'I've another two faint contacts five miles ahead.'

Once more we approached a dimly-lit boat, but were unable to make radio contact. Were we going to spend the whole bloody night wandering from boat to boat in a wild goose chase? In deteriorating weather conditions, the approach to the next boat took an interminably long time as Crash ever so carefully guided the pilots, who had no visual references to work on, down to a safe operating height, in a slow, measured programmed approach from three thousand yards downwind. Third time lucky. This boat was lit from stem to stern. 'Could you try the portable Westminster, Rocky, on channel sixteen?'

Rocky Sharp had the cargo door open, and with the hand-held radio managed to establish that this was in fact, the *Coromandel*, heading south-east into a strengthening wind which by now had risen to thirty-five knots—gale Force Eight.

Shit! Look at the way that bitch is pitching! The *Coromandel* was a moderate-sized stern trawler about 23 metres long, with a high foremast streaming the usual clutter of aerial wires aft to the wheelhouse roof, from which several whip aerials also lashed at the air as the boat rolled heavily in a fifteen to twenty foot swell. The deck amidships was completely enclosed, and the only possible area on which to land a stretcher was the cramped stern space below the wheelhouse, on which stood a huddle of orange-clad fishermen.

Rocky clipped himself to the double-lift harness and disappeared into the night as Crash tried to guide the aircraft into position for a low line drop on to the aft deck. Five or six times Al Falconer tried to maneouvre above the stern as the heaving boat threatened to stuff its whip aerials up our exhausts. Rocky had been dangling precariously beneath the Sea King for almost twenty minutes before Crash gave it up as too risky and hauled him back on board.

'I'm preparing a highline,' he informed the pilot as he deftly attached one end to the winch wire while surveying the scene below through the open door. 'Take it up thirty feet... steady... forward twenty yards... three o-clock, four yards... steady. Forward fifteen yards... half-past two, five yards... holding good position... highline on board and held. I'm lowering the aircrewman now. Forward thirty yards... twenty yards... steady... steady!' The *Coromandel* was certainly not making things easy for Rocky, Crash or Al, as she pitched and yawed and swung her stern in every direction bar the direction of Rocky's outstretched feet. Eventually, at the fourth attempt, guided in by the highline, he was dumped unceremoniously and hauled on board by the crew. The winchwire, with highline still attached, was wound in and its hook quickly attached to the lightweight stretcher which was then slung out and lowered. Below us, the crew and Rocky were gradually hauling in the line to bring the stretcher on board, when the trawler's stern suddenly dipped in a trough at the same time as the highline snagged. It tightened momentarily, then parted at the built-in weak point—one hundred and fifty pound breaking strain—just like that!

There was no fuss. Crash quietly reported the break, hauled up the stretcher, attached a second line, and once more went through the same long, agonising rigmarole before the sandbag was finally grasped and the stretcher lowered again. Unbelievably, the same thing happened, and the stretcher swung free in the gale. 'Highline gone again!' Crash reported, almost laconically. 'Just keep position. I'm going to try and swing it aboard free. I think we can do it... and anyway, we've no highlines left.'

Carefully and coolly, he directed Al Falconer over the ship once more—as I began a soul-searching ponder as to just what in hell's name was I doing here, when most sane civvies of my age were snugly tucked up in bed. The Sea King was juddering, pitching and yawing violently in the hover, almost as badly, as far as I was concerned, squinting out the starboard window, as that bloody boat below us, thumping into heavy seas and making life difficult for everyone—and none more so than Al Falconer. Isolated up front, with rain lashing his windscreen, both he and Adam Carr could see practically nothing below them. Because the fishing boat was so small, by the time they had been talked directly above it by Crash, they could no longer see the bows. The only visual reference they had was the forard masthead, and even that frequently dipped and swayed out of sight. And with the black night and a fifteen foot swell, it was a pilot's nightmare. An edge crept into Al's voice. He was not comfortable flying in these conditions.

'How far is it to Barra Head?' he demanded. 'I'm having a hard job keeping in the hover with no references to go on. It might be better to get the bloody boat into the lee and lift the casualty off from there. As it is this bugger is still steaming directly away from land.'

There was a short pause till Crash replied, 'Twenty miles.'

'How long would it take for them to get there?'

'Anything up to four hours in this weather, and we can't hang around that long. We'll have to go for it.' Hanging around for four hours would have meant a sixty-mile trip north to Benbecula to refuel while the *Coromandel* headed for shelter; plus a four hour delay in getting a critically-ill patient to specialist hospital care. It was a terrible dilemma for the crew which Crash Roberts' coolness decisively resolved. Involved, yet peripheral to the action, I could sense in his slow calm drawl a deliberate attempt to bring out all the best in the flying skills of his pilots.

'We can do it. I've had a good look at the stern of the boat, and it is possible to come upwind and drop the stretcher on board. Just take our time… three o'clock fifteen yards… down six feet. Keep that height… Lookin' good… Lookin' good… forward thirty yards… forward ten yards… Steady! Steady! You're doin' real fine. Stretcher is five yards behind stern in good position. Up six feet… keep steady… nine o'clock three yards… steady… forward two yards… lookin' real good… stretcher going over the stern… Now! Stretcher secured on board. Well done! Slacking off winchwire. Lay off twenty yards to port.'

Inaudibly, but palpably, there was a sigh of relief, as down below, Rocky and the fishermen grabbed the stretcher as it careered over the stern rail, and hauled it inboard. That was the difficult bit over, at least for those on board the aircraft. Down below, however, unbeknown to us, Rocky Sharp was having his own problems. Having managed to land safely on the *Coromandel* unscathed apart from a pair of bruised shins, he had moments later been flung against a pile of nets as the boat rolled violently. Stretching out his right hand to save himself, he had felt a severe pain and looked down to find his hand impaled on an upturned, discarded knife which some brain-filleted bonzo had left lying about. Pulling out the knife, he had been relieved to find he could still waggle his fingers, feel them and grip. His first job then had been to patch himself up with elastoplast strapping, before carrying on preparing the patient and organising his transfer from a cabin to the stretcher outside.

With the unconscious man securely strapped in, and himself clipped to the winch hook, Rocky gave a thumbs-up and Crash, leaning out of the aircraft door, with one hand on the winch lever, snatched the stretcher cleanly from the stern just as it dipped into another trough. Rocky's troubles were not yet over. He had re-attached the broken highline to the stretcher, hoping it would be paid out by the fishermen, and help control the spin of the stretcher during the ascent. But once again it dragged and snagged, and became entangled round his legs. With great presence of mind, he had reached for his diving knife and slashed the taut rope. Now released, the stretcher began to spin alarmingly, and sway with a dangerous pendulum motion below the aircraft. Crash leaned out further and further, grabbing the winch wire with his free hand in a desperate attempt to dampen the pendulum effect.

Behind him I saw Scouse Williams, my medic, who had quietly harnessed up to give a helping hand with the stretcher, suddenly reach out and grab Crash by the belt of his dispatch harness, hauling him back on board just as he was about to overbalance and pitch headfirst out the door. Between the pair of them, they slowly winched up the stretcher the last few feet and pulled it and Rocky to safety.

Joining them in the back, I checked over the patient. He was a big lad. Young, about thirty, semi-conscious and responding to painful stimuli. Rocky said his name was Buchan, Andrew Buchan, and reported no history of injury, just a sudden loss of consciousness lasting half an hour, followed by a slight improvement to his present state. It sounded very like a cerebral haemorrhage, perhaps a subarachnoid. With oxygen running at 15 litres per minute, I got Rocky and Scouse to pack a rucsac underneath the end of the stretcher to raise his head to 10 to 15 degrees and help reduce intracranial pressure. His pulse, blood pressure and oxygen saturation remained stable on the Propaq as we quietly settled down to record fifteen minute monitor readings on the low level run to Glasgow.

'The radar has just packed in!' suddenly announced Crash, just a wee hint of exasperation creeping into that previously unflappable voice. 'Doc, How high can we fly this guy? 'Cos if we have to fly back low level, we can't go through Crinan without radar, and that means going south round the Mull of Kintyre—and that means going dangerously low in fuel, apart from adding an extra hour on to the flight.' We had spent almost one and a half hours hover time over the *Coromandel* and had now been in the air for over three hours, with another hour to run to Glasgow. The aircraft's endurance was something like four and a half hours. This was cutting it a bit fine!

'He has not had a head injury, and is on fifteen litres of oxygen, so there is no reason why we can't go up to four thousand feet if you want to.'

'OK, Doc. That's just what I wanted to hear. Climb to four and a half thousand feet on a heading of one thirty degrees.' I checked the Propaq screen anxiously. The altitude made no difference. In fact, if anything his BP and pulse rate settled as the flight progressed.

It was satisfying to know that here one of the basic tenets of pre-hospital care was being enacted—i.e. the patient was going to reach hospital in at least no worse a condition than when uplifted, and probably a bit better. This was the one main benefit of carrying sophisticated monitoring equipment, compared with the past when we had very little to go on apart from a sensitive middle finger.

We flew on. Andy remained restless. I found that shining a light in his eyes to check his pupils was counter-productive, as he pushed it away and tried to sit up, so I desisted. His other parameters were fine. As we approached Glasgow, it was the crew's turn to get restless. The airport was clamped by thick cloud and fog. A visual flying approach was out of the question. We had no radar, and poor radio comms. Crash spelled out our predicament to Air Traffic Control, who set him on a ground radar controlled approach, gradually talking us down a thousand, then five hundred feet at a time as we flew in over the Cowal Peninsula. Then it was two hundred, then one hundred feet height reductions, till well clear of the Erskine Bridge and the adjacent high tension pylons. Ever so slowly, Al Falconer gently eased the aircraft down through the last few hundred feet to emerge clear of cloud only two hundred feet above the lights of the runway.

It was now four-thirty. We had just made it with thirty minutes fuel left. Andy was quickly transferred to the ambulance with instructions to the crew to keep him on high oxygen all the way to the Southern General. Fortunately, as it turned out, investigations revealed no serious or permanent brain damage, and he was discharged home six days later.

Refuelled, we arrived back at Prestwick at five-thirty, quietly elated at a good job done under dreadful circumstances. Up at sick bay, I had a look at Rocky's hand. The knife had deeply penetrated his left palm, and he was very lucky not to have severed some tendons or nerves. Scouse gave it a good clean before I closed it up with a couple of heavy sutures and grounded him for a week.

Lucky Rocky! Home at six-thirty, I only slept for four hours. I had that talk to give to the retired school teachers—meeting at twelve-thirty for lunch at one! I was tremulous with exhaustion as I sat down to lunch, but the unexpected presence of several old teachers whom I knew, and the presentation itself, soon got my adrenalin going. Which was just as well, for at the close, while busy answering questions and exchanging reminiscences, the bleep sounded—my new message pager.

'Tone only' came up on the screen. That meant *Gannet*—and a SAR!

It was an RTA in Kintyre. Lochgilphead to Southern General helipad… head and chest injuries on a spinal board… fortunately conscious and uncomplicated… broad daylight… ably assisted by Magz Brodie, my right-hand girl—whom I had been delighted to have back with me for a second spell at *Gannet*, after her seadraft on *Illustrious* and a difficult, unhappy tour at Faslane. Unfortunately, due to matters outwith my control, Magz had continued to get the rough end of the stick following her return to Prestwick. Newly promoted to Leading MA, she was struggling to do her own demanding job, *and* cope with all the administrative hassles and responsibilities of a petty officer, because of a series of stupid drafting decisions which had given sick bay a turnover of four POMAs in two years—and now a gapping problem of six months without one. Magz had been under tremendous strain, but, thanks to her resilient, larger-than-life personality, had still managed to fulfil her SAR duties—and give me unstinted support. She deserved a medal!

Out and back in one hour forty minutes. Unlike sick bay, this task had been a relaxed outing for both of us… almost a jolly.

Wish all jobs could be the same!

And if I'm lucky, maybe Helen won't even know I've been away.

'When did you get back, love?'

How did she know?

'Oh, *Gannet* phoned looking for you about twenty past three. Fiona told me when I got back from my Ladies' Lunch at five o'clock.'

Nice as ninepence she was!

Five o'clock! Must have had a lovely lunch.

Scribbled memo in the hall: 'Set the living room fire, and pack the dishwasher.'

Up you, horoscope!

23

12th August 1996

THE GLORIOUS TWELFTH

Rob Smith picked up the phone. 'Yeah, yeah... he's here just now.' He looked up. 'Leading Aircrewman Davies says you and Scouse are out of date for Abandon Aircraft drills... and can you come across to the hangar later on this morning.'

'OK. Tell him we'll be across the back of eleven o'clock. I want to do a kit check anyway.' I'd just acquired a handy wee zip-pouch which looked useful for all the odds and ends lying loose or lost in the depths of my goon suit leg pockets.

I thought I was still in date anyway. It was only a few months since Gerry Flannery had gone over the procedures with me—January, in fact. But this was now mid-August, already! Just where had all the summer gone?

It had been quite a vintage year for survival equipment drills. Like the Abandon Aircraft drills, pool drills were also six-monthly, and I was now a month overdue for them as well. Sea drills were also pending, but 'Woody' Woodbridge, the POSE, had promised me a warm August sea for my bi-annual plunge into the Clyde off the Cumbraes equipped with lifejacket and wee liferaft, from which I would hopefully be plucked to safety by a passing Sea King—if jellyfish and floating Glasgow turds from 'The Cludgie Boat' didn't get me first!

Back in early May, I had gone on a masochistic mission to Yeovilton for another of their bi-annual drills, the dreaded Dunker, and had shivered all of a sleepless night under two thin blankets, in an unheated wartime wooden hut euphemistically called an officer's cabin... perfectly designed for instant hypothermia and ideal acclimatisation training for Arctic Norway—or the Dunker at 0830 next morning!

And the Dunker itself had evolved a few surprises in the two years since my last visit. As well as fitted glass windows—which had to be knocked out before exiting upside down, from twelve feet under water, in the dark—they had also made it a house rule that if any one of the batch of five crewmen doing the sequence of four runs lost his bottle or ballsed it up during an escape, the whole batch had to repeat the evolution. And Sod's Law dictated that one of my group had to do just that, giving me five lung-bursting immersions instead of four!

Getting properly orientated under water wasn't too bad, but punching out the window with the heel of one hand was a bit of a problem till I discovered that a 'Glesca kiss' was much more efficient—reckoning that if I hit the perspex hard with my helmet, my head would go straight through the opening, followed quickly by me—and it worked a treat.

Over the years, Dunker training had proved its worth in ensuring the survival of aircrew in sea-ditching incidents, and this was forcefully and poignantly brought home in the pre-match video, which featured Neil Goodenough describing in graphic detail his own escape using STASS, following the *Gannet* Sea King crash off Islay in November 1993.

Although widely regarded as a boring chore, we were all fully aware that Abandon Aircraft drill, like the other repetitive training sessions, might someday be vital to our survival and had to be taken seriously, though with Scouse Williams and his infectious giggle, it was difficult to do anything seriously. Richie Davies tried hard, as we boarded a spare mark 6 Sea King in Hangar One. Having just got used to the spacious interior of the SAR mark 5, I had forgotten just how claustrophobic, cramped and crowded the mark 6 anti-submarine workhorse was, crammed with sonar gear.

'I want one of you to sit in the jump seat and act out the escape procedures. Doc, could you do it? Scouse has a white shirt on... ' It was a warm day, and Scouse was wearing his number twelves—summer rig, a square-necked, short-sleeved cotton shirt. I quickly sussed Richie's thought processes.

'What! You don't want Scouse to get his cheap white Pusser's shirt dirty, but it's OK for me to get my best navy blue summer blazer covered in oil and grease—and me with a Rotary Club meeting at lunchtime!'

The LACMN, relatively new to *Gannet*, looked nonplussed and a wee bit embarrassed at my apparent outburst—till Scouse started his giggling, and he realised I'd been taking the mickey! He grinned. 'Adopt the new crash posture, Doc.' I curled myself into a ball on the seat, with my left hand grasping the seat under my knees and my right arm tucked, protected, diagonally across my chest. I thought I'd got it right—but I'd got it wrong. My left arm should have been my orientation arm guiding me to the window on my left, and should have been held protected across my chest, with my right arm gripping the seat but ready to release my seat-belt once the ditched aircraft had stabilised in the water. The importance of repetition! We explored all the other emergency exits and the location of their release handles till, duly satisfied, Richie let us go.

It was a beautiful day and, as I sat in my surgery that afternoon, occasionally stealing a glance upwards at a brilliant blue sky framed in the two foot square Velux roof window which was my only sensory contact with the world outside, it was a case of 'Beam me up, Scotty!'

At a quarter to four, with three patients still between me and freedom, the phone rang. 'It's someone from HMS *Gannet*, Doctor Begg.'

'Lt Gilmour, Doc. We've got a man of seventy-five up a mountain with a heart attack. Can you come in please.' Hurriedly scribbling her prescription, I apologised to Mrs Hearton opposite. She was a retired nursing sister herself, whose son was an airline pilot, and I was sure she'd understand as I fled the room in shirt sleeves, leaving jacket and gear behind.

John McArthur, the young Irish LMA, was standing at the apron gate holding my helmet as the red-nosed mark 5 roared in the background. I dived on board with my kit holdall and we were airborne.

'Where's my goonsuit and life-jacket?' I asked as I stripped off in the back, looking for the rucsac containing my flying suit and boots.

'Down there beside you.' said John, pointing to the floor behind me.

'But that red all-in-one is not mine… and I don't wear a troop lifejacket.' John looked bewildered, then embarrassed.

'It was all that was there in your locker, sir, except for a rucsac lying on the floor.'

'Well, that bloody rucsac contained my flying suit with all my bits and pieces, my flash gloves and my boots. How the hell am I going to manage in a peat bog with these on?' I waggled my lightweight fawn calf-leather shoes in the air.

'Sorry, Doc. I haven't flown with you before, and didn't know they had stowed your kit in a rucsac. I thought the red suit was yours.'

'Never mind, John. Just remember to get rid of it back to stores when we return. And hope we don't get tasked to a sea job before the end of this one!' Apart from the missing gloves, boots, and various bits and pieces in their new wee zip-pouch, it was really not much of an inconvenience. Fortunately, I always stowed my stethoscope, torch and scissors pouch in my holdall, and flying overland on a hot sunny day, it was quite pleasantly cool to be clad only in an overall and vest.

The Glorious Twelfth! Down below us on the heather moorlands of Renfrewshire, tweedy gents and gentesses would be blasting away both barrels at *Lagopus lagopus scoticus*, the poor wee red grouse. Up here, at four thousand feet, both barrels of the paraffin budgie's exhausts were getting their own back on *Homo sapiens* as a brace of not so sapient pilots flew with their windows open, and every now and again a bolus of hot fume-laden air would waft through the cabin.

Still, it was breathtakingly beautiful as we crossed the Clyde and flew the length of Loch Lomond, its blue waters speckled with small pleasure craft, the tawny Luss hills speckled with sheep, and to the east, a bit further away, doubtless the path up Ben Lomond was speckled with tourists. Beyond Glen Falloch, the peaks of Beinn Dubhchraig and Ben Oss—a long hard slog from the Crianlarich-

Tyndrum road when I last traversed their summits twenty years ago—looked small and ludicrously easy to climb from this eagle's perspective four thousand feet up.

I was still not quite sure where we were going. One of the few drawbacks of the SAR-designated mark 5 was its inferior comms system. I was plugged into a rear cabin cable which I later discovered was designed simply for emergency communication between aircrewman and pilots. As such, it had no access to all the other radio channels, and so I was unable to eavesdrop, as I usually did in the anti-submarine warfare mark 5 or mark 6, the conversations between aircrew and RCC Kinloss. To make matters worse, the crew were all new to the SAR roster, and I had only flown with them once before, last week, on a quickie medevac during the night from Rothesay to Greenock, a ten-minute transfer requiring minimum communication. They hadn't quite realised how important it was to keep the medical side of the operation involved in any decision-making process. I heard Bridge of Orchy mentioned. I had climbed many of the surrounding mountains. I butted in.

'Could you give me a heads-up on this old guy, where he is, and where you plan to take him?'

Sorry, Doc. He's seventy-five, with chest pain, and is with a seventy-nine year old companion on Beinn Achaladair near Bridge of Orchy. As far as the hospital is concerned, we haven't worked it out yet… could be Vale of Leven, it's probably nearest. Where is Corpach?'

'Near Fort William.'

'Fort William is another option, or maybe Oban. But it will probably be Vale of Leven. It's on our way home. But we'll have to wait and see what RCC have in mind.'

By this time we had overflown Tyndrum and were following the Rannoch road and railway round Beinn Dorain towards Loch Tulla. Here the road and railway parted company, and Gordon McMillan the P1 banked the aircraft to the right, along the line past Achaladair Farm, and headed up a burn which led into a broad corrie terminating in a narrow col between Beinn an Dothaidh and Beinn Achaladair. The first sweep up the lower reaches of the burn proved fruitless.

'They should be on this burn somewhere.' muttered McMillan, as he turned the aircraft round and began to sweep further up the hill. Mountains are vast. Where do you start looking? This was broad brilliant summer daylight, and yet it was difficult to spot two men from the air. Because of the nature of these searches, often for eight or ten hours in appalling weather conditions, poor visibility and minimal winter light, I was seldom if ever called in for mountain jobs. This was my sixtieth SAR, and only my second mountain one. I silently saluted the determination and gritty endurance of aircrew, and my own MAs, searching on short winter days, when these benign-looking hills would suddenly transform into fearsome, featureless, white-out shrouds for unwary climbers, and often a body would lie undiscovered till the spring thaw.

But not today. Two thirds up the burn, just as the corrie began to close in, two small figures huddled together by the mountain path, one in a red shirt lying on his side, his head pillowed on his rucsac. 'The gradient is too steep for a land-on. We'll put Chief Patterson and the MA down first, and then the Doc.' I slipped my stethoscope and the sphygmo into my pockets and clipped the first response satchel to my lifejacket becket, while the other two were winched thirty yards downhill from the casualty. Then I joined them in my fawn calf shoes. Fortunately the path was navigable dry-shod.

Despite his ordeal, climbing down from the high col two hours after his chest pain started—he gave it a pain score of 7 out of 10—and lying on the bare hillside for another two hours while a second septogenarian companion ran three kilometres down to the farm for help, our seventy-five year-old was in remarkable good condition. Once Chief Patterson had directed the helo to circle out of earshot, I had peace to check his BP and pulse. Both were normal. His pain had subsided. I gave him an aspirin to chew. He wanted to stand up, but the effort, or the excitement, made him retch, and he lost a bit of colour. Not so good. With a helicopter transfer and a long distance to go, there was a fair risk of collapse. I felt it better to safeguard venous access, and popped a Venflon into a wrist vein. At least I felt better!

The Chief aircrewman called in the aircraft, and as it roared its approach, John and I crouched over the casualty to protect him from flying grass and a severe buffeting from the downdraught. His seventy-nine-year-old climbing companion caught the corner of my eye as he stood leaning into the blast. What the hell was he doing? Taking photographs of the rescue! Another one for the climbing log! Then I gaped when I looked across and saw where Gordon had landed the Sea King—talked down by Lt Simon Moulton, the observer, onto a slab of sloping rock no bigger than the deck of a type 23 frigate. With the patient on the stretcher, Chief Patterson motioned me onto the aircraft, declining my offers of assistance with the carry. Just as well, for there would not have been room for four of us and the stretcher, on the four-foot-wide platform, edged by a five foot drop, which they had to negotiate to get to the cargo door, which itself was about five feet above ground. Quite a lift! From inside, I dragged the foot of the stretcher to the rear of the aircraft, then helped manhandle our elderly photographer on board and direct him up front.

Then it was a beeline for hospital. Twenty minutes to Vale of Leven, I reckoned, as John and I set up the Propaq to monitor his BP and and oxygen saturation, with the HeartStart also wired up and ready. On oxygen, his saturation levels were good, but my attention was concentrated on his pulse rate which began to dip alarmingly to the mid-forties ten minutes into the flight. Was this an elderly very fit athlete's pulse, or was he developing a potentially dangerous bradycardia? Colourwise he was still fine. In the background, plugged into my one-channel cable, I was distantly aware that his companion was still enjoying his part of the adventure and making the most of it, standing up behind the pilots and pointing out all the mountains—even as far away as Cruachan.

The Sea King throbbed relentlessly on, but I saw nothing apart from these flickering figures on the Propaq screen—47, 44, 42, 46, dropping to a worrying 41—highlighted by an intermittent flashing of the number on the screen. His BP also dropped a little, but his breathing was steady. How long to the Vale? The aircraft banked to starboard and to my relief I saw a stretch of sea with boats on—the

Clyde! A few minutes to specialist help. Bracken-clad hillsides slipped past the window as Gordon made his approach. I hadn't seen these before. We must be coming in from another direction. Then a windsock momentarily appeared as the nose lifted prior to touchdown. They must have upgraded the landing site since last year—it was now a proper concrete helipad. Very posh!

The ambulance was standing by with a young doctor on board. Loading the stretcher for a quick trip to the hospital which I could see a short distance away, I was about to hand the casualty sheet to the doctor when I realised that I did not have our patient's name and address. 'What's your name?' I asked.

'McRoberts,' replied the young doc. John McArthur looked up in surprise.

'I don't mean you.' I laughed. 'It's the patient's details I'm after!'

'Alec Paterson,' came a strong voice from behind a lifted oxygen mask. He was looking a bit better. 'I come from Falkirk.'

'Yew are a long weh from home now,' commiserated the doctor. He was Irish.

'I know yew,' exclaimed John suddenly. The lad looked at him closely.

'I know yew too... Yew were at school with me!'

'Yeah. I haven't seen yew for ten years—since we sat our A-levels!' Gobsmacked by this amazing coincidence, I stepped down from the ambulance at the hospital entrance.

'How are you, Dr Begg? It's been a long time since I've seen you!' The voice came from behind the beard of a big, smiling, medical-looking bloke in a tweed jacket who was standing, arms behind his back, observing the scene from the hospital steps. I looked, and looked again. I knew the face—but it shouldn't be here at Vale of Leven.

'Gordon... Gordon Murchison.' he prompted.

'Yes, I know. I recognised you. But what are you doing down here at the Vale?' Gordon was an Oban GP and part-time anaesthetist who helped run the decompression chamber at Dunstaffnage, and also was the Oban Lifeboat doctor. It was possible that he was here doing an anaesthetic locum, or maybe visiting the Faslane Naval Base 'pot'.

He laughed. 'This is Oban, not Vale of Leven!' I took stock of the last, lost, twenty minutes. The puzzling reference to Cruachan. The bracken-covered hillside. The windsock and the concrete helipad. Head down concentration on the job. The distraction of a dangerously slow pulse-rate—and John's Irish schoolmate. The total bloody absence of communication from my bloody aircrew! What a bloody Charlie I felt… what a wally! I laughed it off, and explained what had happened to Gordon as we wheeled Alec into the security of the resucitation room. He was going to be fine, I was sure of it. His main concern was for his two companions—the one stranded on a Rannoch Moor farm with a car, and no keys—and the other stranded fifty miles away in Oban with the keys, but no car! We reassured him that the police would sort that out very quickly, collected our stretcher, and said goodbye.

Gordon Murchison was waiting by the door. I sang the praises of our Propaq in helping monitor awkward pulse abnormalities in flight. He concurred. 'Yes, it is a great bit of kit. We've got one on the lifeboat now, and it is invaluable.' He paused for effect. 'That reminds me—what happened to your guys a couple of weeks ago, with that diver on Islay?'

'What diver on Islay?' I asked, puzzled.

'The one with the bends that you couldn't get off, and the Oban Lifeboat had to go and take off for you,' he grinned, with a wee hint of triumph in his eye. 'Can the Navy not fly in bad weather like fog, nowadays?'

'Only overland. It's usually OK over the sea. I've flown into Coll on several occasions when the fixed-wing ambulance plane could not land because of fog. The pilots tend to fly above summer fog and drop down below it as they near landfall, to make a visual approach. I hadn't heard about this job. There must have been some approach problem which made a landing too difficult. I'll ask the boys and let you know the answer.'

En route to Prestwick, I did just that. 'Yeah. I remember that job. Can't remember who was duty that day though… about three weeks ago. Might have been the SARO, Andy Holley. Islay was really clamped by fog, and they couldn't find the airport, or see a bloody thing, and had to abort.'

'Even with radar, coming in off the sea?' I persisted.

'Yeah. Flight rules don't allow us to approach land in thick fog unless we can have a visual on the shore at five hundred yards. Any less than that and it would be too late to take avoiding action if we were heading for a pylon or a cliff. Remember, we are up in the air, and need good visual references to tell us where we are—to stop us flying into the ground. Not like these lifeboatmen who can dip their wellies in the water anytime, and know they'll not go down any lower than the trough of the next wave!'

Point taken. I would inform my friend!

24

3rd November 1997

SWAN SONG

'I don't want to hurt your feelings, Doc... but the Surgeon Commander told me that he is now the PMO for *Gannet*—and all the other small Navy shore bases'. The frank eyes in Ronnie Horlock's broad face signalled troubled embarrassment as he broke what he feared might be a terrible shock to me, just a week after sick bay had endured its first Fleet Medical Audit in seventeen years—although we were at least semi-prepared for it by the reverberations and revelations rumbling up from medical centre staff at Culdrose and Yeovilton, who were still reeling from the trauma of their own audits.

'...And he said you won't be asked to do any more SAR flying in your new contract.'

This was news to me! I had certainly mentioned in the passing to the new Director for Naval General Practice, during our interview, that I had almost made myself redundant over the past year, because my MAs were now much more confident than ten years ago; and I had expressed some reluctance about having to go down to Yeovilton for the Dunker yet again in a few months time, if I was only going to have one or two jobs a year.

Better training, enhanced by Dr Roger White's ATLS courses at Crosshouse, coupled with the substantial benefits of now having hard-won, superb monitoring equipment on the SAR Sea King to back them up; plus protocols and guidelines prepared by myself on most emergencies they were likely to face, had instilled in the MAs such a high level of confidence, that there were now very few occasions when they felt they needed medical back-up. The hospitals, too, were making more use of their specialised crash teams, often sending an anaesthetist and ITU nurse to oversee the transfer of critically-ill hospital patients—which was a great relief to a simple GP like myself—and a great advance in patient care. I had had only one callout this year, away back in March, to ferry a heart attack from Rothesay to Greenock. And that had been a waste of time—and was not likely to occur again, since the Scottish Ambulance Service had finally constructed an airstrip at Rothesay for their fixed-wing air ambulance, which was now intended to take over night-time medivacs from the *Gannet* Sea King. At least that was the theory… We would wait and see!

'I think he's jumped the gun here, Ronnie,' I informed him, not yet having had a chance to have a chat with Cdr David Issitt the new Captain, who was due to meet me for the traditional heads of department interview—assuming that I still was 'head' of my department.

'Options for Change', the last Tory government's euphemistic slogan for redundancies and cost-cutting in the services, had been sweeping through the Navy for several years, but up until now, its effect on *Gannet* sick bay had been limited to a chronic shortage of staff due to over-enthusiastic and ill-considered pruning of the medical assistant Branch. Consequently, the Navy was now desperately short of MAs, and some had come—and gone again—before I even learnt their names. Ronnie Horlock was my *fourth* POMA in two years. Although just recently advanced from Killick, he was a big, bulky six-footer, and I hoped his imposing presence and clear idea of how he wanted his sick bay run, would restore some order to the long-term chaos of an almost rudderless administration. Still in the first few weeks of his eighteen months draft, he had been well and truly landed in the deep end, firstly with a couple of Medical Board of Survey reports to write up, and now, out of the blue, this bloody Fleet Medical Audit—in which our sick bay had really done quite well. It was myself who had been left feeling well and truly keel-hauled!

Our auditing Surgeon Commander, fresh home from Hong Kong, had swept into the base with both brooms blazing. And more than the brooms were blazing when, after an hour of seemingly innocuous interview chat, he suddenly dropped the bombshell: 'And now for the bad news. You have been greatly overpaid for the work you do… for years!'

I was gobsmacked, embarrassed by what I felt was a hidden implication that I must have been screwing the system—despite his assurances to the contrary—and bloody angry that all the hard work and commitment I had put into *Gannet* over the past eleven years now appeared to be being devalued. But I contained myself—I always think better on paper—and had spent much of the following week drafting a three-page letter, copies to the Surgeon Commodore, who lived and breathed Fleet Air Arm and who, as my Boss, had always been very supportive in the past, and to the COs of HMS *Gannet* and RAF Prestwick. In it, I pointed out that I had inherited the same contract arrangement as my predecessor Dr Suddie MacKechnie, who had claimed the same approved fees without any questions from Navy paymasters for the seventeen years prior to my taking over in 1989. I also pointed out that I had been tied to the SAR bleep for eleven years, and had been obliged for most of these years to have to find a locum—seldom available—if I wanted away for the day, or a weekend. I had also been prepared to be on call twenty-four hours a day, seven days a week for any problems at the base, and had frequently found myself having to stay in the district on fine weekends due to no one being available to cover me—all away playing golf or cricket! I had always been pleasantly surprised at, and never questioned, the generous levels of MoD remuneration compared with my partners' NHS hospital sessions, but considered this imbalance justified—that these few extra thousands were hard earned—and barely recompensed the full-time duty cover I had willingly given, and the consequent loss of personal freedom I had endured.

And now I faced the indignity of someone telling me that I had been paid this 'excessive' amount of money for a contract of 'only three by three-and-a-half hour sessions per week'! Well, if that was how they now looked at it, in future I would be working for ten and a half hours a week and not a bloody minute longer! And if they wanted out-of-hours cover for the rest of the week, they would have to negotiate separate terms. And what would they do for night cover now that our practice, along with most others in Ayrshire, had opted out of nights on call and were using the Doctors on Call Co-operative? The Navy would have to enter into an additional contract with Ayrshire doctors for cover after 6pm, overnight and at weekends. They might yet find their new deal costing a lot more in the long run, than this crude cost-cutting exercise would save.

The letter was drafted and ready to go, I had got it out of my system, and on reflection, I now felt quite relaxed about the whole thing. My honour vindicated, I could probably look forward to much more free time. This was the big positive aspect which attracted me. I wouldn't need to be available day and night any longer. I could bugger off when I felt like it without having to find a locum, and maybe giving up SAR might not be a bad idea after all. I was approaching fifty-five, and since my cartilage operation twelve months ago, was not quite as agile on rough ground as I had been. And with my longstanding back problem, the thought of carrying fourteen stone casualties across rough ground on the lightweight stretcher was becoming less and less appealing.

And, I had just bought myself *Sula*, a twenty-nine foot Seamaster yacht, realising an ambition I had been nurturing for several years—an ambition sparked off in particular by one memorable SAR, when I had been bewitched by the tranquillity of a beautiful still summer morning, sitting in the cockpit of a yacht becalmed off the Treshnish Isles, while we awaited the return of the Sea King to lift off an ancient mariner with a stroke. Not being a golfer, and with salmon fishing by and large abysmal due to recurring dry summers, sailing the western seaboard and pulling up anchors had suddenly become a compelling and attractive alternative to pulling up weeds within the narrow horizons of our garden. And Helen, surprisingly, had been in full agreement—to the extent of joining Colin, Fiona and myself on a Day Skipper Navigation course. Yes, I day-dreamed… giving up SAR might not be such a wrench after all.

George Hall pushed his head round the door. 'OPSO wants you to give him a ring, sir.' I wonder what Fraser wants, I thought. Maybe to discuss details of a presentation I was due to give next April to the the Ayrshire Practice Managers Group at the behest of Averil Oldfield, our own Practice Manager. Would be a bit of a non-event, now that my flying career was at an end! And by a strange coincidence, Fraser Anderson had also been there at its beginning—flying as a young observer on my first two SARs.

'Thanks for ringing back, Jimmy. I just wanted your advice on a problem. We've just received a signal from *Fort Victoria* about a guy with a back injury. The story is a bit vague, but as far as we can gather, he fell down a ship's ladder three days ago, and is now paralysed from the waist down. The *Fort Victoria* has been exercising west of Kintyre and is making for the Clyde, ETA fifteen-thirty. They don't have a doctor and were talking about keeping him on board till they disembark, and that is what I wanted to discuss with you... Do you think that is a good idea or not?'

It certainly was not! A man with a likely history of a progressive spinal paralysis should be in a specialised spinal unit as soon as possible for assessment. A further four-hour delay could greatly increase the risk of permanent paralysis. He would be better flown direct to the Southern General. I said I would check with the specialist unit there, and phone him back.

'That's fine. Meantime I will signal Fort Victoria and give them a heads-up on the possibility of a casevac, and put the SAR aircraft on standby. Could you attend if required?'

'Well, theoretically, I have been told unofficially that I will not be doing any more SAR flying, but there is nothing in writing, and my old contract is still in operation... and I've never done a deck landing on a fleet auxiliary before!'

'Oh, I haven't heard any dit about your being taken off SAR, so I've no problem with you flying at this end.' That was what I wanted to hear—the chance of an interesting swan song SAR!

I lifted the phone, dialled the A&E department at Southern General, and related the case history as far as we had it, to the duty doctor, who agreed that a direct transfer to the spinal unit would be the best course of action, rather than a local admission to Crosshouse and a possible road transfer later. Fraser was informed, and fifteen minutes later, I had joined young Rob Pointon, my MA, in the SAR crew room.

'I think this is a job for the spinal board if ever there was one, Rob… could you check it is on board'. Arguments about space and weight-saving by various aircrewmen in the past had led to its being offloaded intermittently, and I did not want egg on my face on my last SAR if the spinal board was lying in the hangar as we landed on the RFA!

'Yeah, it's on board, Boss. They are becoming more aware of spinal immobilisation nowadays, and we sometimes find we have to sort out patients we get from the Ambulance Service who have not been properly secured. And we are waiting for that new lightweight nylon spinal board which we ordered through sick bay—that should stop any further argument about weight.'

Initially informed that *Fort Victoria* was west of Mull of Kintyre, I was surprised when, after a quarter of an hour, the aircraft banked to reveal the RFA about five miles south of Sanda, steaming north east into the Firth of Clyde, its huge bulk dwarfing an attendant Frigate which lay a mile off on its starboard quarter. A low pass showed two Sea Kings already parked abreast on the forard end of the flight deck, but with more than enough room for Lt Kirkham to put us down astern. The wind was fifteen knots, the ship twenty thousand tonnes and sitting steady. This was no type 22 frigate with six feet to spare at the front and four at the back. I was quite relaxed. We landed on without a bump.

Crouching low beneath the rotorblade draught, we scurried forard with the lightweight stretcher past the secured Sea Kings to the flight deck doors, to be met by the First Officer and several crew members. My first impression was how much older they all seemed to be compared with the young ratings at *Gannet*—till I remembered that RFAs were crewed by civilians who might spend their whole working lives on one ship. We were directed to the starboard side of the deck where Rob and the stretcher were placed in the centre of a painted oval, from which they were 'beamed down' and disappeared into the bowels of the ship by lift. The rest of us took the long way down via a twisting companionway, to emerge at the stern end of a vehicle corridor which stretched the length of the ship. Empty now, on active service it would be crammed with a column of personnel carriers.

Climbing through a bulkhead door, we were right at the sick bay, where a very competent CPO medic filled us in on our casualty, who had apparently lost his footing on a steep companionway three days previously, and had come sliding down with his spine rattling against each step edge as he did so. Surprisingly, although badly scraped, he had landed on his heels, got up and walked away, and had been able with painkillers to continue his duties. The pain had got worse last night, however, and when he woke up, his legs were numb and he had been unable to move them since.

Thus fully briefed, we continued into the small ward, where our patient, Willie Stott, a bald-headed, heavily-built man about forty, was lying trussed up in a Neil Robertson stretcher, with only his bare toes showing beyond the splintage. Willie confirmed the chief's story, and also that he had previously had back problems. But he was impressively immobilised, and there was no point in transferring him onto our spinal board—after all our pre-planning and forethought! And there was no point in unloosening the straps to do a full neurological examination and possibly aggravate his injury. Nevertheless, I thought I had better go through a few simple tests.

'Can you move your toes?' Immediately he wiggled both his toes up and down.

'Can you feel me nipping your toes?' Affirmative.

Well, at least he's not paralysed. I cringed at the prospect of a looming mega-embarrassment on my last SAR, slinking apologetically into Southern General A&E, after making such a convincing case for a direct helicopter transfer to the spinal unit of a spinal injury patient—who was now walking. But he wasn't walking. The only thing we were certain of, was that he could now move his toes.

And all that meant was that there was now less pressure on his spinal cord. Get a grip! Better safe than sorry!

Carefully loading the Neil Robertson onto the lightweight stretcher, and adding a cervical collar and brow-strapping for the sake of completeness, we popped Willie and Rob on the cargo lift which, with no sides, looked somewhat precarious as it rose slowly above our heads towards the flight deck high above. With the patient on supplementary oxygen, and with little else to do apart from watch in case he started to throw up, the short trip up to the Southern was uneventful, apart from the pilot throwing a couple of wobblies to avoid shitehawks. Fortunately Willie was none the worse.

A young casualty doctor was standing by with the ambulance men as we set down on the helipad, and I filled him in on the details so far, as we drove the few hundred yards to the new A&E department, where Malcolm Gordon, the A&E consultant was waiting, and listened attentively as I repeated the history and findings. Together we lifted the Neil Robertson onto the resuscitation room couch, and very gently the Neil Robertson strapping was loosened to expose Willie's legs. As Mr Gordon leaned over to begin his examination, Willie bent both his knees to assist him! Oops! He seemed to be well on the road to a miraculous recovery… and it was maybe politic for us to be well on our road home. Happily, two days later, Willie was likewise homeward bound.

As the Sea King rose from the helipad, the pilot flew north and banked steeply to port. Below us the Clyde snaked past Govan, and sailing down the Clyde was a procession of small vessels escorting a larger ship with a familiar yellow funnel, and three masts.

The Royal Yacht *Britannia*! On her final voyage round Britain… Leaving her birthplace on the Clyde at the end of her many years of service, about to be decommissioned. The end of an era. As a kindred spirit, I saluted her.

25

UPWARDS AND ONWARDS

Since my 'swan song' flight in November 1997, there have been many changes in the Search and Rescue set-up, both nationally and locally at *Gannet*. SAR has always been an evolving service, driven to improve itself from within by those at the coal-face—or more appropriately the cliff-face—who have encountered serious problems, recognised shortcomings and deficiencies, and striven to correct them.

For many years, inter-service rivalries were keen but often counter-productive, with RAF and Navy patches jealously guarded, and one-upmanship assiduously promoted in the spirit of 'anything you can do, I can do better'. More recently however, the aftermath of the Cold War has led to the paring of lots of military fat, the loss of sundry little military empires, a salutory banging of heads, and the emergence of a commendable increase in tri-service co-operation. On the SAR side, there was one very positive spin-off with the introduction in 1999 of a three-week Advanced Pre-Hospital Care training course for RAF and Royal Navy backseat aircrew, and a major standardisation of medical equipment carried on SAR helos.

This came just at the right time for the future of the SAR service at HMS *Gannet*, which was scheduled for closure as a Royal Naval Air Station in March 2002 as part of the Cold War 'peace dividend'. The newly-named HMS *Gannet* SAR Flight was planned to have a ship's company of 90 personnel, and fly three designated Sea Kings, manned by 20 dedicated SAR aircrew, and a tightly-knit supporting team of maintainers; but the five MAs who had flown as SAR crew medics for the previous twelve years would be drafted elsewhere, leaving the Flight without adequate medical expertise.

Fortunately, the new advanced training course now meant that backseat aircrew would be competent to set up i/v lines, administer morphine, intubate unconscious casualties, and defibrillate cardiac arrests. Once all aircrewmen were fully qualified, the SAR role of the two remaining MAs and the doctor would become purely consultative, advising on any problems outwith the experience of aircrewmen, which might arise during a mission.

Equally fortunately, *Gannet*'s role—unique in the UK—in dealing with a very large annual number of medevacs, had been clearly recognised for many years, and was something for which the SAR Flight was well prepared. *Gannet*'s average of just under 80 medevacs per year, was more than twice that of RNAS Culdrose, and not far short of the aggregate total of 95 for all six RAF Stations. The wealth of accumulated experience, and increasing familiarity with our first-class monitoring equipment, previously operated by MAs and doctor, has greatly strengthened crews' professional confidence in being able to care for seriously ill patients in transit.

Recently, however, *Gannet*'s long-established tradition almost made it a victim of its own success. During the evolving years of SAR, many remote island doctors had come to rely on the availability of an escorting doctor or MA on request, although in reality, this was not something which the MoD or *Gannet* was contractually obliged to provide, but was an extra luxury—a wee bit of 'quality care in the air' from sick bay and the Navy! Late in 2002, a potential crisis of confidence in the service arose.

With no doctor or MA now available, island GPs were being faced with the clinical and ethical dilemma of having to send seriously ill patients off on potentially risky, unescorted trips to hospital in a military helo, on the not-infrequent occasions when adverse weather conditions made evacuation by air ambulance impossible. Down south, remote from the practical realities of island medical emergency evacuations, the MoD's legal department were also concerned about the medico-legal implications of their aircraft being tasked by Ambulance Air Desk to transfer unescorted NHS patients to mainland hospitals.

Why this level of concern should have suddenly arisen after thirty years of delivering much the same service without any questions ever being asked, or ungrateful patients suing the MoD, is a bit of a mystery. And what is the medical difference between transporting an injured patient from an island to hospital, and evacuating an injured climber off a mountain to the same hospital—apart from one being requested by a doctor, and the other by a mountain rescue team medic? Perhaps the answer lies in that unwelcome and nasty import from the USA—the 'suing mentality'—allied to its British oppo—the 'blame everyone but yourself' culture. While this unpleasant double phenomenon is now sadly endemic in mainland urban populations, I would suspect that the rugged independence, stoicism, and self-reliance which have kept our remote highlands and islands populated for thousands of years, would still lead to islanders gladly accepting the chance of a quick aerial trip to hospital unaccompanied, rather than have to wait twenty-four hours for the ferry and a four hour ambulance journey on the mainland. After all, since most helo transfers take considerably less than an hour anyway, all that seemed to be required was for each case to be judged sensibly on its merits, and the relative risks, small or large, professionally assessed.

For several weeks the impasse dragged on, till it reached a stage where island GPs were lobbying their councillors and MPs, and the MoD were involved in discussions with health boards and the Ambulance Service. At one point, it was suggested that *Gannet* should fly to Glasgow to pick up the paramedic from the air ambulance any time it was grounded, and it was felt necessary that a medical escort was required for a patient. After one ludicrous situation in which what should have been a twenty minute there-and-back flight took one and a quarter hours, common sense finally prevailed, and it was agreed that in future, the need for an escort would be left to individual discretion based on transit time, state of patient and aircrew/GP/Air Desk mutual agreement.

The inter-hospital transfer of gravely-ill patients was never an issue in this case, for in recent years, much greater use has been made of escorts by highly trained specialist hospital teams who can be picked up locally or in Glasgow and flown to the requesting hospital—mercifully a far cry from the late 1980s and early 1990s when I might have been called upon with my very limited GP experience! Again all part of the evolving service.

Averaging 250 callouts per year over the past eight years, *Gannet* remains at the forefront of SAR operations, and is consistently one the top three busiest units in the UK. While most missions tend to average two hours, and perhaps a 120-mile round trip, SAR aircrews can still be called upon to extend themselves and their aircraft to the limits of endurance. In 2003, they flew as far as London in one direction, and in another, to a ship 200 miles west of Ireland.

The work of HMS *Gannet* SAR Flight is essentially and totally a dedicated team effort—from the engineering workshops and survival equipment section to sick bay, from the met office and control room to the SAR crew room. While this book's emphasis has naturally been on flying—on 'the glory and glamour bit' and on trusting your life to the skills of pilot, observer and winchman—every time we flew as aircrew, we were all trusting our lives to the team back at Prestwick, to the lads and lasses who serviced our aircraft and our survival equipment, forecast our weather and relayed our communications.

It will continue to be a team effort of highly disciplined, highly skilled and highly motivated young professionals, with whom I have been proud to be associated for so many years. All those who venture out of doors, to the hills or out to sea, or who live and work under the 500-mile-wide umbrella whose spokes are the five giant carbon fibre rotorblades of Rescue 177, should also be proud and grateful for HMS *Gannet*'s dedicated service to the West of Scotland, both now and in the years ahead.

Afterword

Search and Rescue: The Way Forward?

By Lt Cdr Roger Stringer RN,
Commanding Officer at HMS Gannet *SAR Flight*

When Jimmy approached me to write the final chapter of the sequel to *Rescue 177*, I felt very privileged to be asked to make a contribution. Having been involved on and off with operations at HMS *Gannet* for the last twenty years, I am quite well placed to reflect personally on how SAR flying has developed, and what the future holds for what is now very much an integral part of the nation's emergency services—not just the preserve of downed aircrew, mariners in distress and those unfortunate enough to have accidents in the more inaccessible parts of the UK.

In brief, I first served at *Gannet* in the late 1980s with 819 Squadron as a line pilot, before returning as an instructor in 1994. I was then fortunate enough to be reappointed to the squadron in 1998, initially as a Detachment Commander and then as Senior Pilot, until 819 Squadron disbanded late in 2001. I began my current post as Commanding Officer of HMS *Gannet* in December 2004 and, oddly enough, even having amassed close to 6000 flying hours and having served at Prestwick previously, this is the first time that I have been directly involved in the management of SAR in my 24-year flying career.

Those who have read the first volume of *Rescue* 177 will be aware that 819 Squadron was based at Prestwick for support of the nuclear deterrent and the defence of the Clyde. Involvement in SAR was very much an *ad hoc* task, which the command was only too happy to assist with when called upon. The recovery of crashed military aircrew was always at the forefront of its duties, but considering the location of the unit, it only made sense to assist in civilian rescues as directed by the Rescue Co-ordination Centre or Coastguard. Crews were not specifically trained in the finer aspects of SAR operations, although they enthusiastically, and in some cases very courageously, drew on their experiences to good effect. SAR at *Gannet* could only be described as adequate, as too were the machines which were flown. Believe me, a helicopter laden with anti-submarine hunting equipment, which cannot be taken out in a hurry, is not the best machine to use for creeping up the side of a mountain in turbulent winds. Medical equipment was, by today's standards, very poor, and until doctors or medics were routinely carried, a survivor's chances of recovery were limited.

Twenty years ago, the label of 'enthusiastic amateurs', often levelled at us by our RAF counterparts, was probably nearer the mark than we would care to admit. Fortunately, the RN has come a long way since those days, which can be attributed to the work of not only my predecessors, but to all those involved who could cast aside single-service prejudice, mistrust and politics to reach a common goal. The fruits of this co-operation were reflected at a joint SAR conference which I recently attended. Here the RAF, RN, Coastguard and in some areas the air ambulance services, could be seen to be working within a common command structure, employing similar standards and practices and exchanging experiences to reach mutual agreement on a number of what would previously have been thorny issues. I can honestly say, without any doubt, that the UK has, at last, a cohesive SAR organisation that would be able to cope safely and efficiently with most eventualities.

As a relatively junior pilot I can recount one of my early SAR missions as an example of just how poorly we were placed at *Gannet*. Late one September night in 1987 I was called from home by bleeper to come in for a search. The weather that night was pretty awful, and a young man had been reported missing from a small boat at the western end of the Sound of Mull. Well over an hour later, after all the crew had driven in, we launched without a medic (as none were apparently available) to join the operation. On reaching the search area a further hour later in driving rain and winds of over 50 knots, we began sweeping the southern side of the Ardnamurchan peninsula, peering down to the rocky shoreline with only the aircraft's landing lights to assist us, my rear crew hanging out of the cargo door getting drenched, while straining to catch a glimpse of anything in the surf. After nearly two hours of this we were running short of fuel and elected to fly to Connel airfield at Oban in order to use the emergency fuel stored there for these occasions. This consisted of a stock of 56-gallon drums and an electric pump stored in a hut close to the runway. Each barrel had to be tested for water contamination before being manhandled close enough to the aircraft to enable gravity refuelling to take place. Not trusting the reliability of the aircraft's internal battery to start an engine on such a wet night, we elected to shut down the rotors but keep one engine running. The rate at which the fuel could be tested, moved and pumped was only just greater than that used by the remaining running engine. It took over an hour to take on 3000 pounds of fuel (about half the capacity of the Sea King) and all of us had taken a hand in the evolution. Feeling the physical effects of an hour's workout we returned to the search area, this time to place Coastguard search parties along the coast. Most of the volunteers came from Mull, so a rendezvous at a golf course to the north of Tobermory was selected. I had little experience of night landings at unlit field sites and despite having nearly 100 night deck landings to my credit, I did not relish flying into an unlit area near the cliff tops. None of the people on the ground could have made a calculated appraisal of the suitability of the chosen site but I am still here to tell the tale so it must have been OK. All I remember is being half-blinded by an over-enthusiastic Land Rover driver, who thought that turning his headlights onto full beam in the latter stages of my final approach to land would help me not to crash! We came back and forth to the site several times in order to collect more teams and drop them at a number of unlit sites on the Ardnamurchan cliffs that night. The appalling weather did not let up, and nearing dawn we were released by the RCC. We arrived back at Prestwick having logged over six hours of night flying, exhausted, and fit for very little more than a bite of breakfast and bed.

The unfortunate young man was not found that night, nor was any trace of his small boat. I don't recall if his body was ever recovered, but I doubt if it was. How many similar missions were flown by crews from Prestwick in those early years is hard to tell, but with hindsight, how inefficient it was by today's standards. Even if we had found the casualty that night, only rudimentary first aid could have been administered in the helicopter. I even doubt if we could have landed at Oban hospital, since until recently a purpose-built landing site did not exist, and any casualty would have had to be transferred to an ambulance at Connel Airfield.

It was not very long after this incident that, under the supervision of Lt Cdr Roy Lewis, the squadron formed a cadre of dedicated aircrew whose training was specifically tailored to SAR operations. Crews were constituted to maintain a minimum level of appropriate experience, and wherever possible a doctor or medic was flown. Although the luxury of configuring the aircraft primarily for SAR was not an option, due to the squadron's main role of anti-submarine warfare, they were optimised as best they could be, and specialist equipment was sourced from all possible sources. Needless to say, budgets are never flush with surplus funds and are indeed scrutinised by accountants, not operators, and since SAR was not considered to be sufficiently important, the acquisition of kit was by no means easy.

Although the formation of this cadre was a big step forward, it proved quite divisive within the squadron. Despite being all of one company, elevation to SAR duties from within aircrew left some of those not chosen feeling very much second class. Obviously the ASW element of the unit also needed experienced aviators for its primary role, but some quite senior aircrew felt undervalued. Separate crewrooms and working routines did nothing to help the situation, and for some time there was very much a 'Them' and 'Us' division, which needed a degree of careful management to prevent friendly rivalry and banter developing into something more subversive.

When I returned as an instructor in 1992 to 819 Squadron, it had settled into a more cohesive unit with SAR routines. The senior line crews were rotated through SAR duties on about a nine-month cycle, leaving only the junior members to aspire to joining the cadre towards the end of their appointment. This seemed to work well and made for a far more harmonious life all round. The aircraft were still far from suitable, but the level of equipment had improved considerably, and the service provided was a quantum leap from what I had left three years previously. As the squadron instructor I was not rostered for SAR duties, and looking back through my log-book, I only have one entry for a SAR mission in a two year appointment. Unfortunately it was for the search for POACMN Jim Scott following his ditching in November 1993.

I remember that night vividly. I was woken by a phone call shortly after 2 AM. It was the other instructor on the squadron, Lt Mike Swales who was the duty supervising officer. My immediate thought when I heard his voice was that I had overslept and missed the brief for an early morning exercise against a submarine. Despite being half asleep, his opening words of 'We've lost an aircraft, Roger,' will always stay with me. Driving into Gannet a few minutes later, I couldn't get out of my head the stark reality of having an aircraft crash into the sea at night with your close friends in it. Incidentally I was to have taken over that aircraft later when it returned from that serial. Arriving at the crash site just south of Islay at first light, low cloud, drizzle and a very poor visual horizon was, at times, very disorientating. I believe the poor weather was not a contributory factor to the accident, but it certainly made searching for Jim and any wreckage difficult. Understandably, the accident left the squadron quite dazed for some time afterwards, and the fact that Jim's body was never recovered didn't help.

My next appointment to 819 Squadron in 1998 saw little change to the routines established earlier for SAR but it was evident that operations were undoubtedly slicker. A succession of innovative and forward-thinking officers, who were nominated to lead the SAR element of the unit (SAROs), had left their respective marks. Equipment levels were considerably better, training more specialised and focussed and co-operation with the RAF and Coastguard noticeably improved. Doc Begg had by now hung up his flying boots, but in addition to the medical staff flying in support of missions, the rear crew were now receiving medical training enabling them to administer more than basic first aid.

During this time I flew a number of routine SAR missions, although as a Detachment Commander and latterly Senior Pilot (Second in Command of the Squadron), I was not part of the regular SAR crews. Whilst flying with these crews I saw at first hand a markedly different approach. Gone was the second division 'make do as best we can' attitude. These were properly trained, adequately resourced young men and women, finally flying aircraft fit for the purpose. The Sea King mark 5s, albeit old, were fitted out with proper stowage for the plethora of kit now carried, and the sonar, previously used for ASW, had finally been removed, not only freeing up more cabin space, but reducing the basic weight of the aircraft by some 1200 pounds. This gave greater performance and higher thrust margins, so very vital in the mountains where even in relatively benign conditions one often needs the extra power to counteract the effects of sudden downdrafts, or allow landings to be safely made at higher altitudes. Remote refuelling sites were all now equipped with purpose-built diesel pumps with generator back up. Fuelling from these sites was now a routine part of operations away from base and not seen as a last resort for emergency use only.

However, even with this level of equipment the squadron was still lacking in one vital area, night-vision goggles (NVGs). These vital pieces of equipment had been used both on front line operations and by RAF SAR crews for some considerable time. Unlike our other RN colleagues flying from RNAS Culdrose in Cornwall, whose main trade is offshore, crews from HMS *Gannet* are regularly tasked inland into the mountains. By day the hazards in this often unforgiving environment are clear, but by night, inland operations are severely limited by an inability to see. Techniques had been developed over the years to enable overland SAR, but the transition from height to low level, especially in the hills, was always treacherous and was only flown by the most experienced of crews. A number of lengthy written requests for NVGs from a succession of SAROs were unsuccessful. Funds were never released from the budgets allocated for equipment procurement, the main argument cited being that NVGs for SAR were not seen as having a high enough priority over other projects. It was rumoured that some senior officers held the opinion that the use of goggles was seen as unnecessary for the task. How true this was is still open to debate, but some night vision aids were supplied. These, however, were far from effective and were really only used in assisting the rear crew with night searches. Flying with NVGs is not simply a matter of attaching the goggles to one's helmet and hoping they turn night into day. One's field of view is greatly reduced, and because one is looking into two tubes that only project a two-dimensional image onto the eye, depth perception is near impossible to judge accurately. It is a much more exacting and perishable skill, and specific training must be completed before one can safely fly using the equipment. Additionally the whole cockpit and instrument lighting have to be changed too. Failing to do this renders the goggles next to useless. Clearly this was not a quick fix but there seemed to be more and more hurdles being put in the way by those who were against procuring the equipment, and there were some in the squadron who thought that only an accident would make them see sense.

Inevitably it happened. Fortunately lives were not lost, but had it not been for the timely call of the aircrewman who was sweeping a powerful handheld lamp from the cargo door and the subsequent swift reactions of the flying pilot, it might have been a different story. One dark winter's night the duty crew were scrambled to a job in Glencoe. Assessing the weather before launching they elected to transit at low level north up the coast before heading inland, following firstly Loch Etive and then Glen Etive, thereby making their way eventually to the eastern end of Glencoe. The flight was uneventful until they turned into Loch Etive. Remaining at low level and relying on the aircraft's lights, they made their way eastwards following the shores of the loch. They were so far inland the observer was now unable to use his radar for navigation, and the pilots were using their map to progress further inland. Following the shoreline religiously, they were unaware that they had strayed into a rapidly narrowing valley, having followed a burn that flowed into the loch. Sweeping a lamp out of the rear door, the crewman suddenly saw trees very close under the aircraft and a steep rocky cliff face looming quickly out of the darkness. Unaware of this until the crewman called out, the crew were seconds from impacting the hillside. Hauling the helicopter towards the loch and applying a huge amount of power to initiate a climb, the crew shot skywards. Gathering their composure some 4000 feet higher, they had fortunately not only found a hole in the clouds, but narrowly averted a crash. Needless to say, that was the end of their participation in the mission that night, and they returned to Prestwick quite shaken up.

Although this was not a pivotal moment, it did go some way to strengthening the argument for the procurement of NVGs. Some criticism was levelled at the crew following that night, but in their defence the incident served to highlight the fallibility of the prescribed techniques being used, and how easily something could have happened before.

I too had been tasked that winter to a job on the west coast of Arran, where a group of elderly walkers had just walked too far up a valley and as darkness fell realised their predicament. Electing to remain where they were, one of them who was still fit left the hill to raise the alarm. It was an overcast moonless night, and when we reached the scene towards midnight it was drizzling. After receiving a brief from the local mountain rescue team, we began a search up the valley that climbed up from the coast and dog-legged before reaching a plateau some 1800 feet high.

Faced with a difficult choice when it came to searching, we could either attempt the difficult manoeuvre of hover-taxiing backwards up the valley and leaving a downhill escape dead ahead, or conventionally flying nose into the valley, but leaving sufficient height and room for a 180-degree valley turn should we need to escape in a hurry. I have the utmost trust in my rear crew who will clear the blind areas of view when manoeuvring in tight spaces, but like most helicopter pilots, I do not like flying backwards at the best of times, let alone in the dark. So I elected to do the latter, and fortunately on the first foray into the valley located the party of walkers tucked into the hillside, sheltering by a small sheep enclosure. Unfortunately the wind at the top of the valley was blowing nearly in the opposite direction to what it was on the coast, some 1000 feet lower. This meant that we had to return into the valley as we had done initially, but then fly past the walkers, execute a tight turn a few hundred feet beyond them and then descend back down the valley and establish a hover into wind at their position, as landing next to them was out of the question due to the steepness of the ground. This would be relatively simple in daylight, but the same manoeuvre at night using only the aircraft's lights was tricky. Unlike car headlights which shine directly ahead, the Sea King's forward-facing floodlights are biassed downwards. An additional, trainable landing light helps, but only gives a pencil beam of light and only becomes really effective in the last hundred yards or so. Once in the hover, the walkers could be winched up, which was a relatively easy evolution. When all of them were onboard, I began to transition to forward flight.

My intention was to maintain visual contact with the valley side and creep back down towards the coast. Within seconds of leaving the hover I completely lost all visual references with the surface, the aircraft was still descending but I could not judge any proximity to the terrain below, and I could see nothing but blackness. My co-pilot was no better placed. I had no option but to initiate a rapid climb inside the confines of the narrow valley, maintaining heading and hoping to pop out of the valley and into Kilbrennan Sound. About 800 feet later and still in the climb, we saw the lights of Catacol appearing below us on the west coast of Arran. Clearly, had we been using goggles that night, the whole evolution of searching and manoeuvering within the valley would have been so much easier and safer.

I left the squadron in December 2001 shortly after 819 Squadron had disbanded. HMS *Gannet* was to be a much smaller establishment, no longer responsible for the defence of the Clyde and additional fleet tasking in Scotland, but now with the sole task of SAR for an area stretching north from the Lakes to the Nevis Range, and west from the Borders to 200 miles out to sea, including Northern Ireland and many of the Western Isles. During the next three years, *Gannet* SAR Flight, as it was to be known, underwent a number of difficult teething problems. This was understandable, considering its heavy reliance on a parent unit some 600 miles away, and its need to convince the rest of the world that it was now unable to take on all the additional tasks which 819 Squadron, with its greater number of aircraft and staff, had done in the past.

I was delighted and privileged to be appointed to command the *Gannet* SAR Flight from December 2004, and arriving back following my refresher courses I found the place much changed and in a very sound state. Far from the gaze of senior supervisors, a remote unit can easily gain the reputation for going a bit native. My predecessor had gone a long way to dispel the myth that Prestwick was an easy-going little flying club that worked by its own rules and was a cushy number for all. By contrast it had been the busiest SAR unit in the country for two years running, and had achieved a very high degree of operational efficiency with very limited assets. His major coup however was that the Flight was now fully equipped with NVGs. The whole establishment seemed a highly disciplined, professional and cohesive group, focussed on their primary task.

Notwithstanding the greater degree of specialist flying training, one must not lose sight of the fact that SAR operations remain inherently dangerous. Even the most experienced of operators can be caught out. A few months before my tenure as CO began, a serious incident occurred in the Lake District during a rescue that could have been considered as just another routine job.

On a day with no clouds in the sky and hardly a breath of wind, perhaps one of the more experienced crews of Rescue 177 was scrambled to a walker who had fallen onto a ledge about 100 feet below the summit of Pike of Stickle. Once on scene the crew elected to winch the crewman to the casualty before collecting three MRT members from the valley floor. The winching position was tight into the cliff edge, but not abnormally close. Having returned to the position to winch down the MRT, the flying pilot perceived he was in exactly the same position as he had been some minutes before. The first team member was winched successfully, but during the second transfer, just as he was removing the winch strop, the rotors struck the cliff face at a point behind the pilot's right shoulder. The helicopter dived away, dragging the helpless MRT member some 80 feet down the mountainside before he could free himself fully, breaking both wrists in the process. Usually if a winch malfunction occurs a cable cut facility is operated, but the vibration caused by the now unbalanced rotors was so severe that the observer could not identify the cut switch. Descending rapidly into the valley, the pilot (on exchange from the German navy) managed to select the only flat area available, and carried out a near-perfect forced landing. The remaining MRT member on board the aircraft was not aware of anything wrong!

In this case the injuries sustained were fortunately minor, the aircraft was soon flying again, and the only major hit was professional pride. The root cause of the incident was attributed to a combination of adverse light and the similar colours of the vegetation and rotor disc—an easy mistake, but remember these were very experienced operators. Needless to say, the subsequent enquiry made some recommendations that have been incorporated into standard procedures, but it still remains a sobering reminder to practising aircrew of their mortality.

Once I had settled back into the daily routine, my initial positive observations were further confirmed by the relationship with the Air Rescue Co-ordination Centre (ARCC), which was much improved. Daily dialogue between the duty controllers, and a far from parochial approach by their proactive Commanding Officer, Sqn Ldr Nick Barr, had done a great deal to allay any misconceptions that *Gannet*'s participation in SAR was not taken seriously. Additionally the exchange posting of a senior RAF crewman to the Flight also further helped this now healthy working ethos.

As I mentioned earlier, Jimmy Begg had long since ceased to fly with us on SAR missions, but I was pleased to see him maintaining an active part on the establishment as the resident Aviation Medicine doctor. The foundations laid by him in those very early days had allowed a steady development of the clinical care available in the aircraft, and a service comparable with the civilian air ambulances. A high proportion of tasking from the ARCC was in response to medical emergencies, or the transfer from outlying areas of patients already in NHS care needing a higher level of immediate treatment. Although a very good air ambulance service exists in Scotland, the weather is often not suitable for their single pilot operated light helicopters to respond. They are very well-equipped, and carry two specifically trained paramedics; therefore in order to be able to respond and maintain the appropriate NHS protocols both the equipment and the qualifications of military SAR aircraft and crews have had to be brought up to the same standard. The RAF has established an Air Medical College, graduates of which receive NHS accreditation. All rear crew now undergo training to a basic care level, and all aircrewmen undergo advanced training to enable the use of specialist equipment and the administration of controlled drugs. This is a first for the military, as medics throughout all three services do not receive the equivalent of civilian accreditation. Without the pioneering work undertaken by Jimmy, and his dogged persistence over the years, the Flight would not have been well placed to keep pace with the developments going on outwith routine naval medical practice.

So as I lie in bed at night, I do not lose sleep worrying that my crews are ill-prepared. I am confident that the crews from *Gannet* can launch into the worst of Scottish weather, properly equipped and highly trained so as not to compromise their own safety, and that when they arrive on scene they are very well placed to recover personnel and administer a high level of clinical care. Inter-Service training and co-operation is at an unprecedented high, so the future should seem bright. However, change is now on the horizon.

So far I have failed to mention the third element of UK airborne SAR. The recent and very popular TV show 'Seaside Rescue' has shown the invaluable contribution the Coastguard (HMCG) make to the organisation. For nearly two decades, four helicopter units operated under a Bristow Helicopters contract have operated from Sumburgh, Stornoway, Lee-on-Solent and Portland. Naturally, these civilian units are able to operate at a fraction of the cost of their military counterparts, and therefore it made economic sense to review the whole of the UK SAR organisation with a view to awarding a Private Finance Initiative (PFI) contract to industry. The Sea Kings and S-61Ns used by the military and Bristows respectively are very reliable, but are fast nearing the end of their useful life. Replacing these aircraft with a modern common fleet under one contractor is the current proposal, and by 2012 the new system is expected to come into force. The present location of SAR bases is very much a legacy of our homeland defence, with all the units being embedded within current or former military establishments. The long-term future of some remains very much in the balance. Therefore, being included in the SAR harmonisation project (SAR H) are proposals for the rationalising of where the future bases will be. Historical data will be used and the range, performance and response times of the new helicopters taken into account; and I have little doubt that the current twelve SAR units, six RAF, four HMCG and two RN, will inevitably be reduced in number.

It is planned that a number of military aircrew will still be employed within the units, as the skill sets gained from SAR operations are invaluable back on the frontline but as yet the proportion and distribution of these personnel has yet to be finalised. One option is to make the personnel manning these units fully integrated; the other is to maintain the single service enclaves similar to what we have at present. With the majority of personnel being civilian, it is obvious that if the latter option is taken, by default, the number of military bases will reduce.

As to the future management of this all-encompassing organisation, the jury is still out. The RAF has a large SAR organisation that is part of 2 Group. The ARCC, with the exception of one RN and one HMCG post, is manned by RAF personnel and therefore the RAF has a keen interest in maintaining primacy. The Coastguard has seven Maritime Rescue Centres around our coast and can in certain situations launch ARCC assets directly, so rightly believes it should be a major stakeholder in the future organisation. If total integration were to be achieved, then a single National Rescue Co-ordination Centre would be the ultimate solution where subject matter experts could co-ordinate appropriate action in the event of land, air and maritime emergencies. Within this set-up, elements from the Police, Fire and Ambulance services could provide a totally integrated response. I believe this sways the balance towards a civilian-run management team, assisted by suitably experienced military and emergency service personnel.

As an aside, during a recent conference, one area of humorous contention with regard to future SAR was what colour and livery the helicopters would sport. Many conventional colours including orange, red, yellow, blue with white and red were all suggested. However one senior delegate thought he had found the solution at his local DIY superstore. He had mixed the combination of all the above at the specialist paints counter and come up with, as he described it, 'a mucky pink!'

As a suitable conclusion, I think that with the progress made within SAR over the time spanned by the two volumes of *Rescue 177*, we are not far from having an ideal set-up. Admittedly one will always be behind technology and advances in medicine, but considering where we were twenty years ago the whole organisation is in very good shape. Long gone are those days where we launched with the very best of intent, full of optimism but perhaps not best placed to deliver a wholly effective service. Response times are shorter, crew flying skill levels are higher, medical training is of a very high standard and now NHS accredited, equipment is fit for purpose and an unprecedented degree of harmonisation exists between all the controlling agencies. Personnel from the RNLI, Ambulance Service and Mountain Rescue Teams who train with us regularly are all now far better placed to facilitate swift and efficient rescues. Of course there will always be those occasions where man and machine will be tested to the limit, but what would have counted as a difficult operation in those early days is now just routine. However one must never forget the single most important factor in all of this: the individual. And by that I mean everyone. It is all too easy to single out the aircrew, lifeboat crews and emergency service personnel who are in much demand by the media following newsworthy rescues, but one must not forget that the organisation would not function without those unsung men and women who work tirelessly behind the scenes. Without the selfless, modest and courageous contribution from all those involved at the forefront of SAR, none of this would be possible. What we have in place is second to none, and anyone who has contributed in any way has every right to be proud of his or her achievements.

(August 2006)

Jackspeak Glossary: Naval Terms and Acronyms

Admiralty Surgeon and Agent—A civilian doctor who is appointed, in towns all over the country, often ports, to look after any *Jacks* taken ill on home leave, and provide reports to their ship or shore base on their fitness to travel. A now defunct relic of the old days of the mighty Navy.

aircrewman—See *LACMN* and *POACMN.*

arse-up ducks—Any duck, swan or goose.

ASW—Anti-submarine warfare.

ATC—Air Traffic Control.

AWOL—Absent without leave.

Back-seat crew—Always the observer and aircrewman, plus an MA or doctor if carried.

bag and mask—Method of delivering oxygen to a patient's lungs via a mask and an inflatable bag which is gently squeezed.

BASICS—The British Association of Immediate Care Schemes—a voluntary doctors' scheme to provide training and expert pre-hospital medical care at road accidents and major incidents. Founded in the early 1970s by pioneering GPs in England, it has expanded UK-wide, and provides a valuable service, especially in areas remote from major hospitals. Since the 1990s, ambulance paramedics now do much of this work.

becket—A strong loop sewn into a piece of safety equipment.

bone dome—Flying helmet.

Bootnecks/Booties—Royal Marines.

bowser—Fuel tanker.

burning and turning—Describes a helicopter with engines firing, blades rotating, and ready for take off.

cab—A shorter name for a helicopter than chopper or helo.

Captain—The title of the Commanding Officer of a Shore Base, or Aircraft. The officer in command may be anything from a Lieutenant to a Commodore. E.g. the Captain at HMS *Gannet*—a Shore Establishment (or Stone Frigate)—held the rank of Commander. On his 'ship' were one or two squadrons, each commanded by a CO holding the rank of Lieut. Commander. The Captain of each Sea King might be a Lieutenant, or a Lieut. Commander—or even a Captain or a Major if the most senior officer on board came from Canada, the USA, or Germany. And he could be either the pilot or the observer. All very confusing!

Captain's Table—Formal appearance before the Commanding Officer for promotion or demotion, commendation or court martial, honourable release, or dishonourable discharge.

Casevac—Injured casualty evacuation.

CBs—Cumulonimbus thunder clouds.

Channel 16—The Maritime Distress Safety and Calling Radio Frequency on which Coastguards and all ships maintain a constant listening watch.

Chief—Any CPO.

Chief Tiff—Chief Petty Officer Air Engineering Artificer.

Chinook—Very large twin rotor troop-carrying helicopter.

CINCFLEET—Commander-in-Chief Fleet.

CMP—Civilian Medical Practitioner: the designation of a civilian doctor whether working part-time and alone in a small military unit, or in a full-time post alongside the staff of Service Medical Officers on large bases.

CO—Commanding Officer.

Cocker's P—The annual cocktail party held in the wardroom for all those and such as those in the community.

COMClyde—Commodore Clyde. The Senior Officer based in Faslane.

companionway—Entry into a ship's cabin.

CPO—Chief Petty Officer.

CPR—Cardio-pulmonary resuscitation.

Crab—Navy nickname for anything RAF. The first uniforms issued to the RAF in 1918 came from a cancelled batch ordered by the Tsar of Russia. Their grey/blue colour was similar to that of mercuric oxide jelly or 'crabfat' used at the time to treat body lice—and the name stuck.

Destroyer—Fast escort warship used mainly for the air defence of a convoy or fleet.

dispatch harness—Heavy webbing belt attached to the winchman and the roof of a Sea King to prevent him falling out of the aircraft's open door when directing a winching.

dit—A story or account of an incident or event.

Doc—Nickname for the MA in charge of a sick bay on board a ship without a doctor. On a big ship, the doctor would be the Quack, and the MA the Doc. On SAR sorties, I was referred to as Doc, and, on one memorable occasion, my POMA became 'Baby Doc'.

dockyard omelette/pizza—The visual aftermath of a vigorous *huey.*

Doppler—The forward, sideways, and upwards motion-sensing equipment within the aircraft.

downbird—A helicopter which has made a precautionary or emergency landing, and requires attention from the Maintainers.

Drills—Six monthly Pool or Wet Drills practising with inflatable one man and ten man dinghies in Ayr Baths; and also Abandon Aircraft Drills in the hangar. In addition there were yearly Sea Drills in the Firth of Clyde, swimming to and boarding a ten man life raft, then a one man dinghy from which the occupant was winched up into a Sea King.

Dunker—The dreaded helicopter underwater escape training tank at Yeovilton, in which all aircrew have to pass their Dunker Drills every two years to keep in date.

dunking—Dipping the aircraft sonar in the sea to listen for submarines.

embuggerance factor—An extra little something sent to try us, and make our day!

endurance—The number of hours a Sea King can remain airborne without having to refuel. Normally around four and a half hours. See *range.*

ETA—Estimated time of arrival.
FAA—Fleet Air Arm.
Faslane—UK Northern Naval base, Firth of Clyde—HMNB (Clyde).
Ferrex—Rescue exercise involving a ferry.
fin—The conning tower of a submarine.
First Lieutenant—See *XO.*
flash-up—Start aircraft engines.
F/Med 4—The Tri-Service patient's Medical Record folder.
FONAC—Flag Officer Naval Air Command (now changed to Flag Officer Maritime Air—*FOMA*).
FOSNI—Flag Officer Scotland and Northern Ireland.
Frigate—Fast warship used mainly in an anti-submarine role.
goffered—Swamped by a big wave.
goon bag/suit—Supposedly dry cotton ventile immersion survival suit with rubber neck and wrist seals.
heads-up—A briefing or early warning of a potential problem.
helo—Helicopter.
HIFR—Helicopter inflight refueling procedure.
highline transfer—A winching done from a great height, involving first the lowering of a sandbag on a thin line attached to the winch hook, which is held from below to control the movement of the person on the end of the winchwire, or the stretcher.
HMS *Gannet*—Several Royal Navy warships bore this name before it was finally bestowed on an ASW helicopter base. HMS *Gannet* moved to Prestwick from Northern Ireland in 1971, following the onset of 'The Troubles', and occupied the site of the former wartime and post war US Air Force base on the northern perimeter of Prestwick Airport, till it was decommissioned in March 2003. As from April 2003, the name lives on as HMS *Gannet* SAR Flight, with its three designated SAR Sea Kings.
huey—A noisy retch, or *technicolour yawn.*
hunter-killer—A class of nuclear submarine whose function is to seek out and destroy enemy submarines or ships—as distinct from the 'Bombers' equipped with ballistic nuclear missiles.
ICU—Intensive Care Unit in a major hospital.

Jack—Shortened version of Jack Tar—generic name for all Royal Navy sailors.

Jimmy—The XO or First Lieutenant of a ship.

jolly—A carefree jaunt in a helicopter.

Jossman—The Master-at-Arms.

jump seat—The bulkhead seat at the front of a Sea King, just behind the pilots, and close to the front entrance door.

Killick—Any leading hand.

knot—Nautical mile—approx 2000 yards. Thus, a 30 knot wind = 34 mph.

LACMN—Leading aircrewman. Usually trained Sonar Operators on anti-submarine Sea Kings. Some are also trained as SAR Divers. Now all designated SAR aircrewmen have to undertake advanced paramedical training to equip them to deal with most inflight emergencies. See *POACMN*.

lightweight stretcher—Anything but! A rugged tubular metal basket stretcher used in the transfer of casualties to the helo.

LMA—Leading Medical Assistant.

Lynx—The small twin-engined helicopter carried by frigates and destroyers.

MA—Medical Assistant. Till recently, *MAQs* were female MAs, separately governed by QUARNNS (Queen Alexandra Royal Naval Nursing Service). Trained to man and administer sick bays on ship and shore bases, MAs look after all medical records, pharmacy, immunisation programmes, first aid training courses, and emergency packs. They are given training in basic diagnostic skills, and allowed to prescribe a limited number of basic drugs. MAs are also highly skilled in pre-hospital emergency care. See *LMA* and *POMA*.

Maintainers—Aircraft engineering ground crew.

Master-at-Arms—The MAA is in charge of base policing and discipline, together with his team of Regulators.

Medevac—Evacuation of a medical case—usually a transfer from a lowland or highlands and islands country cottage hospital, to a major city hospital.

MRT—Mountain Rescue Team.

Navex—Navigational exercise.

Neil-Robertson stretcher—A wrap-round slatted rescue stretcher with multiple straps which can be used for vertical stretchering of a casualty from a confined space, e.g. a submarine.

Nimrod—RAF long-range ASW jet aircraft based on the design of the old Comet passenger jet. From RAF Kinloss they provide *top cover* support for exposed, long-distance helicopter SARs.

Northwood—CINCFLEET HQ.

Observer—The Navigator and operational tactician of the Sea King, who is in charge of flight operations and communications. Is also cross-trained with the aircrewman to operate the winch, or go down the wire himself. Observers now undergo extended medical training to equip them for their SAR role.

Oggie—Native of Cornwall.

OOD—Officer of the Day or Duty Officer.

oppo—A sailor's buddy or mate.

OPSO/OIC Ops—The Operations Officer.

Ops Room—Operations room.

ovies—Flying or Maintainers' overalls.

paraffin budgie—A helicopter—which always smells of paraffin!

Perishers—Final 'pass or perish' course for potential Royal Navy Submarine Commanding Officers, usually conducted in the waters of the Scottish Sea Exercise Areas.

Pilot, Left-hand—The co-pilot or P2, who occupies the left-hand seat in a Sea King, shares the flying, and also keeps tabs on fuel levels and instruments while the P1 is in the hover over a casualty.

Pilot, Right-hand—The P1 pilot who will fly the Sea King during a rescue, because the cargo door from which the winchman gives his directions is situated on the right side of the aircraft.

playmate—One of a pair of helicopters on an exercise together.

PLB—Personal Locator Beacon—attached to a PLP and giving out a signal for searching aircraft.

PLP—Personal Life Preserver—put more simply, an inflatable lifejacket.

PO—Petty Officer.

POACMN—Petty Officer aircrewman.

POMA—Petty Officer Medical Assistant. NCO usually in charge of a Sick Bay on board a Frigate or Destroyer, where there is no doctor on board. Larger ships will have full medical facilities with doctors, operating theatres, and wards.

PO(SE)—Petty Officer Survival Equipment.

pot—Hyperbaric recompression chamber.

Preggevac—Transfer of a pregnant patient to hospital.

PSP—Personal Survival Pack: a yellow plastic case containing an inflatable one-man dinghy and other survival aids, on which Sea King aircrew sit, attached by straps, during flight, and which is supposed to go out of the aircraft window with them during an escape from a sinking helo.

Pusser—Describes anything to do with the Navy, especially anything of inferior quality, e.g. kit issue. Derives from the old Purser—the Paymaster or Supply Officer.

Quack—A Navy doctor.

RAF Kinloss—United Kingdom's Rescue Coordination Centre, and home of the RAF Nimrod force.

RAF Lossie—RAF Lossiemouth, home of the Crab Sea King SAR Flight.

range—Maximum number of miles radius from base that a Sea King can travel, hover over casualty, and return safely on a full tank of fuel. Normally around 200 to 250-mile radius, or 400 to 500-mile round trip. The maximum fuel load is about 5200lb, or 520 gallons of kerosene, and the fuel consumption is about 1 mile per gallon! This range can be considerably extended by means of refuelling stops.

rat-arsed—Blind drunk.

rat-bags—Packed meals.

RCC—Rescue Coordination Centre. Now there is only one Centre for the UK, based at RAF Kinloss, covering an area from the Faroes to the Bay of Biscay and half of the North Sea. Prior to 1997 there were two centres, one at Plymouth, Cornwall for the Southern sector, and the other at Pitreavie, Fife, known as 'Edinburgh Rescue', which covered the Northern Sector.

Reggie—Regulator—or 'Crusher'—member of the MAA's team.

RFA—Royal Fleet Auxiliary—supply ships for the Royal Navy.
RNAS—Royal Navy Air Station.
RNLI—Royal National Lifeboat Institution.
RNR—Royal Naval Reserve. Officers and ratings who have left the Service have the opportunity to join the Reserve for a specified time, and usually spend 2-3 weeks per year on service duties.
RTA—Road traffic accident.
SAR—Search and Rescue.
SAR Cell—The name given to the unit within 819 Sqn, HMS *Gannet*, which undertook SAR duties, and which was superseded by the *SAR Flight* in April 2003 when HMS *Gannet* was decommissioned.
SAR Crew—Pilot, co-pilot and observer, who are all Officers, and an aircrewman who is an NCO. Till recently, HMS Gannet Sea Kings also flew with an MA as aircrew, and also a doctor when his services were required. From 2003, the extended-trained aircrewmen will replace the MAs who are being phased out.
SAR Flight—Dedicated Search and Rescue Unit, comprising perhaps three specially equipped Sea King helicopters with back-seat crews specially trained for mountain, sea, and medical casualties. All backed up by a full team of aircraft maintainers, SE Section, stores, admin, etc.
SARO—Search and Rescue Officer. The Lieut. Commander in charge of SAR operations in a SAR Flight.
Sea King—Built by Westlands to an original Sikorski design, this twin-engined helicopter has had an ASW role for the Royal Navy and a Commando carrier role for the Royal Marines for over thirty years. A smaller cousin of the Coastguard's Sikorski 61, it is also the designated SAR aircraft for both the Royal Navy and RAF.
SE Section—Survival Equipment Section, whose job is to inspect and maintain all items of survival kit, and supervise all aircrew survival training.
shitehawks—Usually seagulls.
shout—A SAR callout.
SNLR—Services no longer required. Dishonourable discharge.

SOBS—Senior Observer of a Squadron.

SPLOT—Senior Pilot of a Squadron.

Squadron—819 Squadron, Fleet Air Arm, based at HMS *Gannet*, RNAS Prestwick, initially comprised nine ASW Sea King helicopters, with a ship's company of around 350 personnel. Later, an extra one, then two, designated SAR aircraft were added to the squadron assets.

STASS—Short Term Air Supply System: a small cylinder of compressed air attached to a PLP, giving an extra 1-2 minutes underwater breathing time for aircrew escaping from a sinking helicopter.

Stokes Litter—See *lightweight stretcher.*

stone frigate—A Royal Navy Shore Establishment such as HMS *Gannet*.

stoofed—An aircraft crash.

strop—Heavy webbing loop with sliding toggle passed under the armpits and used to winch people to or from a helicopter. Just don't raise your arms!

Subby—Sub-lieutenant.

technicolour yawn—A spectacular vomit.

tits-up—Broken down and useless.

top cover—Support from 6 miles high, given by RAF Nimrods skilled at locating stricken ships, dropping liferafts, and providing weather, locational guidance, and communications relay, for searching SAR helos on long-range missions.

tube—ASW aircrew nickname for a submarine.

VF—Ventricular Fibrillation. A terminal heart flutter following a cardiac arrest, which can be converted back to a normal rhythm using a defibrillator.

Wafu—Service nickname for anyone associated with the FAA—supposed to stand for 'wet and flippin useless'

Watch Bill—Schedule of the whole ship's company, detailing the general working routine of the ship, each man's place of work, special sea duties, etc.

wet—A brew, a mug of tea.

Wessex—Replaced in 1988 by the Sea King as the Royal Navy and RAF rescue helicopter, mainly because of lack of range, radar, and a second pilot. Some are still used as workhorses by the RAF.

Winchman—The aircrewman or observer in charge of winch operations from the rear door of the Sea King, directing the pilot via the intercom.

Wren—Member of the Women's Royal Naval Service, formerly the organisational backbone of the old Navy. Now disbanded in favour of an equal opportunities service (almost) where women can now serve at sea in front-line ships and aircraft, and there is meant to be no obvious distinction between the sexes—except the obvious!

WO—Warrant Officer.

XO—The Jimmy, Executive Officer, or First Lieutenant of a ship—second in command to the captain of a ship or shore establishment.

yawing—An unpleasant sideways movement of aircraft or boat.